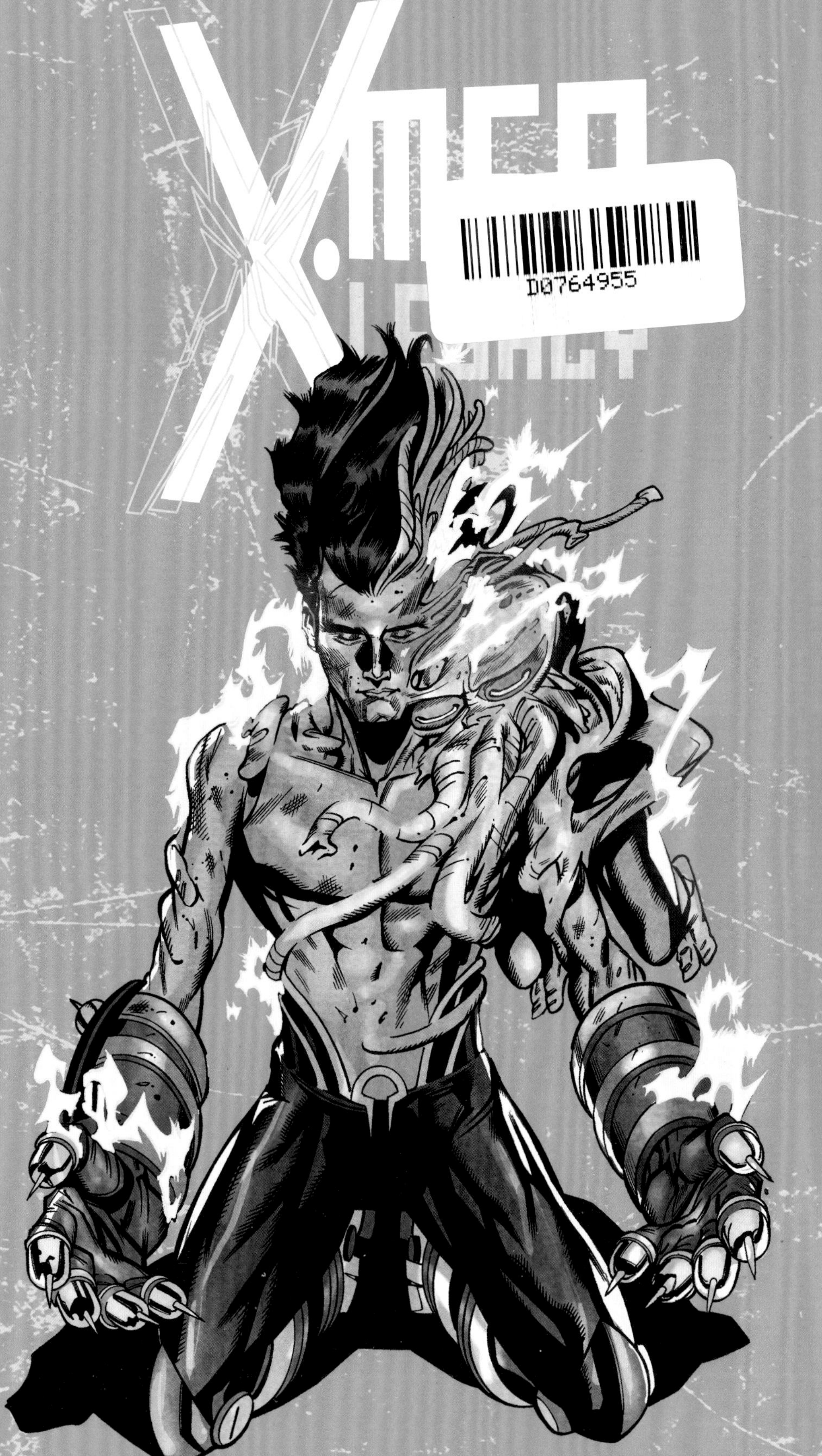

FOR WE ARE MANY

FOR WE ARE MANY

writer **SIMON SPURRIER**

pencilers **TAN ENG HUAT** (#19-20, #23-24) & **KHOI PHAM** (#21-22)

inkers **CRAIG YEUNG** (#19-20, #23-24) with **ED TADEO** (#20)
& **KHOI PHAM** (#21-22) with **JAY LEISTEN** (#21)

color artists **JOSE VILLARRUBIA** (#19-20, #23-24)
& **RACHELLE ROSENBERG** (#21-22)

letterer **VC'S CORY PETIT**

cover art **MIKE DEL MUNDO**

assistant editor **XANDER JAROWEY**

editor **DANIEL KETCHUM**

x-men group editor **NICK LOWE**

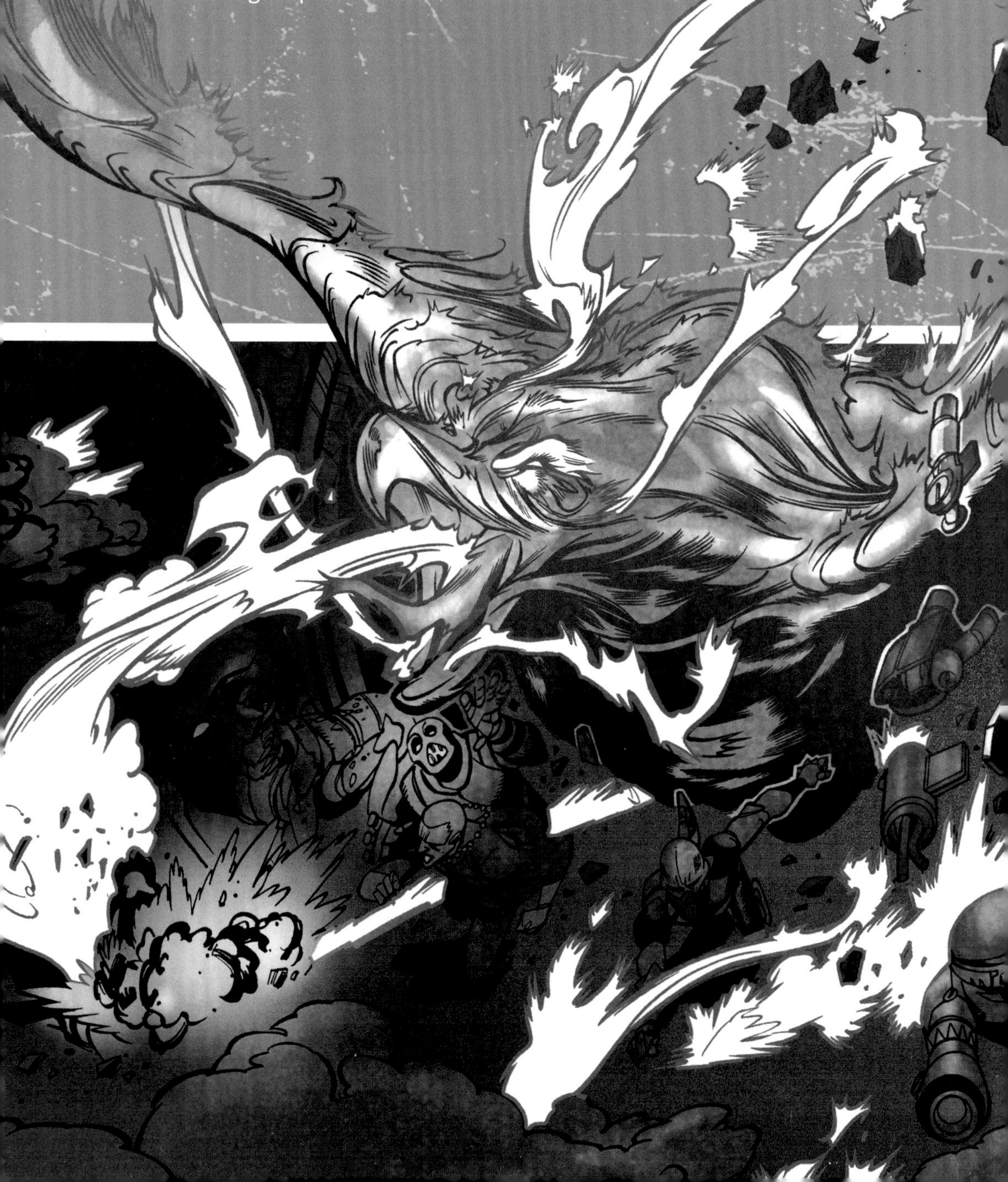

Collection Editor: Alex Starbuck
Editors, Special Projects: Mark D. Beazley & Jennifer Grünwald
Senior Editor, Special Projects: Jeff Youngquist
SVP Print, Sales & Marketing: David Gabriel
Book Designer: Jeff Powell & Rodolfo Muraguchi

Editor in Chief: Axel Alonso
Chief Creative Officer: Joe Quesada
Publisher: Dan Buckley
Executive Producer: Alan Fine

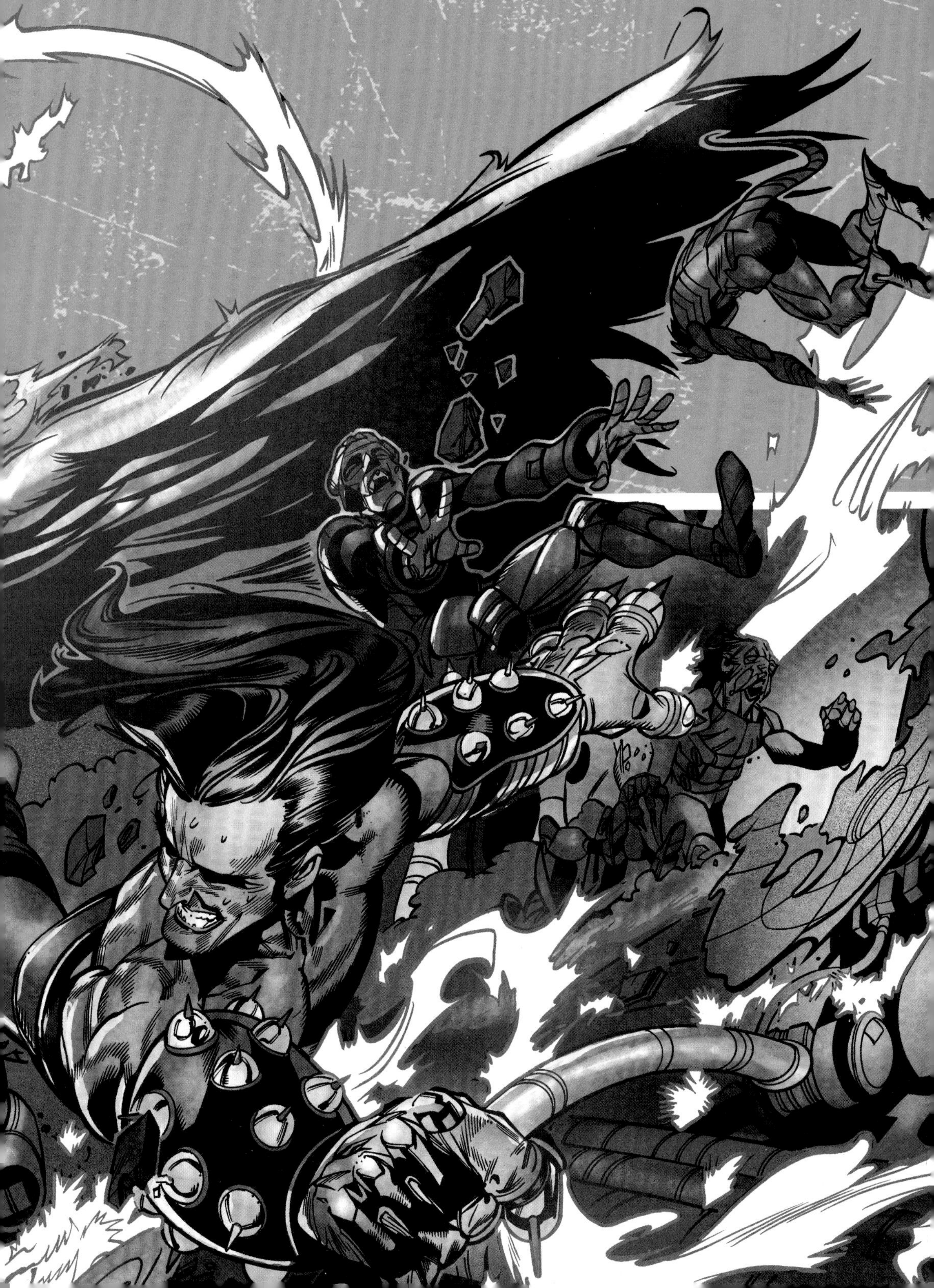

X·MEN LEGACY

CHARLES XAVIER'S MUTANT SON DAVID HALLER WOULD BE NEARLY
OMNIPOTENT IF HE COULD LOCK HIS MULTIPLE PERSONALITIES
AWAY IN AN EFFECTIVE MENTAL PRISON. BUT THAT TASK SEEMS
INSURMOUNTABLE IN THE WAKE OF HIS FATHER'S UNTIMELY DEATH.
NOW, DAVID FIGHTS TO KEEP HIS MIND AND POWERS UNDER CONTROL
AS HE WORKS TO UPHOLD HIS FATHER'S LEGACY.

Previously

ATTEMPTING TO DRAW THE MURDEROUS LUCA ALDINE OUT IN THE
OPEN, DAVID STAGED A CONFLICT BETWEEN HIMSELF AND THE
UNCANNY X-MEN WITH THE HELP OF HIS YOUNG LOVE, BLINDFOLD.
ONCE LUCA APPEARED, DAVID SPRUNG HIS TRAP, HOLDING LUCA IN
A STASIS BUBBLE. HOWEVER, ALL WAS NOT AS IT SEEMED, AS THE
TELEPATHIC MEMBERS OF THE UNCANNY X-MEN HAD LET LOOSE A
POISON IN DAVID'S MIND, CONSUMING HIM WITH HIS OWN FEARS AND
INSECURITIES AND CAUSING HIS MIND TO SELF-DESTRUCT. AS IT DID,
THE DARK SHADE OF PROFESSOR XAVIER LURKING IN HIS PSYCHE
MANAGED TO ESCAPE HIS MENTAL PRISON, LEAPING OUT AND TAKING
POSSESSION OF LUCA.

X-MEN LEGACY VOL. 4: FOR WE ARE MANY. Contains material originally published in magazine form as X-MEN LEGACY #19-24. First printing 2014. ISBN# 978-0-7851-5432-7. Published by MARVEL WORLDWIDE, INC., a subsidiary of MARVEL ENTERTAINMENT, LLC. OFFICE OF PUBLICATION: 135 West 50th Street, New York, NY 10020. Copyright © 2013 and 2014 Marvel Characters, Inc. All rights reserved. All characters featured in this issue and the distinctive names and likenesses thereof, and all related indicia are trademarks of Marvel Characters, Inc. No similarity between any of the names, characters, persons, and/or institutions in this magazine with those of any living or dead person or institution is intended, and any such similarity which may exist is purely coincidental. **Printed in Canada**. ALAN FINE, EVP - Office of the President, Marvel Worldwide, Inc. and EVP & CMO Marvel Characters B.V.; DAN BUCKLEY, Publisher & President - Print, Animation & Digital Divisions; JOE QUESADA, Chief Creative Officer; TOM BREVOORT, SVP of Publishing; DAVID BOGART, SVP of Operations & Procurement, Publishing; C.B. CEBULSKI, SVP of Creator & Content Development; DAVID GABRIEL, SVP Print, Sales & Marketing; JIM O'KEEFE, VP of Operations & Logistics; DAN CARR, Executive Director of Publishing Technology; SUSAN CRESPI, Editorial Operations Manager; ALEX MORALES, Publishing Operations Manager; STAN LEE, Chairman Emeritus. For information regarding advertising in Marvel Comics or on Marvel.com, please contact Niza Disla, Director of Marvel Partnerships, at ndisla@marvel.com. For Marvel subscription inquiries, please call 800-217-9158. **Manufactured between 2/28/2014 and 4/7/2014 by SOLISCO PRINTERS, SCOTT, QC, CANADA.**

10 9 8 7 6 5 4 3 2 1

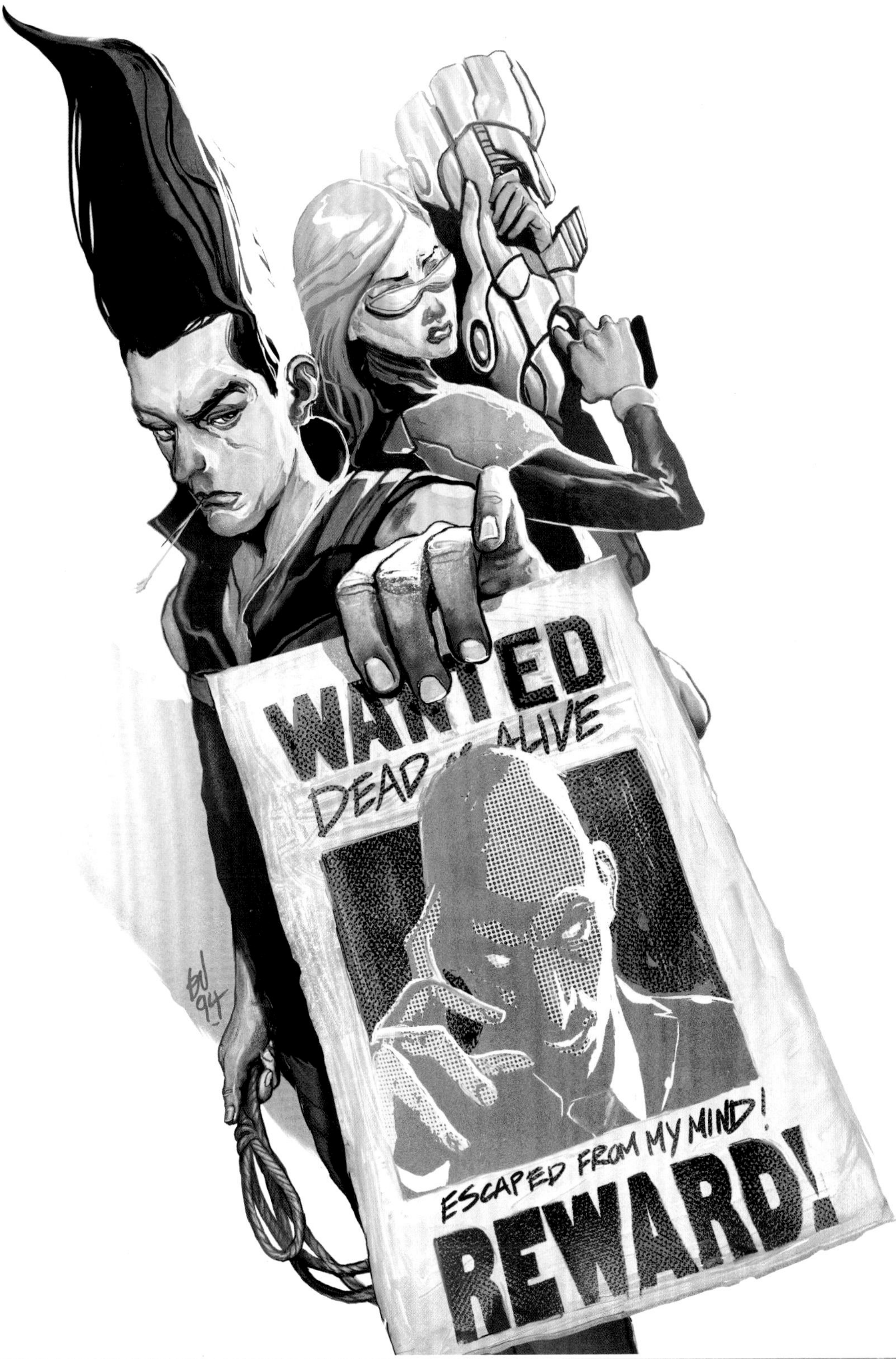
WANTED
DEAD
ALIVE
ESCAPED FROM MY MIND!
REWARD!

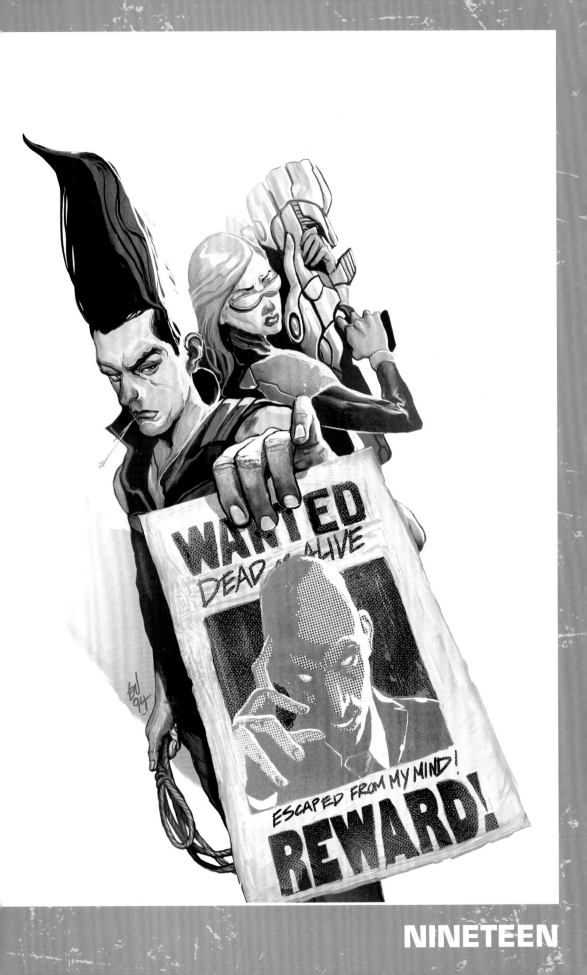

NINETEEN

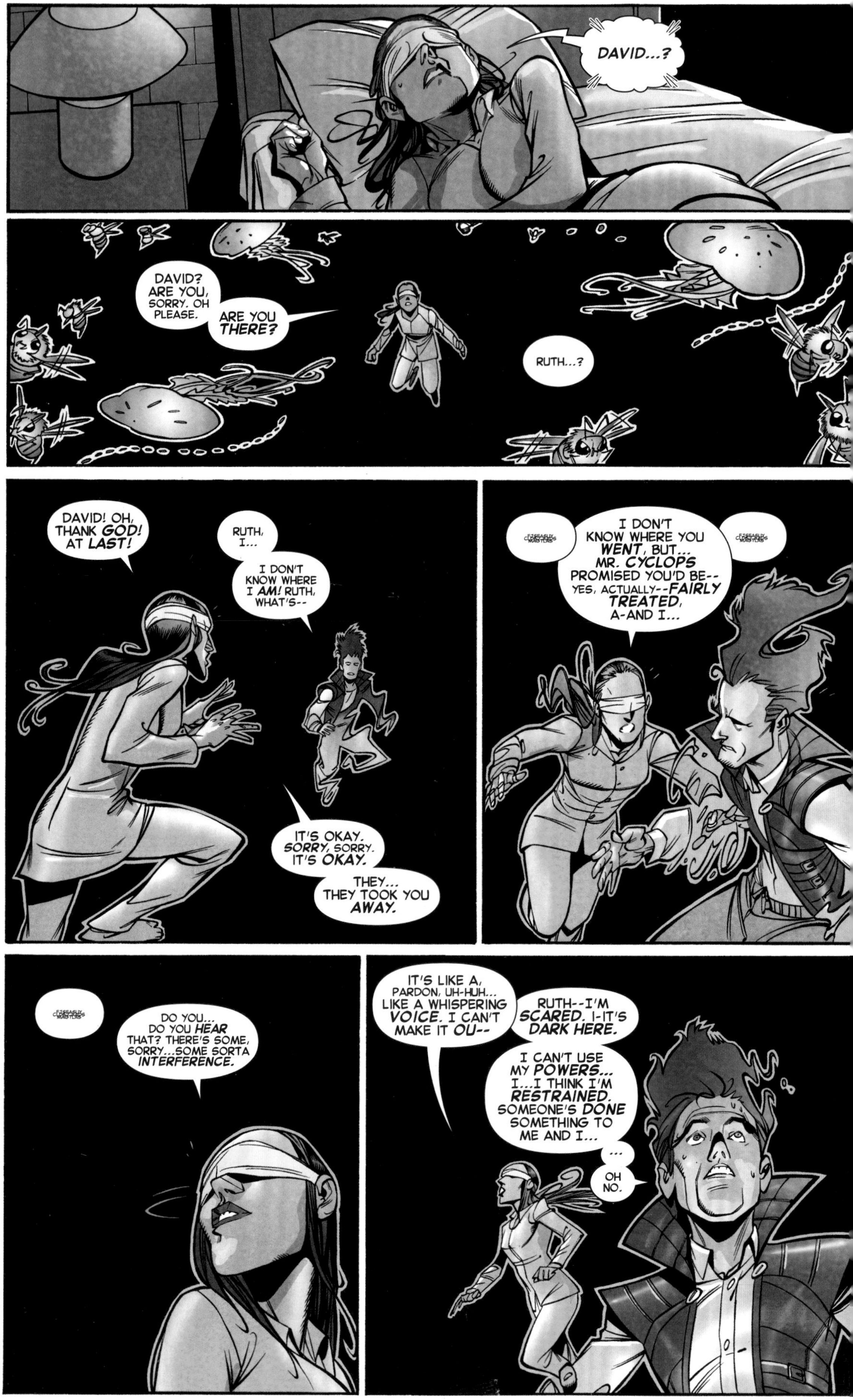
DAVID...?
DAVID? ARE YOU, SORRY. OH PLEASE.
ARE YOU THERE?
RUTH...?
DAVID! OH, THANK GOD! AT LAST!
RUTH, I...
I DON'T KNOW WHERE I AM! RUTH, WHAT'S--
IT'S OKAY. SORRY, SORRY. IT'S OKAY.
THEY... THEY TOOK YOU AWAY.
I DON'T KNOW WHERE YOU WENT, BUT... MR. CYCLOPS PROMISED YOU'D BE-- YES, ACTUALLY--FAIRLY TREATED, A-AND I...
DO YOU... DO YOU HEAR THAT? THERE'S SOME, SORRY...SOME SORTA INTERFERENCE.
IT'S LIKE A, PARDON, UH-HUH... LIKE A WHISPERING VOICE. I CAN'T MAKE IT OU--
RUTH--I'M SCARED. I-IT'S DARK HERE.
I CAN'T USE MY POWERS... I...I THINK I'M RESTRAINED. SOMEONE'S DONE SOMETHING TO ME AND I...
...
OH NO.

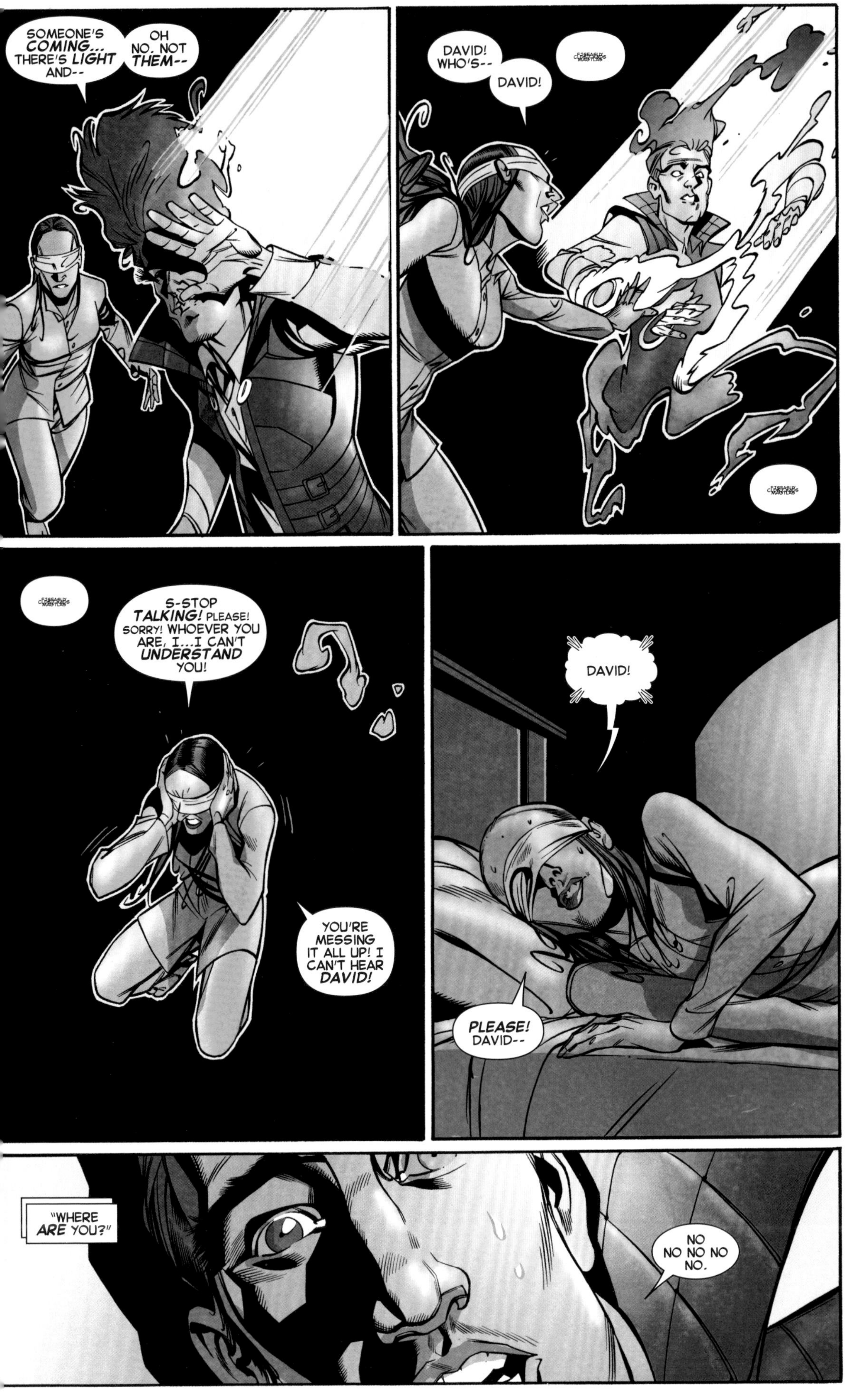
SOMEONE'S COMING... THERE'S LIGHT AND--
OH NO. NOT THEM--
DAVID! WHO'S--
DAVID!
S-STOP TALKING! PLEASE! SORRY! WHOEVER YOU ARE, I...I CAN'T UNDERSTAND YOU!
YOU'RE MESSING IT ALL UP! I CAN'T HEAR DAVID!
DAVID!
PLEASE! DAVID--
"WHERE ARE YOU?"
NO NO NO NO NO.

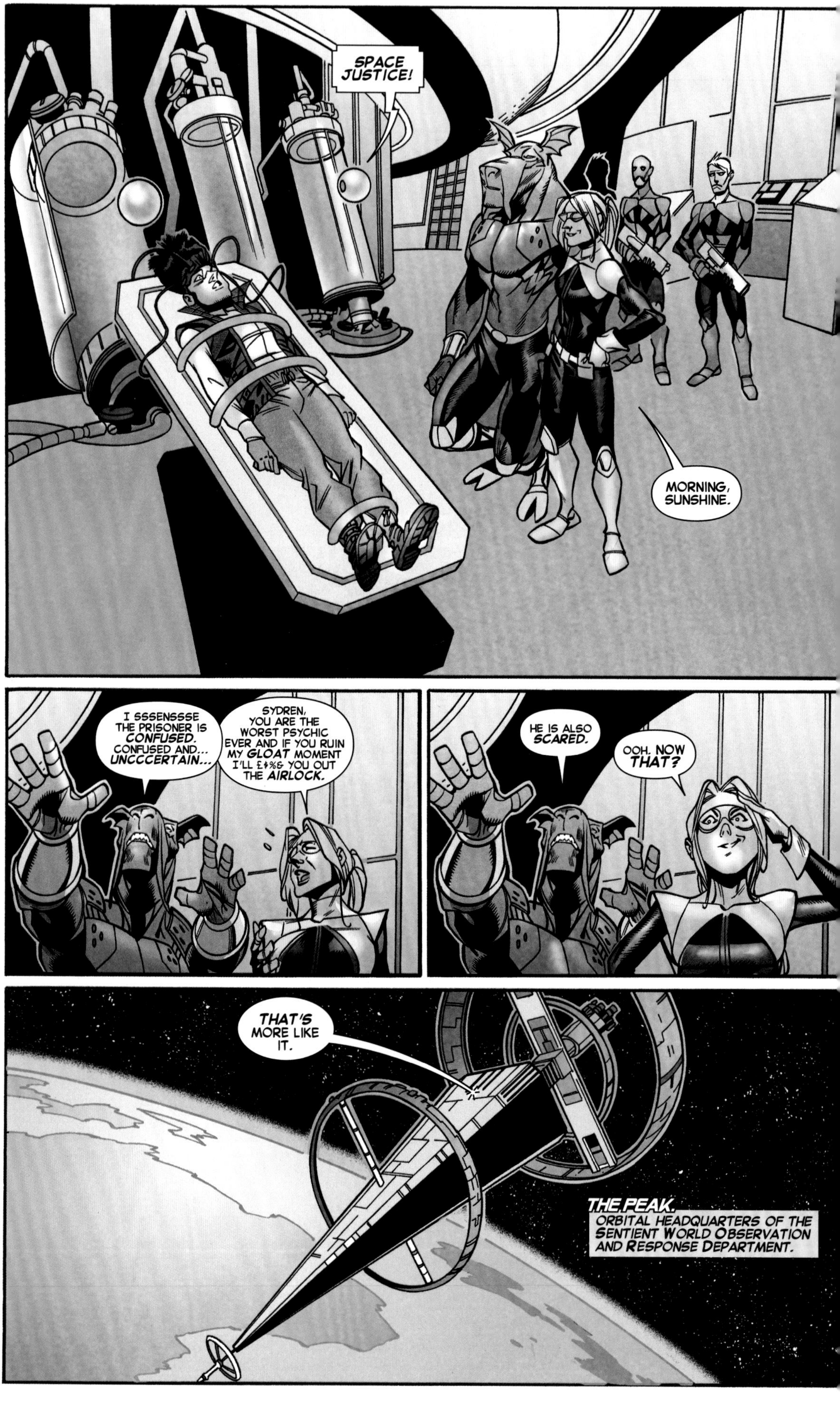
SPACE JUSTICE!
MORNING, SUNSHINE.
I SSSENSSSE THE PRISONER IS CONFUSED. CONFUSED AND... UNCCCERTAIN...
SYDREN, YOU ARE THE WORST PSYCHIC EVER AND IF YOU RUIN MY GLOAT MOMENT I'LL £¢%& YOU OUT THE AIRLOCK.
HE IS ALSO SCARED.
OOH. NOW THAT?
THAT'S MORE LIKE IT.
THE PEAK.
ORBITAL HEADQUARTERS OF THE SENTIENT WORLD OBSERVATION AND RESPONSE DEPARTMENT.

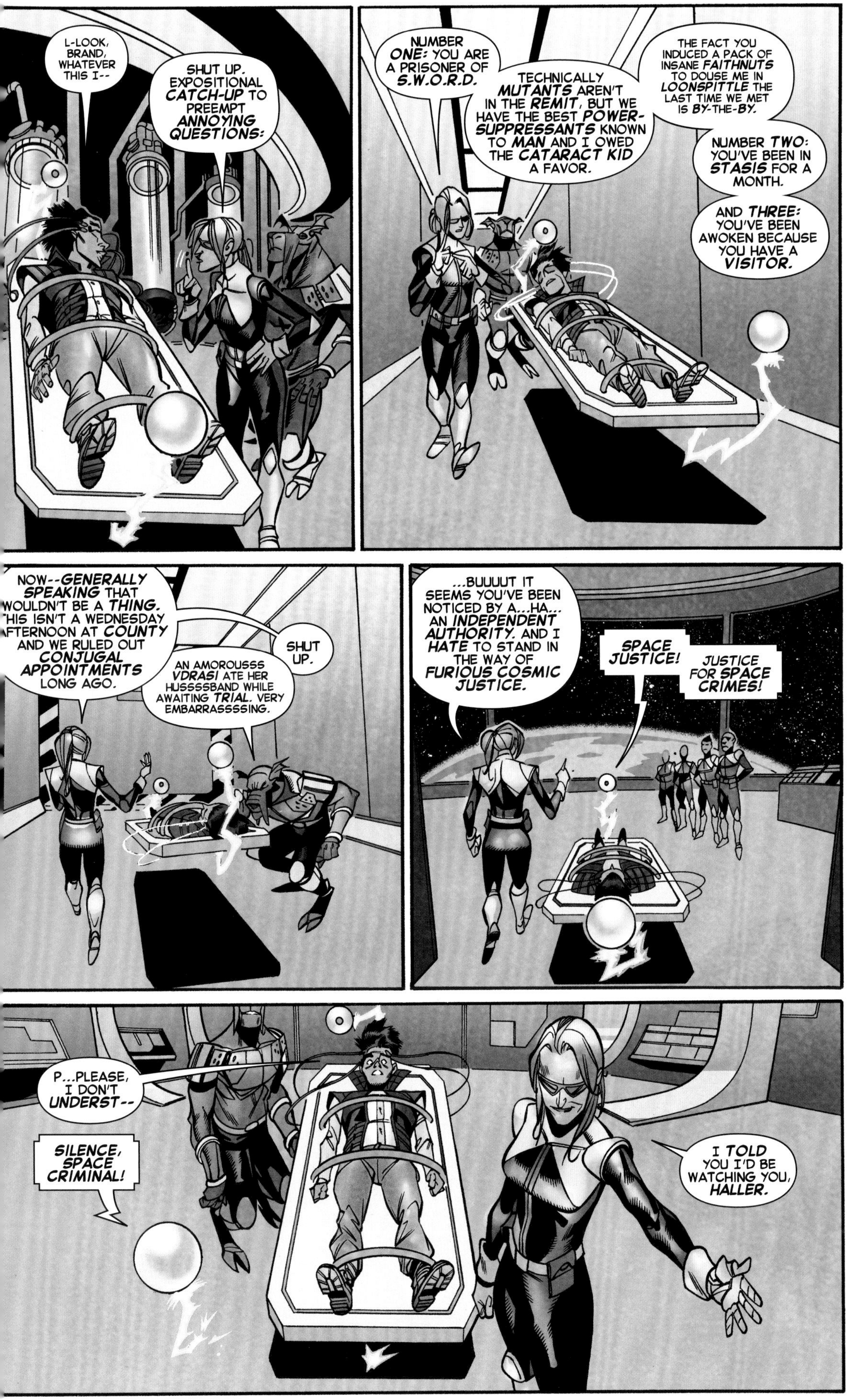

L-LOOK, BRAND, WHATEVER THIS I--
SHUT UP. EXPOSITIONAL CATCH-UP TO PREEMPT ANNOYING QUESTIONS:
NUMBER ONE: YOU ARE A PRISONER OF S.W.O.R.D.
TECHNICALLY MUTANTS AREN'T IN THE REMIT, BUT WE HAVE THE BEST POWER-SUPPRESSANTS KNOWN TO MAN AND I OWED THE CATARACT KID A FAVOR.
THE FACT YOU INDUCED A PACK OF INSANE FAITHNUTS TO DOUSE ME IN LOONSPITTLE THE LAST TIME WE MET IS BY-THE-BY.
NUMBER TWO: YOU'VE BEEN IN STASIS FOR A MONTH.
AND THREE: YOU'VE BEEN AWOKEN BECAUSE YOU HAVE A VISITOR.
NOW--GENERALLY SPEAKING THAT WOULDN'T BE A THING. THIS ISN'T A WEDNESDAY AFTERNOON AT COUNTY AND WE RULED OUT CONJUGAL APPOINTMENTS LONG AGO.
SHUT UP.
AN AMOROUSSS VDRASI ATE HER HUSSSSBAND WHILE AWAITING TRIAL. VERY EMBARRASSSSING.
...BUUUUT IT SEEMS YOU'VE BEEN NOTICED BY A...HA... AN INDEPENDENT AUTHORITY. AND I HATE TO STAND IN THE WAY OF FURIOUS COSMIC JUSTICE.
SPACE JUSTICE!
JUSTICE FOR SPACE CRIMES!
P...PLEASE, I DON'T UNDERST--
SILENCE, SPACE CRIMINAL!
I TOLD YOU I'D BE WATCHING YOU, HALLER.

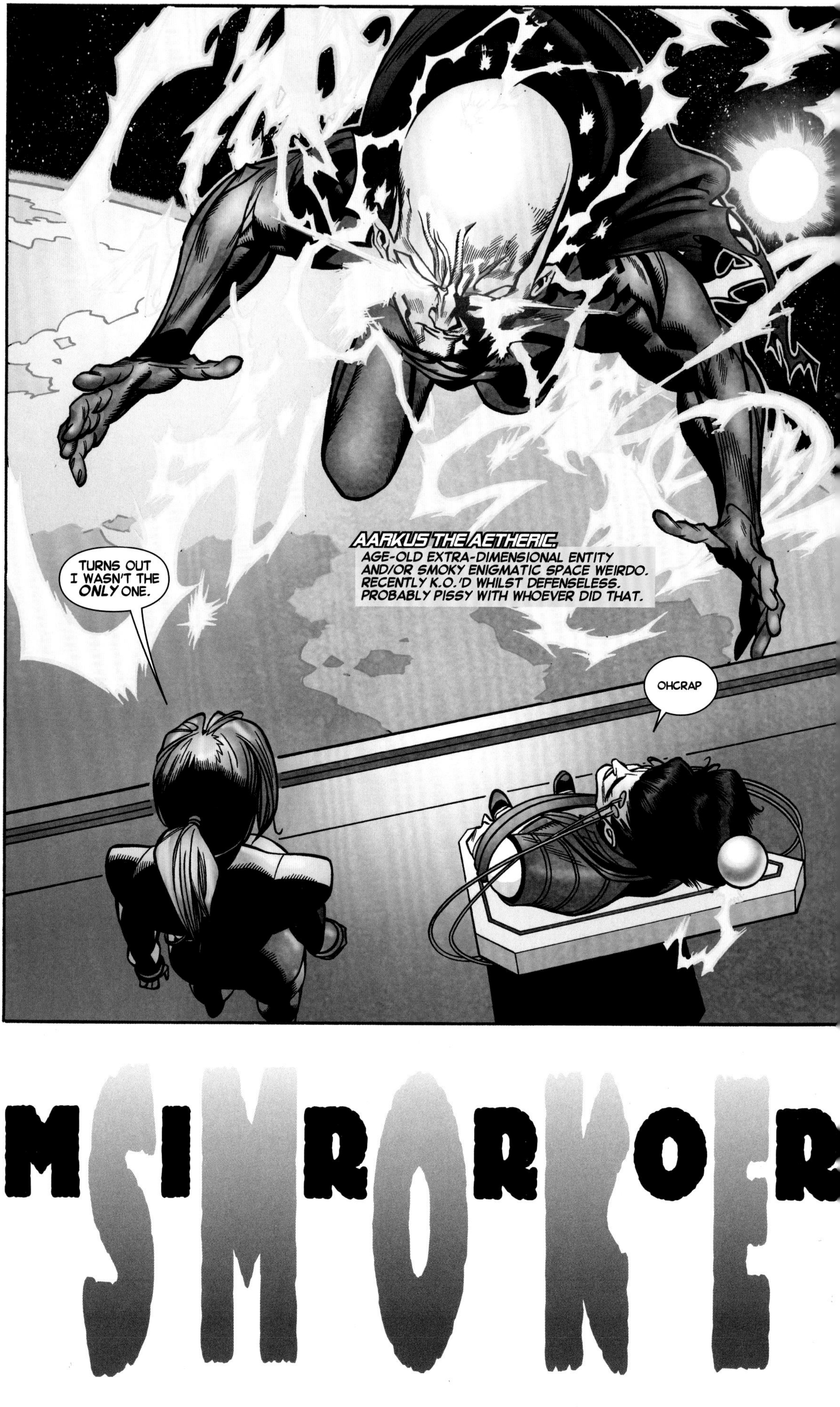
AARKUS THE AETHERIC.
AGE-OLD EXTRA-DIMENSIONAL ENTITY AND/OR SMOKY ENIGMATIC SPACE WEIRDO. RECENTLY K.O.'D WHILST DEFENSELESS. PROBABLY PISSY WITH WHOEVER DID THAT.
TURNS OUT I WASN'T THE ONLY ONE.
OHCRAP
MIRROR
SMOKE

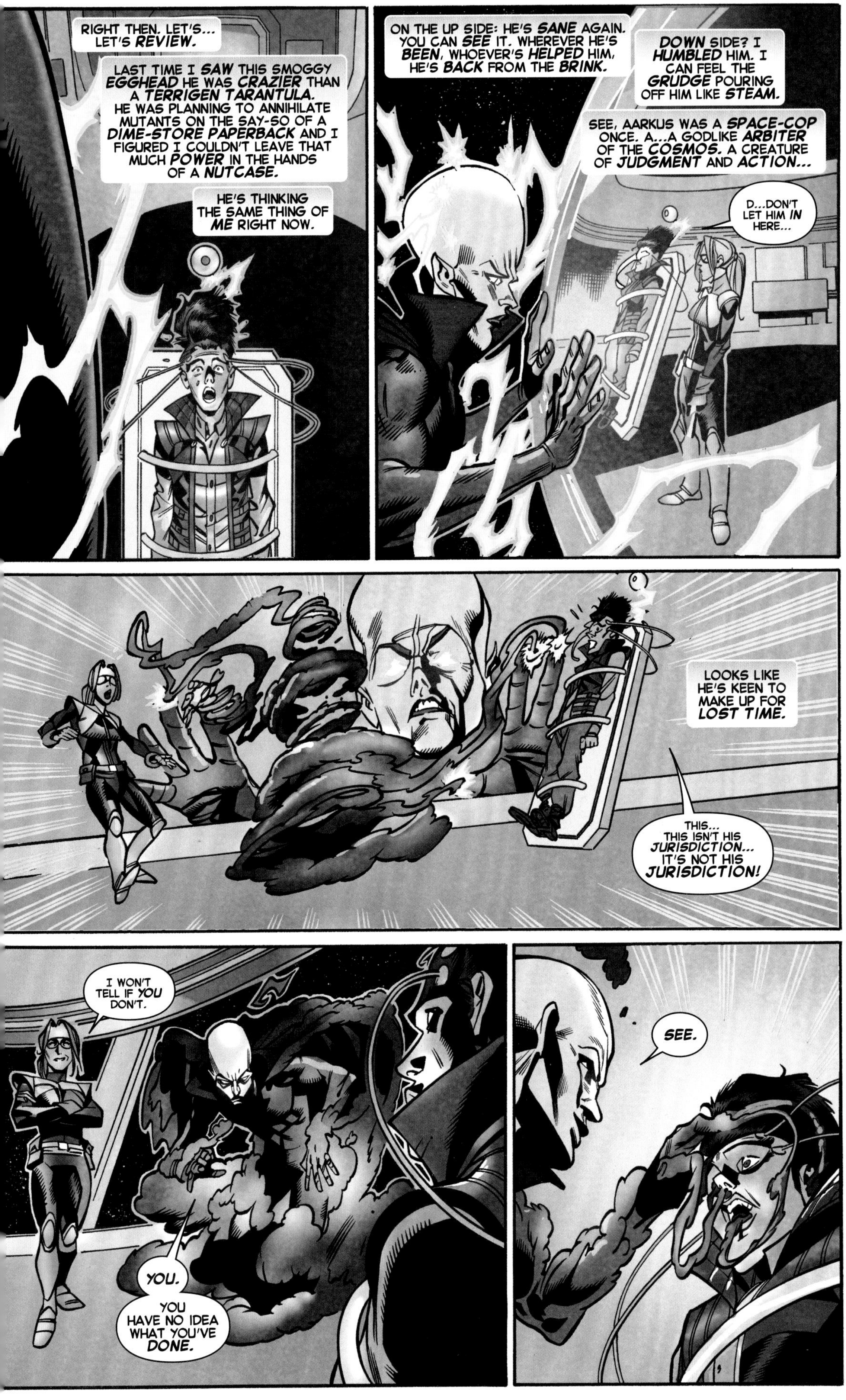

RIGHT THEN. LET'S... LET'S REVIEW.
LAST TIME I SAW THIS SMOGGY EGGHEAD HE WAS CRAZIER THAN A TERRIGEN TARANTULA. HE WAS PLANNING TO ANNIHILATE MUTANTS ON THE SAY-SO OF A DIME-STORE PAPERBACK AND I FIGURED I COULDN'T LEAVE THAT MUCH POWER IN THE HANDS OF A NUTCASE.
HE'S THINKING THE SAME THING OF ME RIGHT NOW.
ON THE UP SIDE: HE'S SANE AGAIN. YOU CAN SEE IT. WHEREVER HE'S BEEN, WHOEVER'S HELPED HIM, HE'S BACK FROM THE BRINK.
DOWN SIDE? I HUMBLED HIM. I CAN FEEL THE GRUDGE POURING OFF HIM LIKE STEAM.
SEE, AARKUS WAS A SPACE-COP ONCE. A...A GODLIKE ARBITER OF THE COSMOS. A CREATURE OF JUDGMENT AND ACTION...
D...DON'T LET HIM IN HERE...
LOOKS LIKE HE'S KEEN TO MAKE UP FOR LOST TIME.
THIS... THIS ISN'T HIS JURISDICTION... IT'S NOT HIS JURISDICTION!
I WON'T TELL IF YOU DON'T.
YOU.
YOU HAVE NO IDEA WHAT YOU'VE DONE.
SEE.

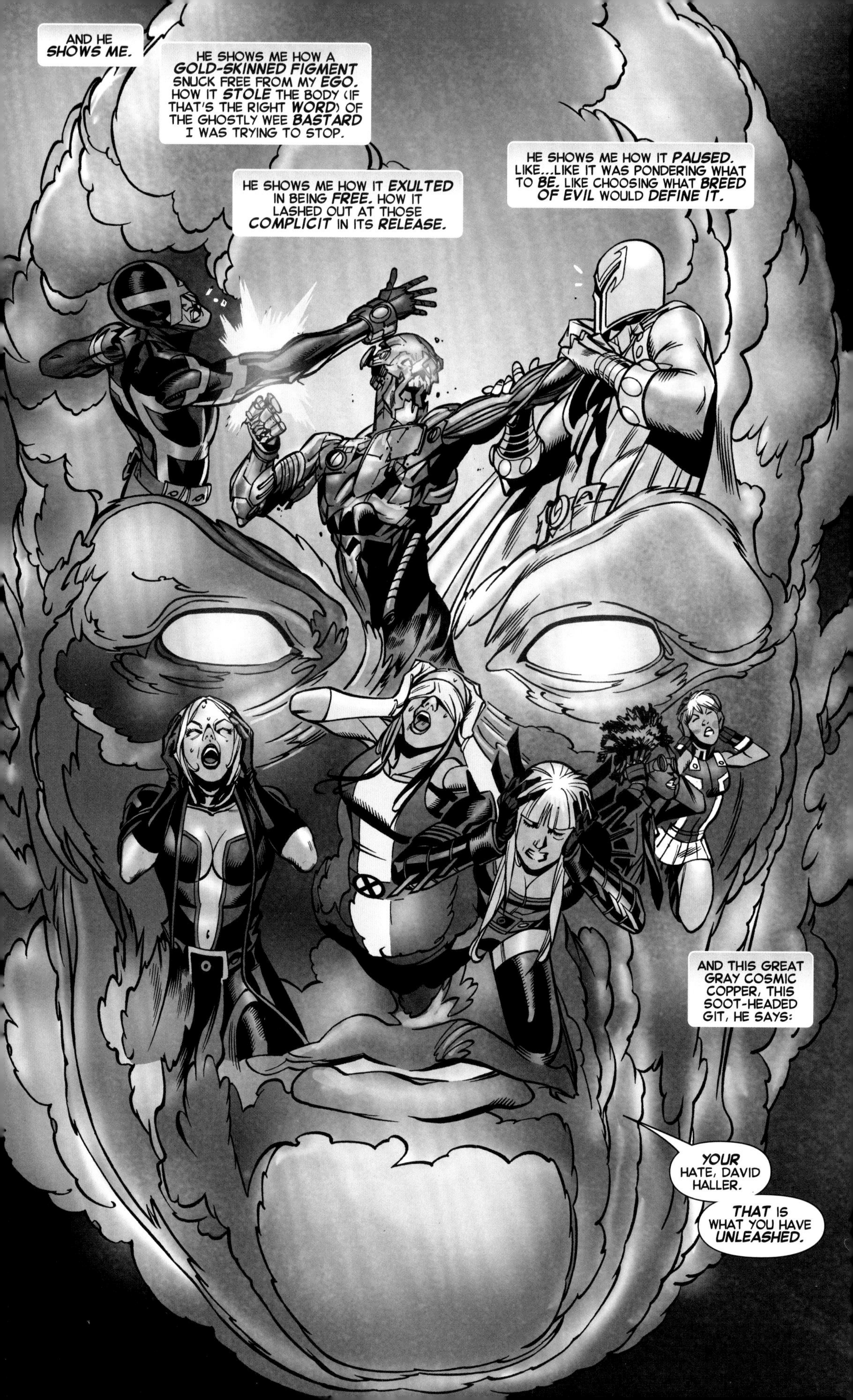

AND HE SHOWS ME.
HE SHOWS ME HOW A GOLD-SKINNED FIGMENT SNUCK FREE FROM MY EGO. HOW IT STOLE THE BODY (IF THAT'S THE RIGHT WORD) OF THE GHOSTLY WEE BASTARD I WAS TRYING TO STOP.
HE SHOWS ME HOW IT EXULTED IN BEING FREE. HOW IT LASHED OUT AT THOSE COMPLICIT IN ITS RELEASE.
HE SHOWS ME HOW IT PAUSED. LIKE...LIKE IT WAS PONDERING WHAT TO BE. LIKE CHOOSING WHAT BREED OF EVIL WOULD DEFINE IT.
AND THIS GREAT GRAY COSMIC COPPER, THIS SOOT-HEADED GIT, HE SAYS:
YOUR HATE, DAVID HALLER.
THAT IS WHAT YOU HAVE UNLEASHED.

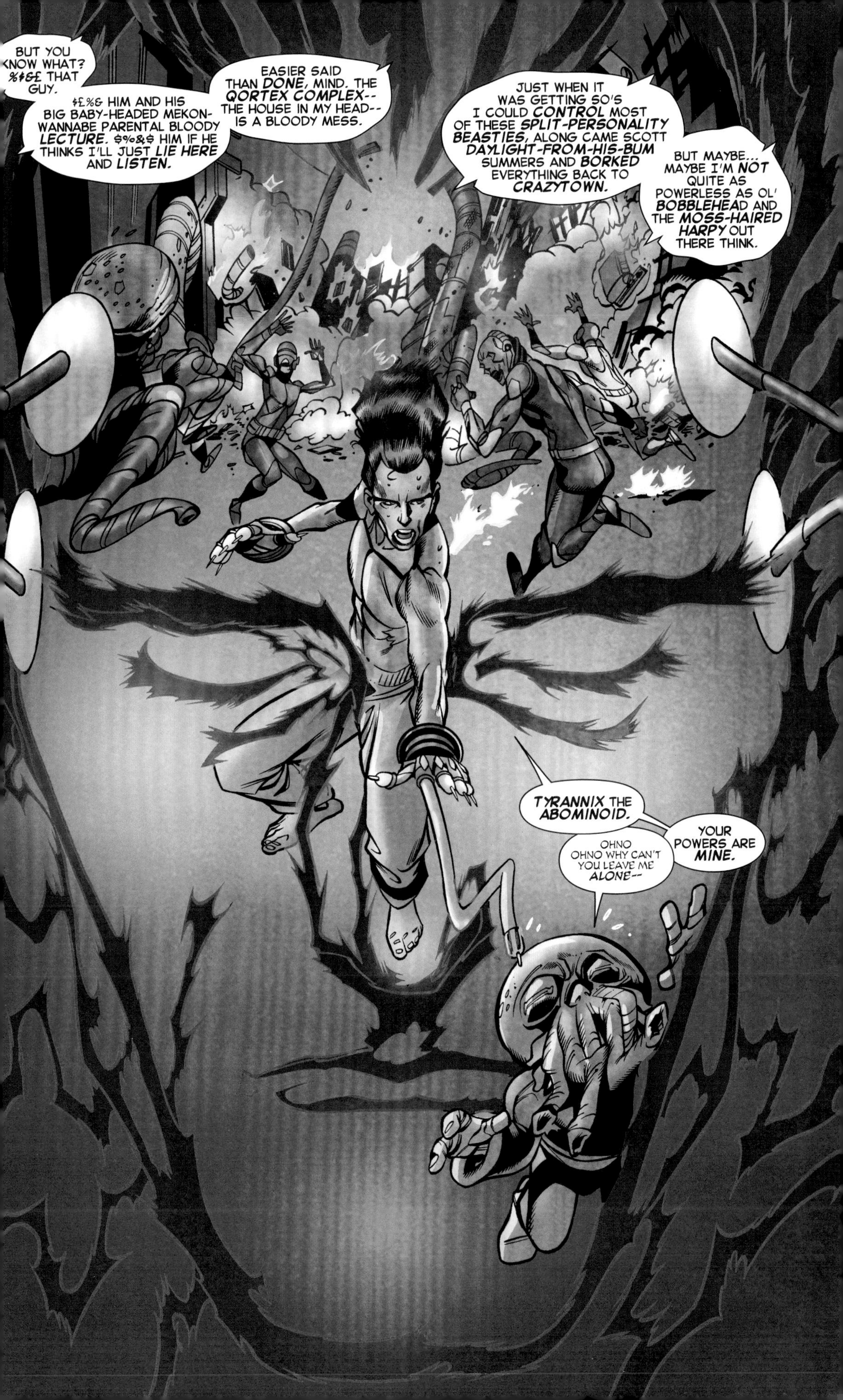

BUT YOU KNOW WHAT? %$&£ THAT GUY.
$£%& HIM AND HIS BIG BABY-HEADED MEKON-WANNABE PARENTAL BLOODY LECTURE. $%&$ HIM IF HE THINKS I'LL JUST LIE HERE AND LISTEN.
EASIER SAID THAN DONE, MIND. THE QORTEX COMPLEX-- THE HOUSE IN MY HEAD-- IS A BLOODY MESS.
JUST WHEN IT WAS GETTING SO'S I COULD CONTROL MOST OF THESE SPLIT-PERSONALITY BEASTIES, ALONG CAME SCOTT DAYLIGHT-FROM-HIS-BUM SUMMERS AND BORKED EVERYTHING BACK TO CRAZYTOWN.
BUT MAYBE... MAYBE I'M NOT QUITE AS POWERLESS AS OL' BOBBLEHEAD AND THE MOSS-HAIRED HARPY OUT THERE THINK.
TYRANNIX THE ABOMINOID.
YOUR POWERS ARE MINE.
OHNO OHNO WHY CAN'T YOU LEAVE ME ALONE--

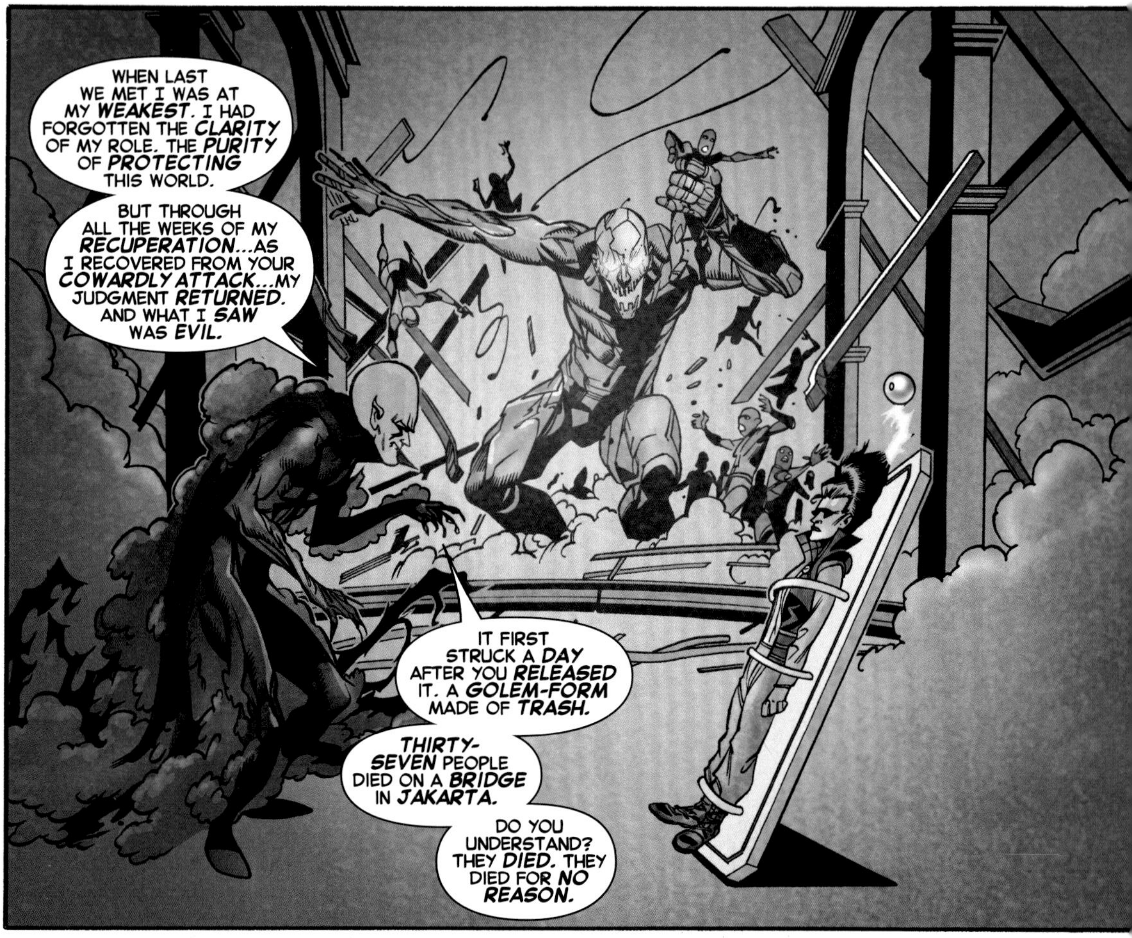
WHEN LAST WE MET I WAS AT MY WEAKEST. I HAD FORGOTTEN THE CLARITY OF MY ROLE. THE PURITY OF PROTECTING THIS WORLD.
BUT THROUGH ALL THE WEEKS OF MY RECUPERATION...AS I RECOVERED FROM YOUR COWARDLY ATTACK...MY JUDGMENT RETURNED. AND WHAT I SAW WAS EVIL.
IT FIRST STRUCK A DAY AFTER YOU RELEASED IT. A GOLEM-FORM MADE OF TRASH.
THIRTY-SEVEN PEOPLE DIED ON A BRIDGE IN JAKARTA.
DO YOU UNDERSTAND? THEY DIED. THEY DIED FOR NO REASON.

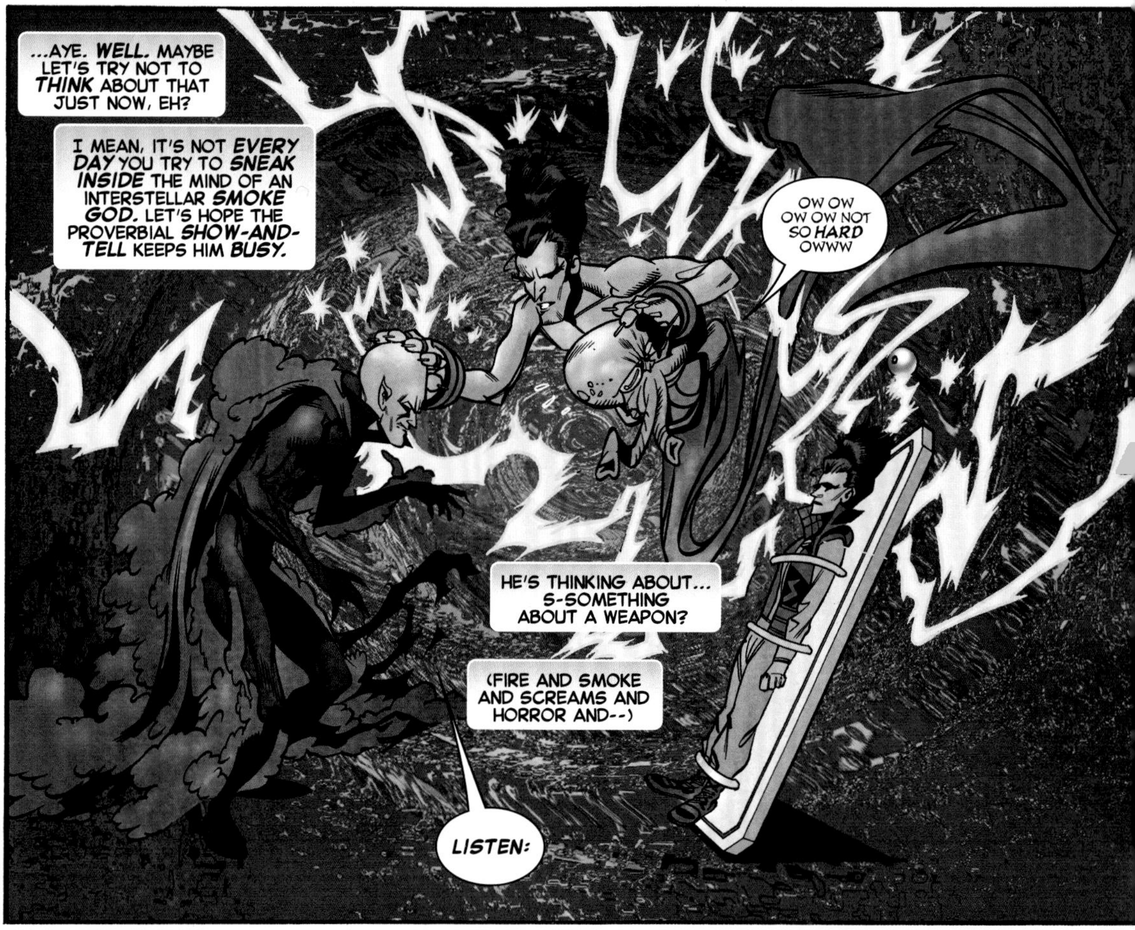
...AYE. WELL. MAYBE LET'S TRY NOT TO THINK ABOUT THAT JUST NOW, EH?
I MEAN, IT'S NOT EVERY DAY YOU TRY TO SNEAK INSIDE THE MIND OF AN INTERSTELLAR SMOKE GOD. LET'S HOPE THE PROVERBIAL SHOW-AND-TELL KEEPS HIM BUSY.
OW OW OW OW NOT SO HARD OWWW
HE'S THINKING ABOUT... S-SOMETHING ABOUT A WEAPON?
(FIRE AND SMOKE AND SCREAMS AND HORROR AND--)
LISTEN:

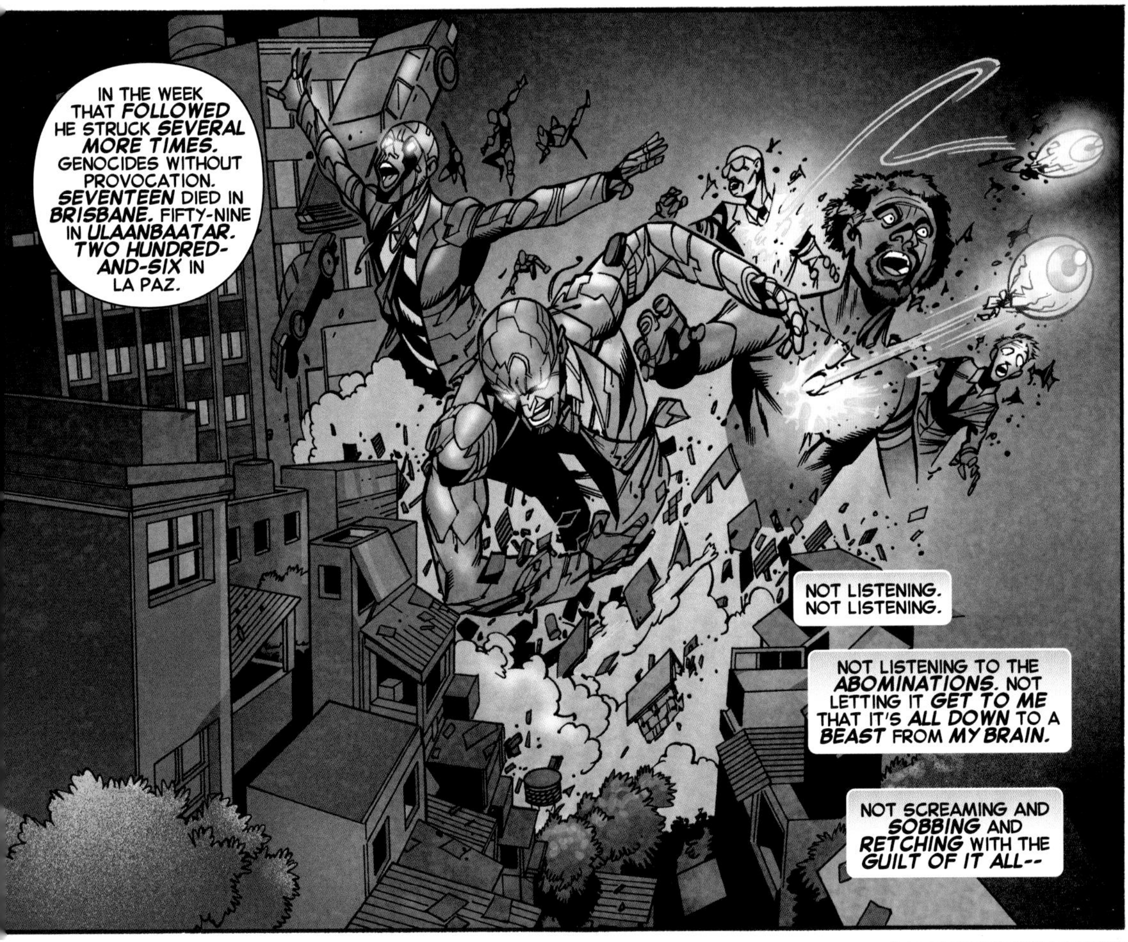
IN THE WEEK THAT FOLLOWED HE STRUCK SEVERAL MORE TIMES. GENOCIDES WITHOUT PROVOCATION. SEVENTEEN DIED IN BRISBANE. FIFTY-NINE IN ULAANBAATAR. TWO HUNDRED-AND-SIX IN LA PAZ.
NOT LISTENING. NOT LISTENING.
NOT LISTENING TO THE ABOMINATIONS. NOT LETTING IT GET TO ME THAT IT'S ALL DOWN TO A BEAST FROM MY BRAIN.
NOT SCREAMING AND SOBBING AND RETCHING WITH THE GUILT OF IT ALL--

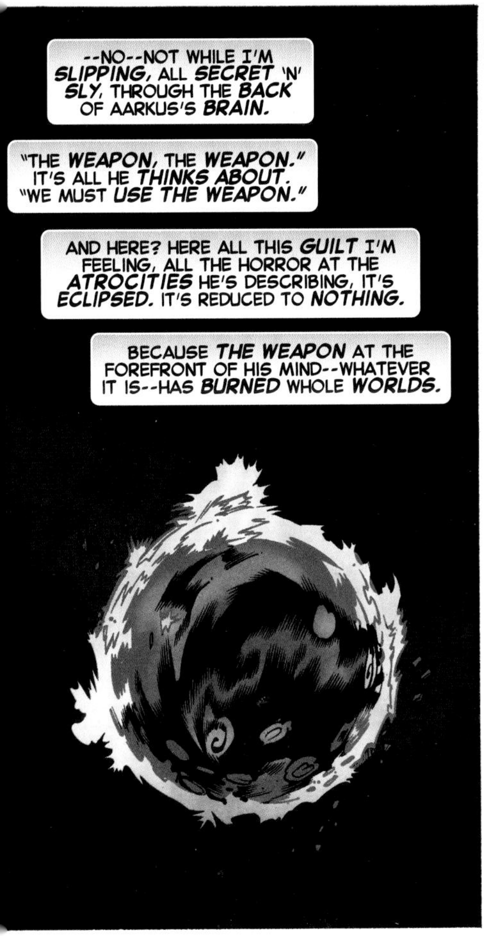
--NO--NOT WHILE I'M SLIPPING, ALL SECRET 'N' SLY, THROUGH THE BACK OF AARKUS'S BRAIN.
"THE WEAPON, THE WEAPON." IT'S ALL HE THINKS ABOUT. "WE MUST USE THE WEAPON."
AND HERE? HERE ALL THIS GUILT I'M FEELING, ALL THE HORROR AT THE ATROCITIES HE'S DESCRIBING, IT'S ECLIPSED. IT'S REDUCED TO NOTHING.
BECAUSE THE WEAPON AT THE FOREFRONT OF HIS MIND--WHATEVER IT IS--HAS BURNED WHOLE WORLDS.

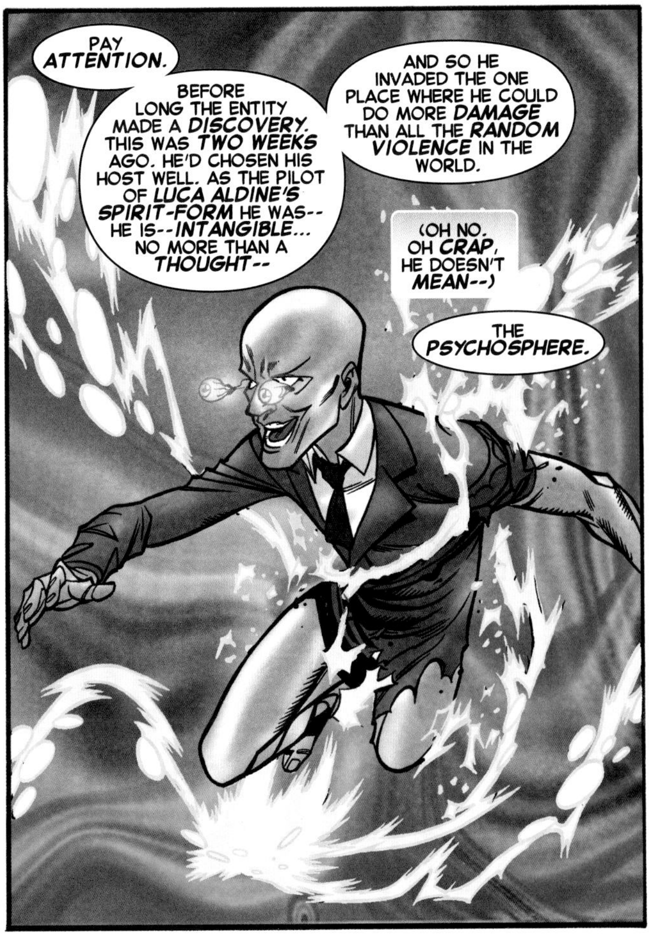
PAY ATTENTION.
BEFORE LONG THE ENTITY MADE A DISCOVERY. THIS WAS TWO WEEKS AGO. HE'D CHOSEN HIS HOST WELL. AS THE PILOT OF LUCA ALDINE'S SPIRIT-FORM HE WAS-- HE IS--INTANGIBLE... NO MORE THAN A THOUGHT--
AND SO HE INVADED THE ONE PLACE WHERE HE COULD DO MORE DAMAGE THAN ALL THE RANDOM VIOLENCE IN THE WORLD.
(OH NO. OH CRAP, HE DOESN'T MEAN--)
THE PSYCHOSPHERE.

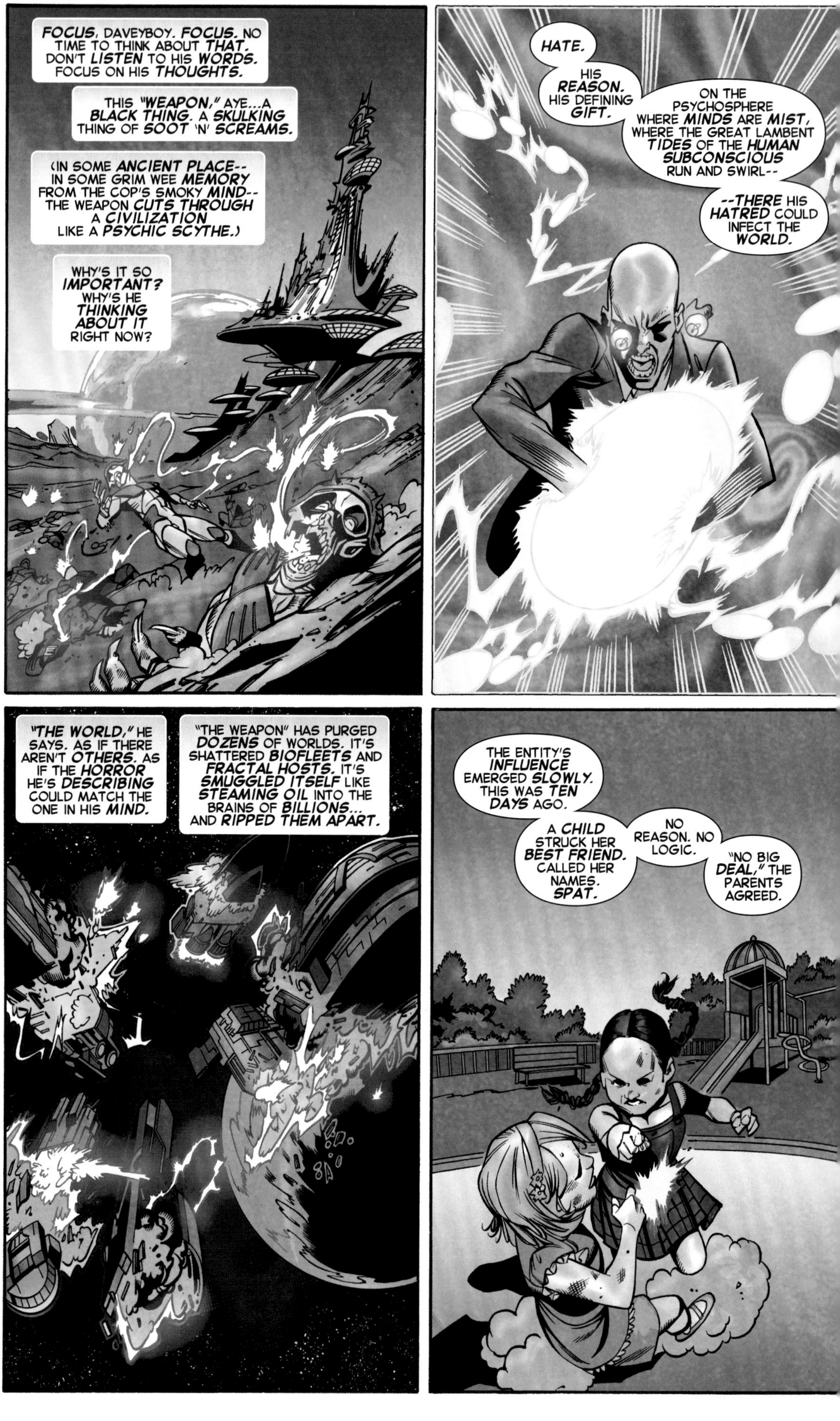
FOCUS, DAVEYBOY. FOCUS. NO TIME TO THINK ABOUT THAT. DON'T LISTEN TO HIS WORDS. FOCUS ON HIS THOUGHTS.
THIS "WEAPON," AYE...A BLACK THING. A SKULKING THING OF SOOT 'N' SCREAMS.
(IN SOME ANCIENT PLACE--IN SOME GRIM WEE MEMORY FROM THE COP'S SMOKY MIND--THE WEAPON CUTS THROUGH A CIVILIZATION LIKE A PSYCHIC SCYTHE.)
WHY'S IT SO IMPORTANT? WHY'S HE THINKING ABOUT IT RIGHT NOW?
HATE.
HIS REASON. HIS DEFINING GIFT.
ON THE PSYCHOSPHERE WHERE MINDS ARE MIST, WHERE THE GREAT LAMBENT TIDES OF THE HUMAN SUBCONSCIOUS RUN AND SWIRL--
--THERE HIS HATRED COULD INFECT THE WORLD.
"THE WORLD," HE SAYS. AS IF THERE AREN'T OTHERS. AS IF THE HORROR HE'S DESCRIBING COULD MATCH THE ONE IN HIS MIND.
"THE WEAPON" HAS PURGED DOZENS OF WORLDS. IT'S SHATTERED BIOFLEETS AND FRACTAL HOSTS. IT'S SMUGGLED ITSELF LIKE STEAMING OIL INTO THE BRAINS OF BILLIONS... AND RIPPED THEM APART.
THE ENTITY'S INFLUENCE EMERGED SLOWLY. THIS WAS TEN DAYS AGO.
A CHILD STRUCK HER BEST FRIEND. CALLED HER NAMES. SPAT.
NO REASON. NO LOGIC.
"NO BIG DEAL," THE PARENTS AGREED.

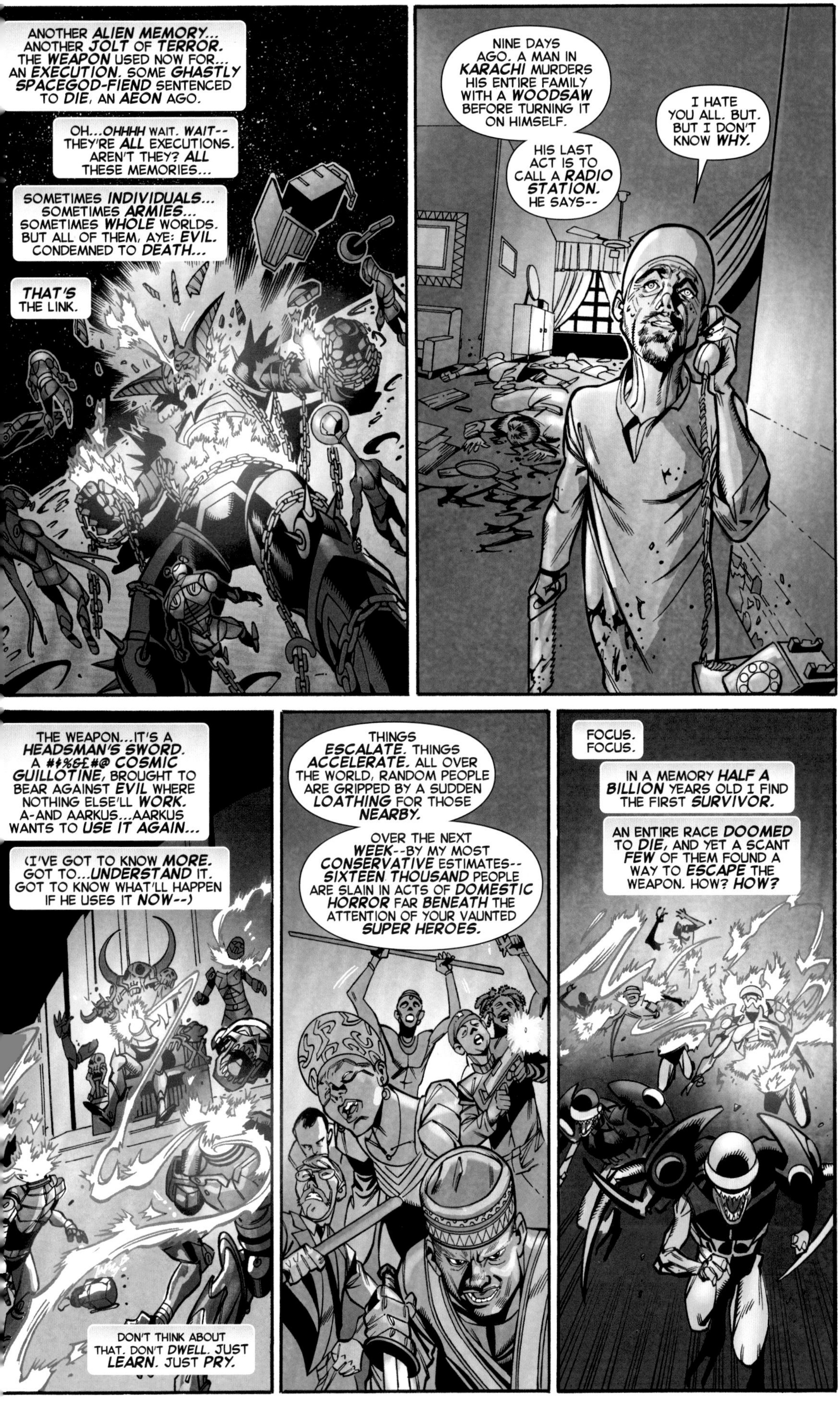
ANOTHER ALIEN MEMORY... ANOTHER JOLT OF TERROR. THE WEAPON USED NOW FOR... AN EXECUTION. SOME GHASTLY SPACEGOD-FIEND SENTENCED TO DIE, AN AEON AGO.
OH...OHHHH WAIT. WAIT-- THEY'RE ALL EXECUTIONS. AREN'T THEY? ALL THESE MEMORIES...
SOMETIMES INDIVIDUALS... SOMETIMES ARMIES... SOMETIMES WHOLE WORLDS. BUT ALL OF THEM, AYE: EVIL. CONDEMNED TO DEATH...
THAT'S THE LINK.
NINE DAYS AGO, A MAN IN KARACHI MURDERS HIS ENTIRE FAMILY WITH A WOODSAW BEFORE TURNING IT ON HIMSELF.
HIS LAST ACT IS TO CALL A RADIO STATION. HE SAYS--
I HATE YOU ALL. BUT. BUT I DON'T KNOW WHY.
THE WEAPON...IT'S A HEADSMAN'S SWORD. A #$%&£#@ COSMIC GUILLOTINE, BROUGHT TO BEAR AGAINST EVIL WHERE NOTHING ELSE'LL WORK. A-AND AARKUS...AARKUS WANTS TO USE IT AGAIN...
(I'VE GOT TO KNOW MORE. GOT TO...UNDERSTAND IT. GOT TO KNOW WHAT'LL HAPPEN IF HE USES IT NOW--)
DON'T THINK ABOUT THAT. DON'T DWELL. JUST LEARN. JUST PRY.
THINGS ESCALATE. THINGS ACCELERATE. ALL OVER THE WORLD, RANDOM PEOPLE ARE GRIPPED BY A SUDDEN LOATHING FOR THOSE NEARBY.
OVER THE NEXT WEEK--BY MY MOST CONSERVATIVE ESTIMATES-- SIXTEEN THOUSAND PEOPLE ARE SLAIN IN ACTS OF DOMESTIC HORROR FAR BENEATH THE ATTENTION OF YOUR VAUNTED SUPER HEROES.
FOCUS. FOCUS.
IN A MEMORY HALF A BILLION YEARS OLD I FIND THE FIRST SURVIVOR.
AN ENTIRE RACE DOOMED TO DIE, AND YET A SCANT FEW OF THEM FOUND A WAY TO ESCAPE THE WEAPON. HOW? HOW?

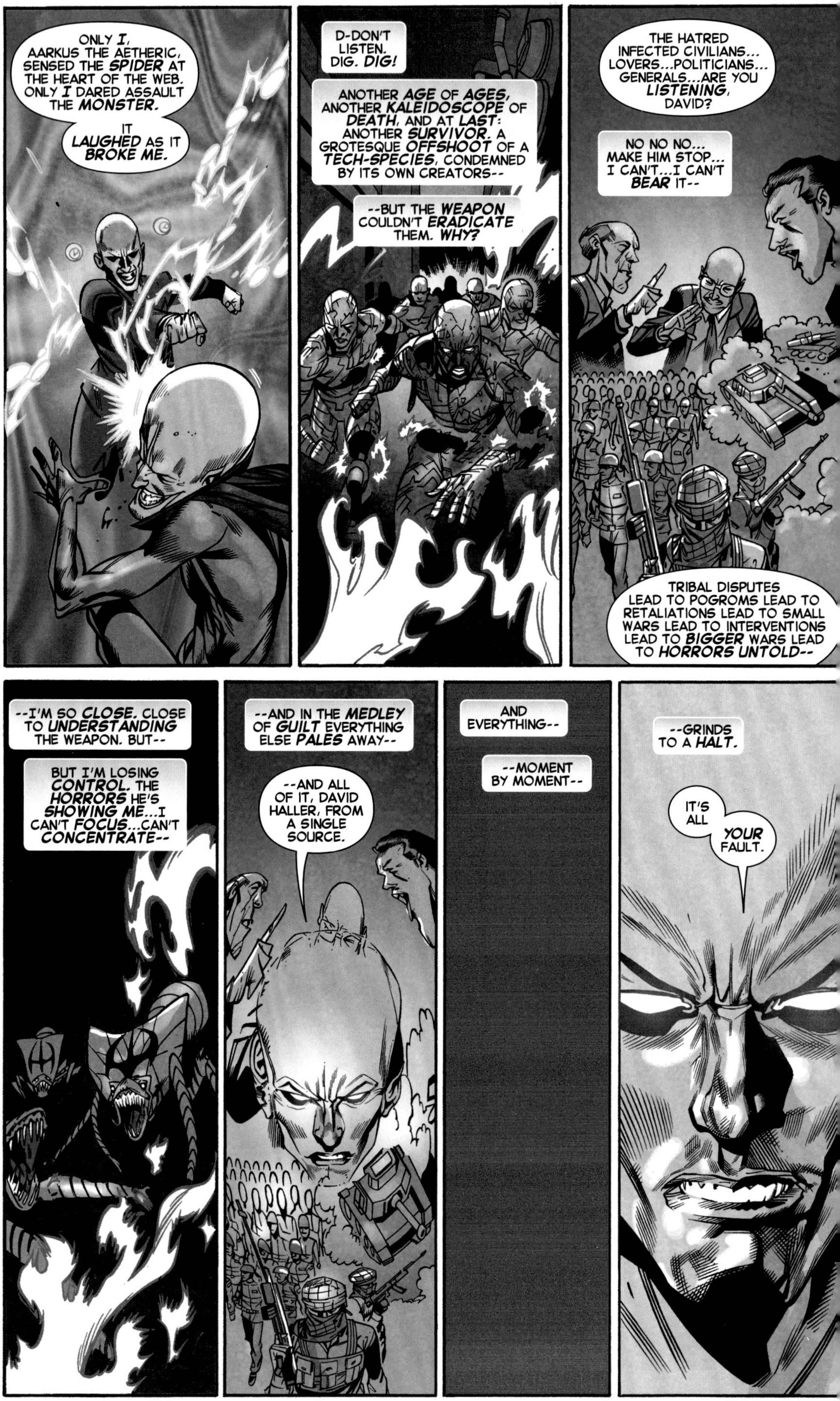

ONLY I, AARKUS THE AETHERIC, SENSED THE SPIDER AT THE HEART OF THE WEB. ONLY I DARED ASSAULT THE MONSTER.
IT LAUGHED AS IT BROKE ME.
D-DON'T LISTEN. DIG. DIG!
ANOTHER AGE OF AGES, ANOTHER KALEIDOSCOPE OF DEATH, AND AT LAST: ANOTHER SURVIVOR. A GROTESQUE OFFSHOOT OF A TECH-SPECIES, CONDEMNED BY ITS OWN CREATORS--
--BUT THE WEAPON COULDN'T ERADICATE THEM. WHY?
THE HATRED INFECTED CIVILIANS... LOVERS...POLITICIANS... GENERALS...ARE YOU LISTENING, DAVID?
NO NO NO... MAKE HIM STOP... I CAN'T...I CAN'T BEAR IT--
TRIBAL DISPUTES LEAD TO POGROMS LEAD TO RETALIATIONS LEAD TO SMALL WARS LEAD TO INTERVENTIONS LEAD TO BIGGER WARS LEAD TO HORRORS UNTOLD--
--I'M SO CLOSE. CLOSE TO UNDERSTANDING THE WEAPON. BUT--
BUT I'M LOSING CONTROL. THE HORRORS HE'S SHOWING ME...I CAN'T FOCUS...CAN'T CONCENTRATE--
--AND IN THE MEDLEY OF GUILT EVERYTHING ELSE PALES AWAY--
--AND ALL OF IT, DAVID HALLER, FROM A SINGLE SOURCE.
AND EVERYTHING--
--MOMENT BY MOMENT--
--GRINDS TO A HALT.
IT'S ALL
YOUR FAULT.

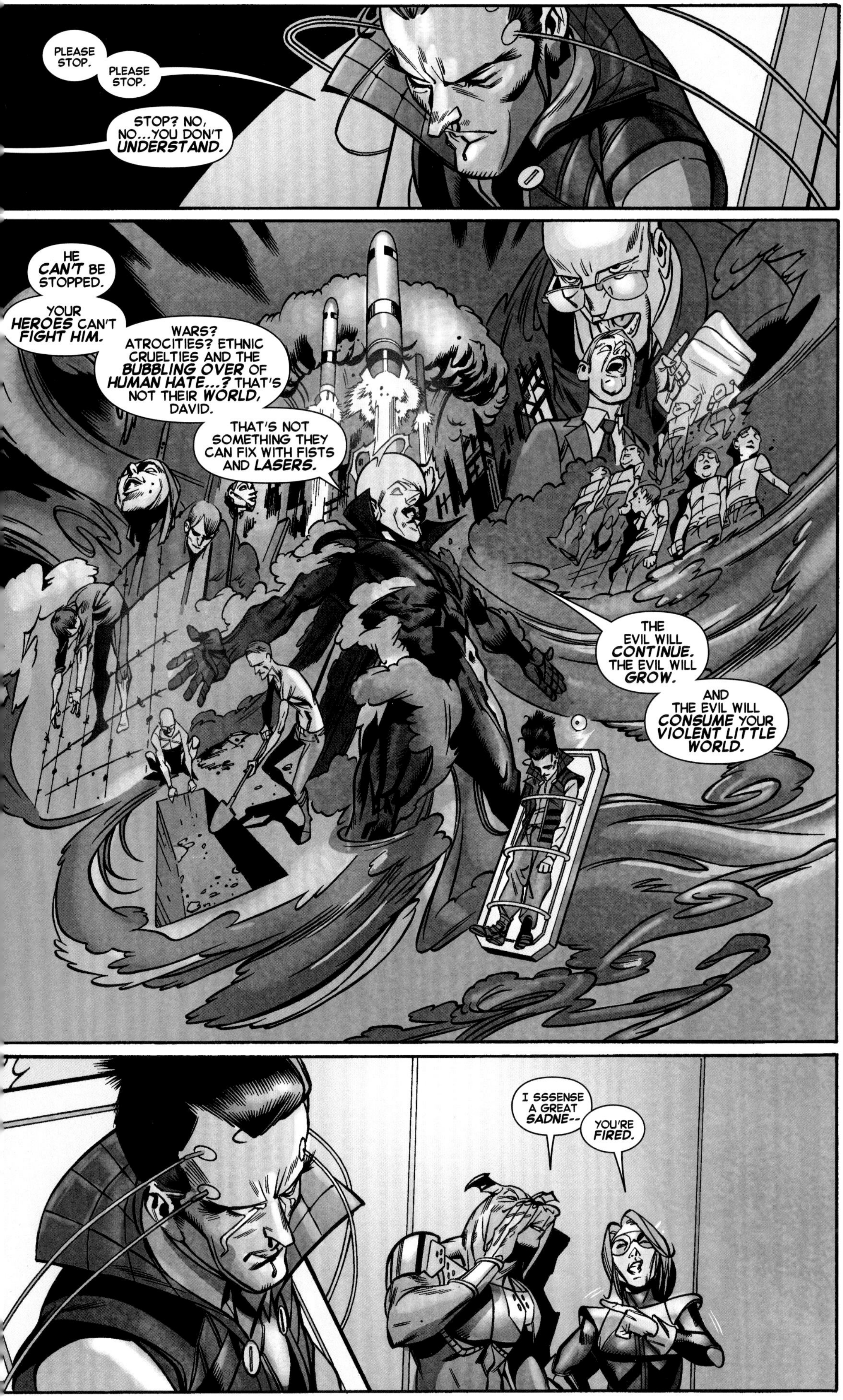

PLEASE STOP.
PLEASE STOP.
STOP? NO, NO...YOU DON'T UNDERSTAND.
HE CAN'T BE STOPPED.
YOUR HEROES CAN'T FIGHT HIM.
WARS? ATROCITIES? ETHNIC CRUELTIES AND THE BUBBLING OVER OF HUMAN HATE...? THAT'S NOT THEIR WORLD, DAVID.
THAT'S NOT SOMETHING THEY CAN FIX WITH FISTS AND LASERS.
THE EVIL WILL CONTINUE. THE EVIL WILL GROW.
AND THE EVIL WILL CONSUME YOUR VIOLENT LITTLE WORLD.
I SSSENSE A GREAT SADNE--
YOU'RE FIRED.

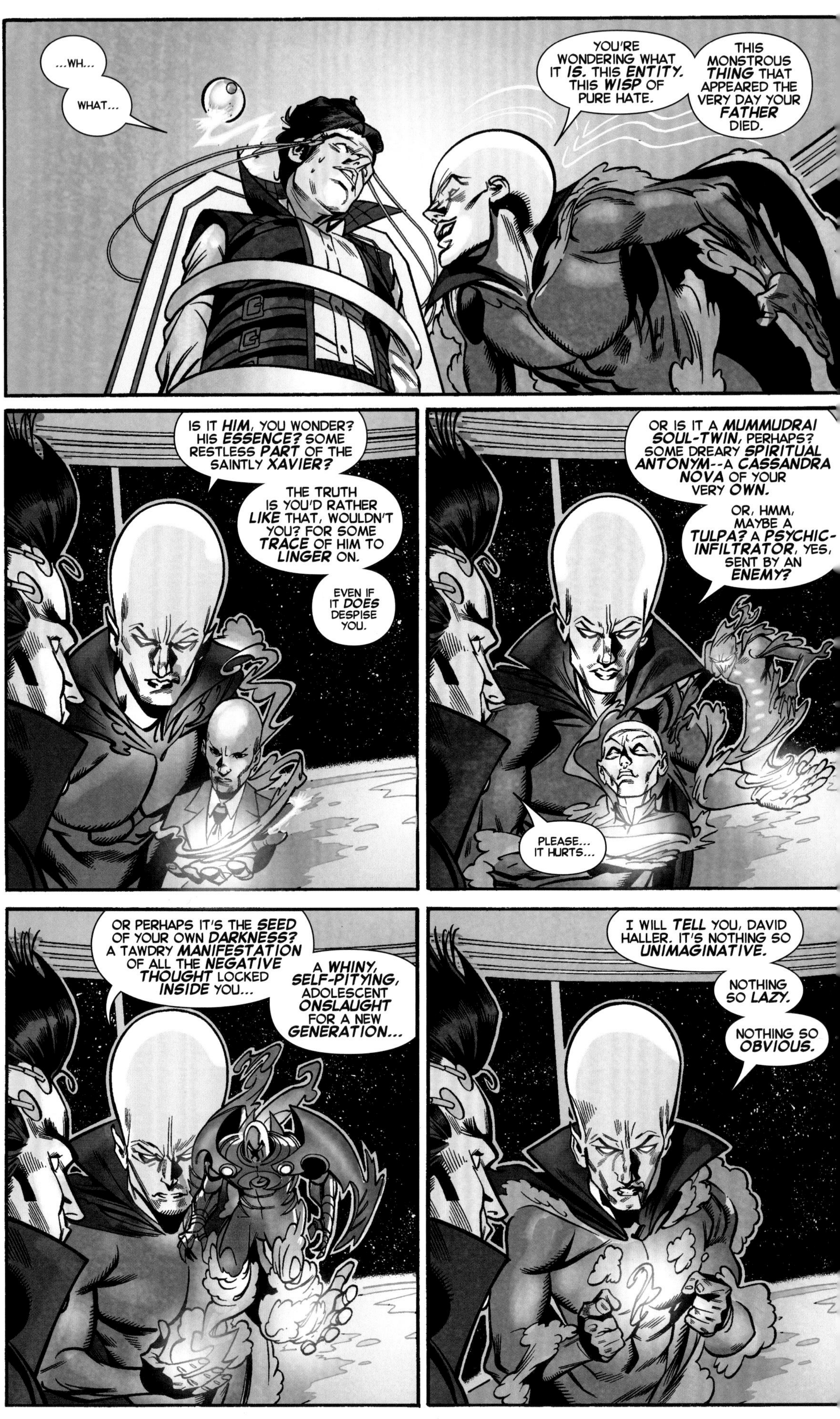
...WH...
WHAT...
YOU'RE WONDERING WHAT IT IS. THIS ENTITY. THIS WISP OF PURE HATE.
THIS MONSTROUS THING THAT APPEARED THE VERY DAY YOUR FATHER DIED.
IS IT HIM, YOU WONDER? HIS ESSENCE? SOME RESTLESS PART OF THE SAINTLY XAVIER?
THE TRUTH IS YOU'D RATHER LIKE THAT, WOULDN'T YOU? FOR SOME TRACE OF HIM TO LINGER ON.
EVEN IF IT DOES DESPISE YOU.
OR IS IT A MUMMUDRAI SOUL-TWIN, PERHAPS? SOME DREARY SPIRITUAL ANTONYM--A CASSANDRA NOVA OF YOUR VERY OWN.
OR, HMM, MAYBE A TULPA? A PSYCHIC-INFILTRATOR, YES, SENT BY AN ENEMY?
PLEASE... IT HURTS...
OR PERHAPS IT'S THE SEED OF YOUR OWN DARKNESS? A TAWDRY MANIFESTATION OF ALL THE NEGATIVE THOUGHT LOCKED INSIDE YOU...
A WHINY, SELF-PITYING, ADOLESCENT ONSLAUGHT FOR A NEW GENERATION...
I WILL TELL YOU, DAVID HALLER. IT'S NOTHING SO UNIMAGINATIVE.
NOTHING SO LAZY.
NOTHING SO OBVIOUS.

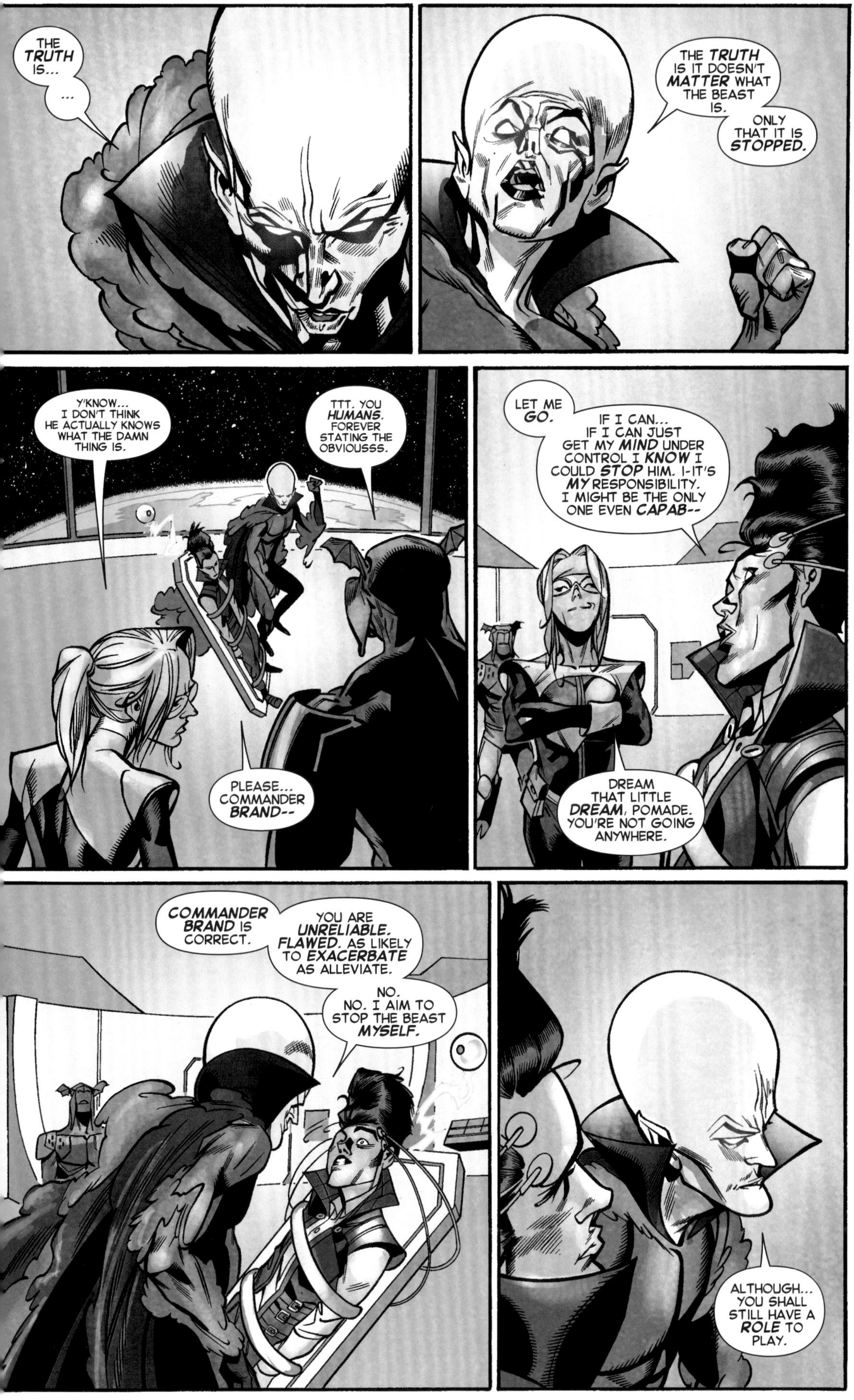

THE TRUTH IS...
...
THE TRUTH IS IT DOESN'T MATTER WHAT THE BEAST IS.
ONLY THAT IT IS STOPPED.
Y'KNOW... I DON'T THINK HE ACTUALLY KNOWS WHAT THE DAMN THING IS.
TTT. YOU HUMANS. FOREVER STATING THE OBVIOUSSS.
PLEASE... COMMANDER BRAND--
LET ME GO.
IF I CAN... IF I CAN JUST GET MY MIND UNDER CONTROL I KNOW I COULD STOP HIM. I-IT'S MY RESPONSIBILITY. I MIGHT BE THE ONLY ONE EVEN CAPAB--
DREAM THAT LITTLE DREAM, POMADE. YOU'RE NOT GOING ANYWHERE.
COMMANDER BRAND IS CORRECT.
YOU ARE UNRELIABLE. FLAWED. AS LIKELY TO EXACERBATE AS ALLEVIATE.
NO. NO. I AIM TO STOP THE BEAST MYSELF.
ALTHOUGH... YOU SHALL STILL HAVE A ROLE TO PLAY.

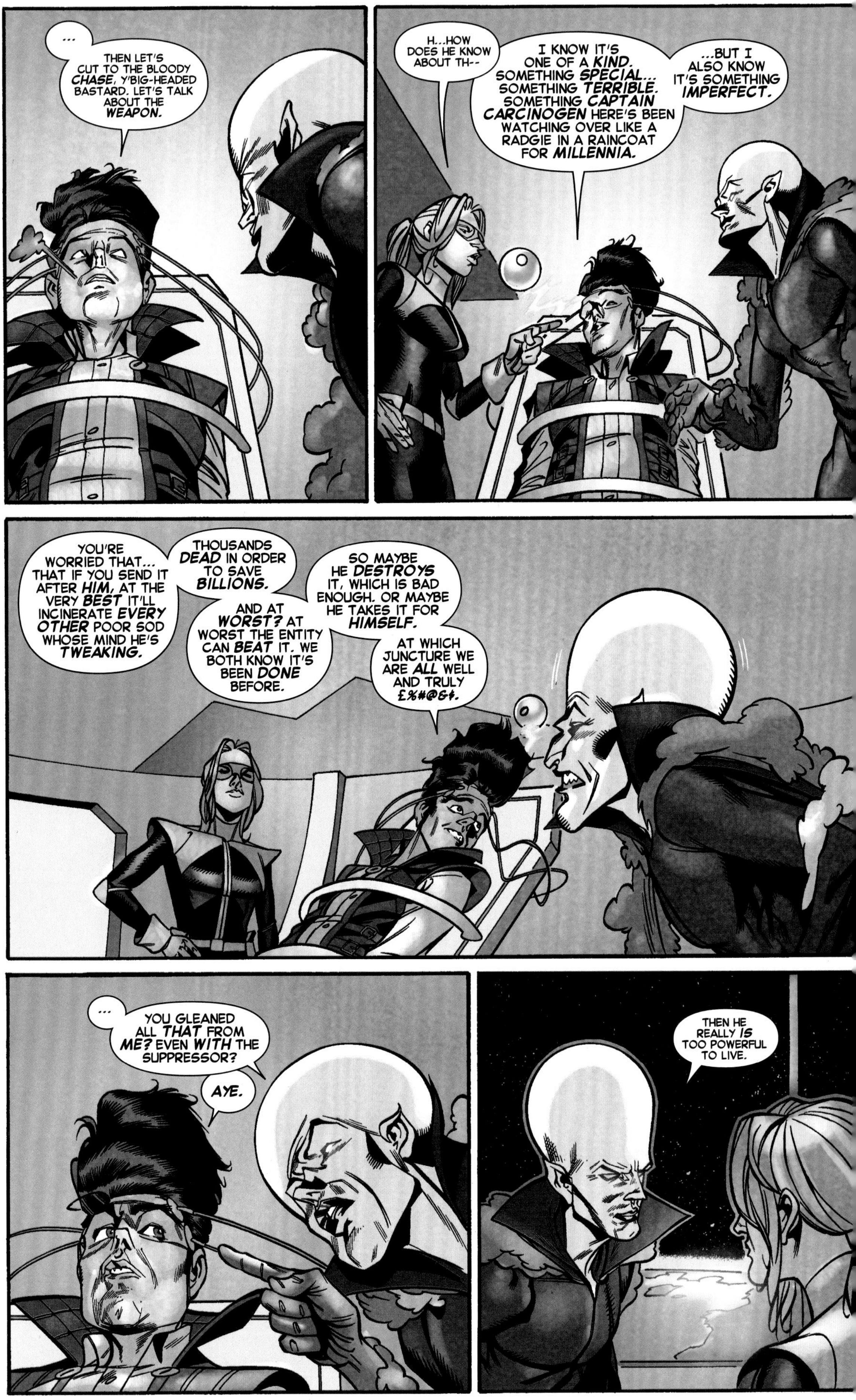
...
THEN LET'S CUT TO THE BLOODY CHASE, Y'BIG-HEADED BASTARD. LET'S TALK ABOUT THE WEAPON.
H...HOW DOES HE KNOW ABOUT TH--
I KNOW IT'S ONE OF A KIND. SOMETHING SPECIAL... SOMETHING TERRIBLE. SOMETHING CAPTAIN CARCINOGEN HERE'S BEEN WATCHING OVER LIKE A RADGIE IN A RAINCOAT FOR MILLENNIA.
...BUT I ALSO KNOW IT'S SOMETHING IMPERFECT.
YOU'RE WORRIED THAT... THAT IF YOU SEND IT AFTER HIM, AT THE VERY BEST IT'LL INCINERATE EVERY OTHER POOR SOD WHOSE MIND HE'S TWEAKING.
THOUSANDS DEAD IN ORDER TO SAVE BILLIONS.
AND AT WORST? AT WORST THE ENTITY CAN BEAT IT. WE BOTH KNOW IT'S BEEN DONE BEFORE.
SO MAYBE HE DESTROYS IT, WHICH IS BAD ENOUGH. OR MAYBE HE TAKES IT FOR HIMSELF.
AT WHICH JUNCTURE WE ARE ALL WELL AND TRULY £%#@&¢.
...
YOU GLEANED ALL THAT FROM ME? EVEN WITH THE SUPPRESSOR?
AYE.
THEN HE REALLY IS TOO POWERFUL TO LIVE.

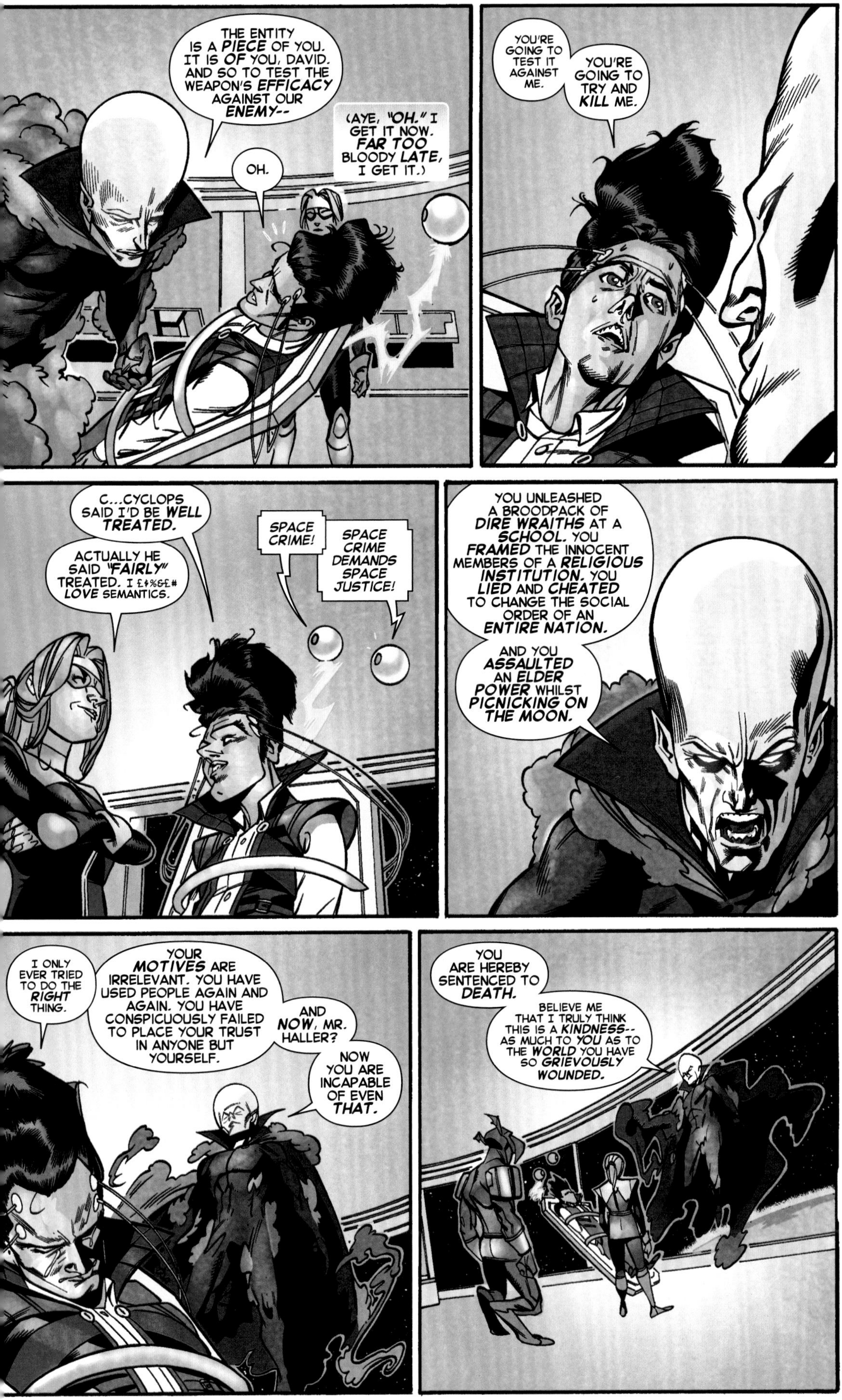
THE ENTITY IS A PIECE OF YOU. IT IS OF YOU, DAVID. AND SO TO TEST THE WEAPON'S EFFICACY AGAINST OUR ENEMY--
OH.
(AYE, "OH." I GET IT NOW. FAR TOO BLOODY LATE, I GET IT.)
YOU'RE GOING TO TEST IT AGAINST ME.
YOU'RE GOING TO TRY AND KILL ME.
C...CYCLOPS SAID I'D BE WELL TREATED.
ACTUALLY HE SAID "FAIRLY" TREATED. I £$%&£# LOVE SEMANTICS.
SPACE CRIME!
SPACE CRIME DEMANDS SPACE JUSTICE!
YOU UNLEASHED A BROODPACK OF DIRE WRAITHS AT A SCHOOL. YOU FRAMED THE INNOCENT MEMBERS OF A RELIGIOUS INSTITUTION. YOU LIED AND CHEATED TO CHANGE THE SOCIAL ORDER OF AN ENTIRE NATION.
AND YOU ASSAULTED AN ELDER POWER WHILST PICNICKING ON THE MOON.
I ONLY EVER TRIED TO DO THE RIGHT THING.
YOUR MOTIVES ARE IRRELEVANT. YOU HAVE USED PEOPLE AGAIN AND AGAIN. YOU HAVE CONSPICUOUSLY FAILED TO PLACE YOUR TRUST IN ANYONE BUT YOURSELF.
AND NOW, MR. HALLER?
NOW YOU ARE INCAPABLE OF EVEN THAT.
YOU ARE HEREBY SENTENCED TO DEATH.
BELIEVE ME THAT I TRULY THINK THIS IS A KINDNESS-- AS MUCH TO YOU AS TO THE WORLD YOU HAVE SO GRIEVOUSLY WOUNDED.

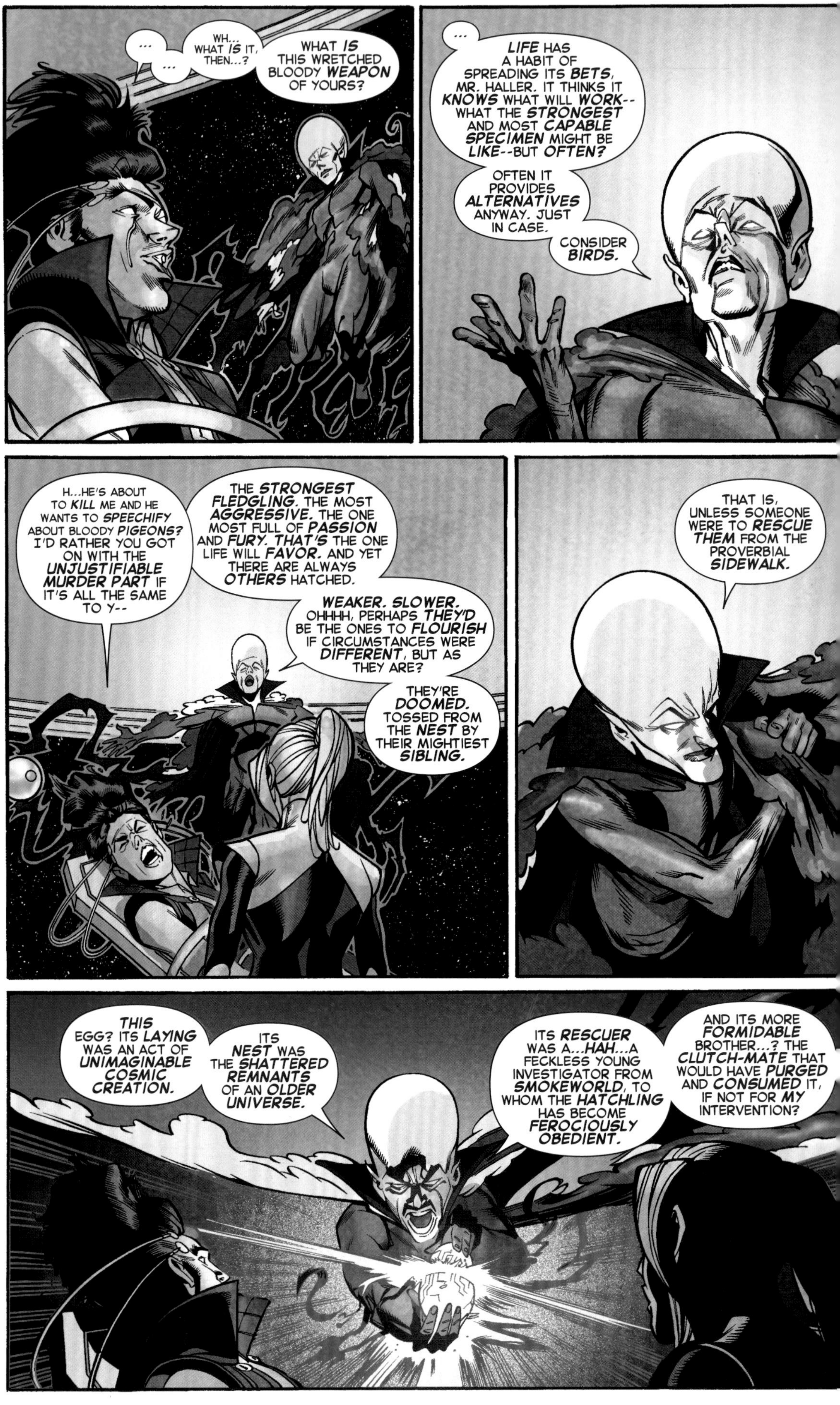
...
...
WH... WHAT IS IT, THEN...?
WHAT IS THIS WRETCHED BLOODY WEAPON OF YOURS?
...
LIFE HAS A HABIT OF SPREADING ITS BETS, MR. HALLER. IT THINKS IT KNOWS WHAT WILL WORK--WHAT THE STRONGEST AND MOST CAPABLE SPECIMEN MIGHT BE LIKE--BUT OFTEN?
OFTEN IT PROVIDES ALTERNATIVES ANYWAY. JUST IN CASE.
CONSIDER BIRDS.
H...HE'S ABOUT TO KILL ME AND HE WANTS TO SPEECHIFY ABOUT BLOODY PIGEONS? I'D RATHER YOU GOT ON WITH THE UNJUSTIFIABLE MURDER PART IF IT'S ALL THE SAME TO Y--
THE STRONGEST FLEDGLING. THE MOST AGGRESSIVE. THE ONE MOST FULL OF PASSION AND FURY. THAT'S THE ONE LIFE WILL FAVOR. AND YET THERE ARE ALWAYS OTHERS HATCHED.
WEAKER. SLOWER. OHHHH, PERHAPS THEY'D BE THE ONES TO FLOURISH IF CIRCUMSTANCES WERE DIFFERENT, BUT AS THEY ARE?
THEY'RE DOOMED. TOSSED FROM THE NEST BY THEIR MIGHTIEST SIBLING.
THAT IS, UNLESS SOMEONE WERE TO RESCUE THEM FROM THE PROVERBIAL SIDEWALK.
THIS EGG? ITS LAYING WAS AN ACT OF UNIMAGINABLE COSMIC CREATION.
ITS NEST WAS THE SHATTERED REMNANTS OF AN OLDER UNIVERSE.
ITS RESCUER WAS A...HAH...A FECKLESS YOUNG INVESTIGATOR FROM SMOKEWORLD, TO WHOM THE HATCHLING HAS BECOME FEROCIOUSLY OBEDIENT.
AND ITS MORE FORMIDABLE BROTHER...? THE CLUTCH-MATE THAT WOULD HAVE PURGED AND CONSUMED IT, IF NOT FOR MY INTERVENTION?

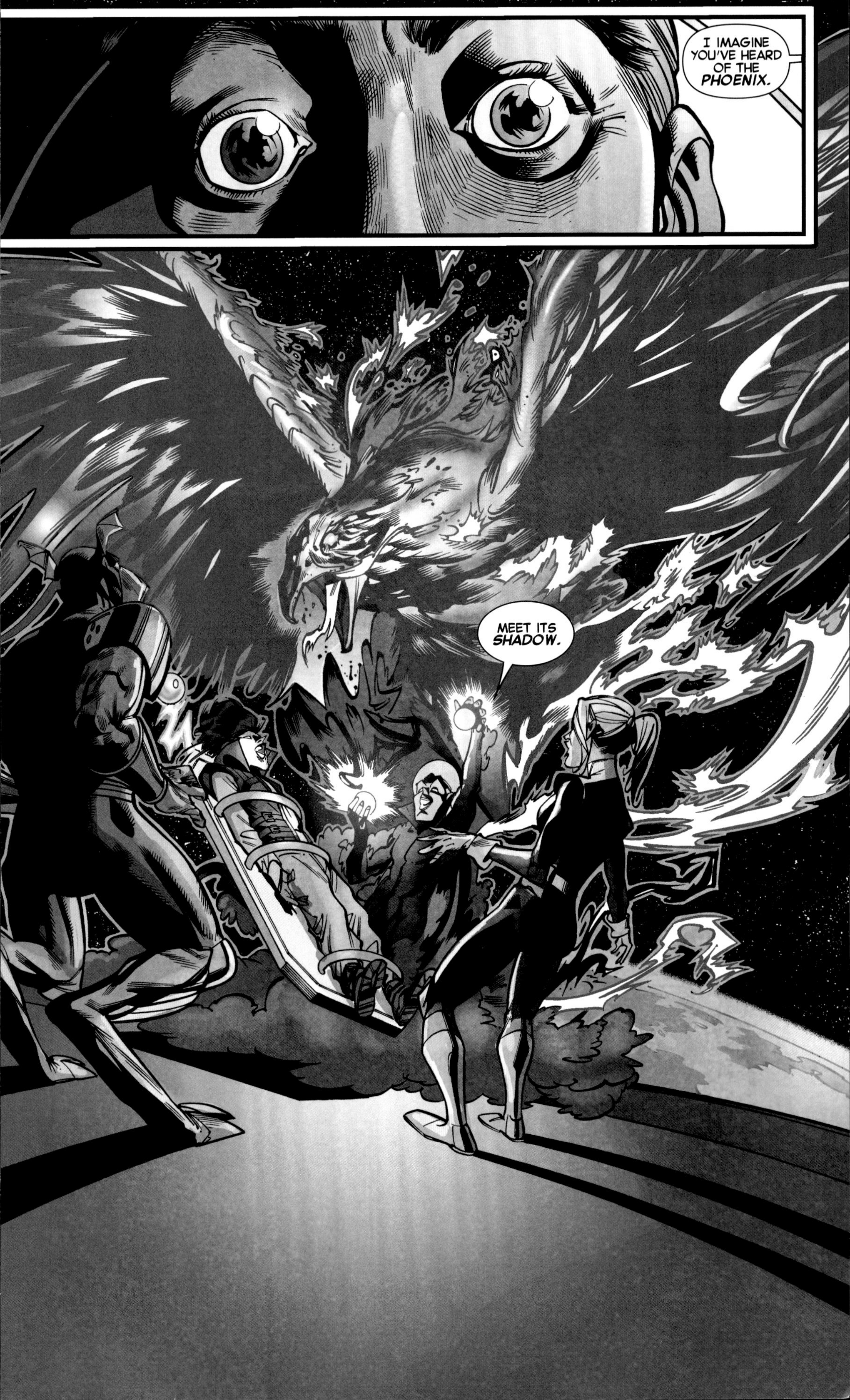
I IMAGINE YOU'VE HEARD OF THE PHOENIX.
MEET ITS SHADOW.

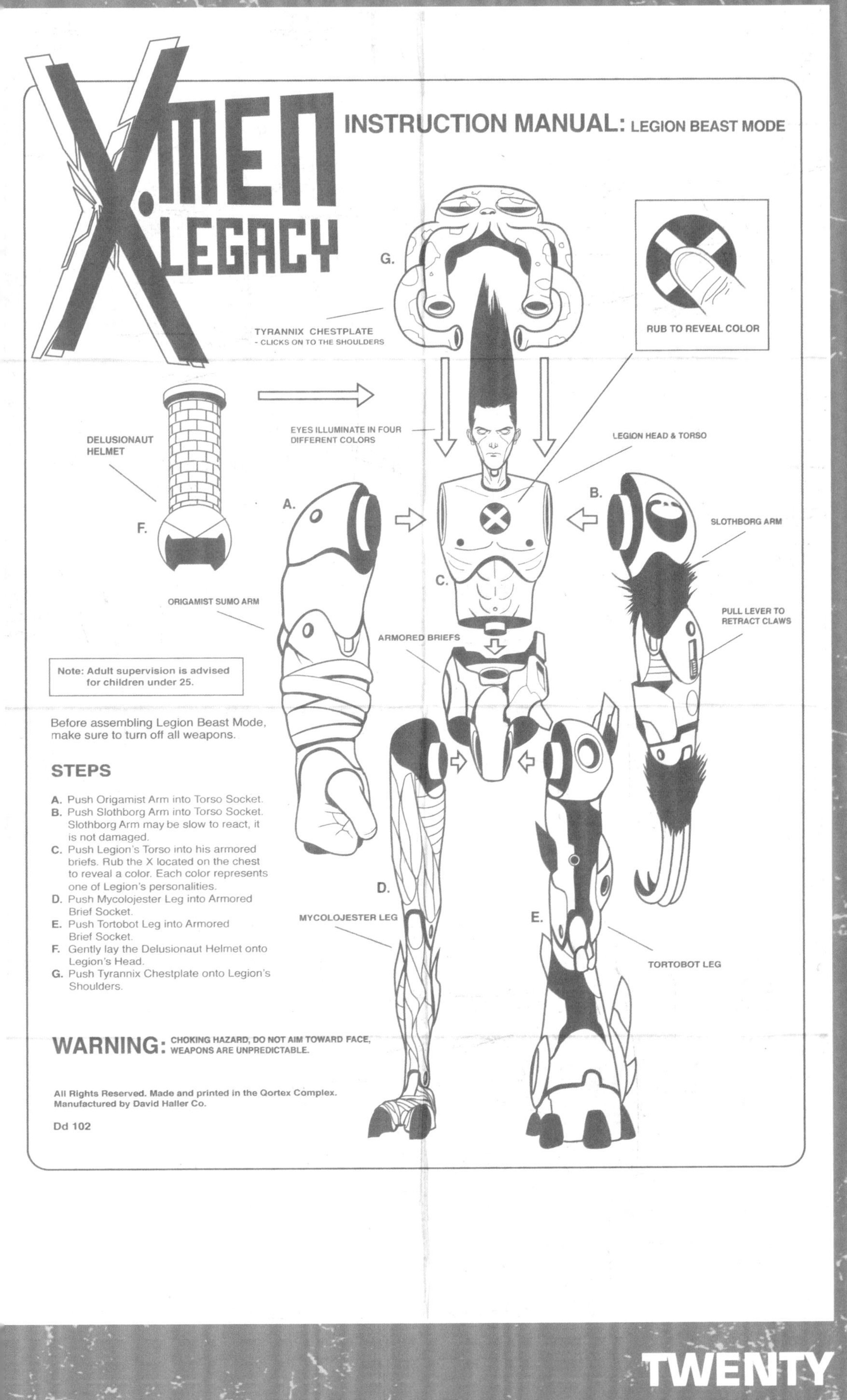
X-MEN LEGACY
INSTRUCTION MANUAL: LEGION BEAST MODE
G.
TYRANNIX CHESTPLATE
- CLICKS ON TO THE SHOULDERS
RUB TO REVEAL COLOR
EYES ILLUMINATE IN FOUR DIFFERENT COLORS
DELUSIONAUT HELMET
LEGION HEAD & TORSO
F.
A.
B.
SLOTHBORG ARM
C.
ORIGAMIST SUMO ARM
PULL LEVER TO RETRACT CLAWS
ARMORED BRIEFS
Note: Adult supervision is advised for children under 25.
Before assembling Legion Beast Mode, make sure to turn off all weapons.
STEPS
A. Push Origamist Arm into Torso Socket.
B. Push Slothborg Arm into Torso Socket. Slothborg Arm may be slow to react, it is not damaged.
C. Push Legion's Torso into his armored briefs. Rub the X located on the chest to reveal a color. Each color represents one of Legion's personalities.
D. Push Mycolojester Leg into Armored Brief Socket.
E. Push Tortobot Leg into Armored Brief Socket.
F. Gently lay the Delusionaut Helmet onto Legion's Head.
G. Push Tyrannix Chestplate onto Legion's Shoulders.
D.
MYCOLOJESTER LEG
E.
TORTOBOT LEG
WARNING: CHOKING HAZARD, DO NOT AIM TOWARD FACE, WEAPONS ARE UNPREDICTABLE.
All Rights Reserved. Made and printed in the Qortex Complex.
Manufactured by David Haller Co.
Dd 102
TWENTY

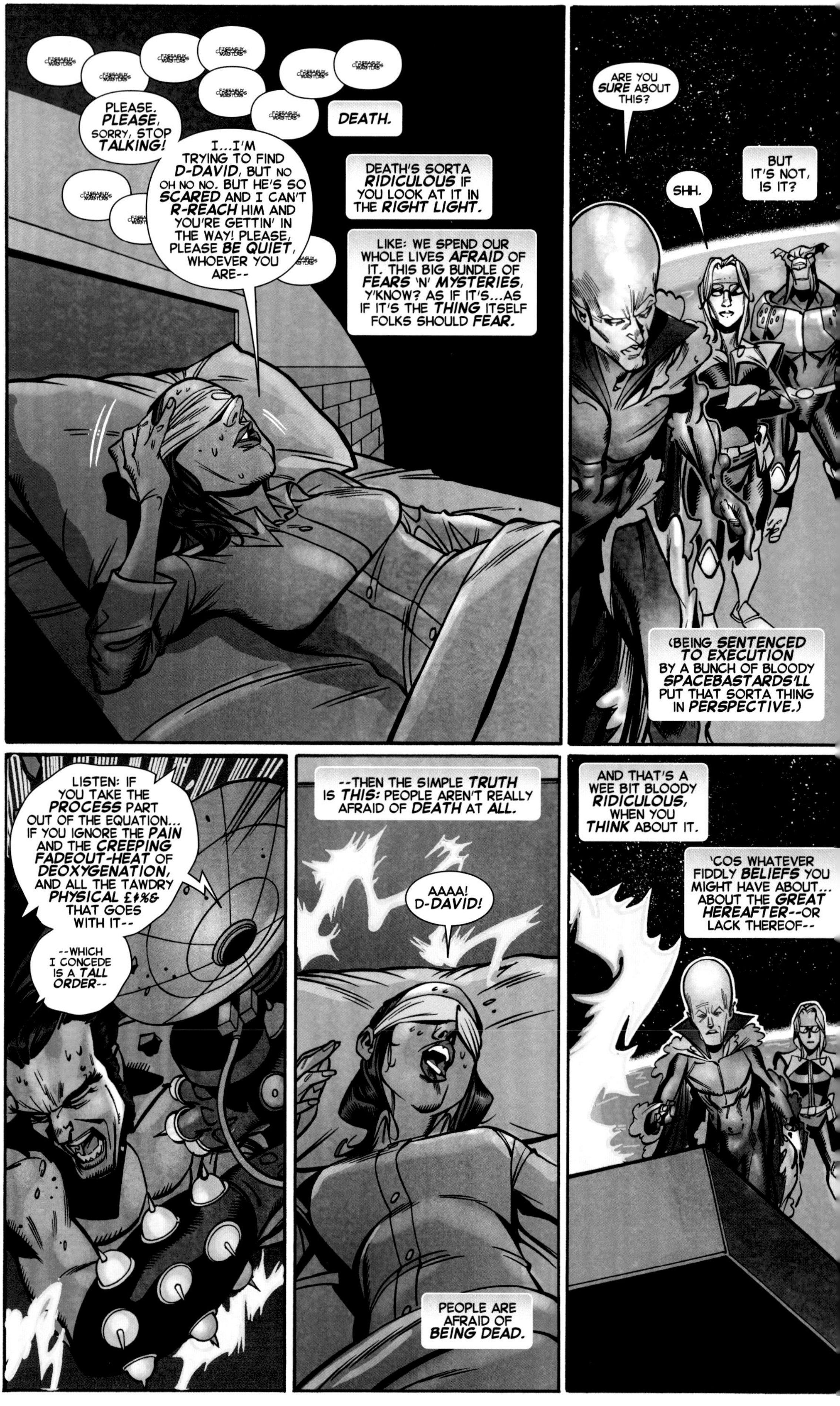

PLEASE. PLEASE, SORRY, STOP TALKING!
DEATH.
I...I'M TRYING TO FIND D-DAVID, BUT NO OH NO NO. BUT HE'S SO SCARED AND I CAN'T R-REACH HIM AND YOU'RE GETTIN' IN THE WAY! PLEASE, PLEASE BE QUIET, WHOEVER YOU ARE--
DEATH'S SORTA RIDICULOUS IF YOU LOOK AT IT IN THE RIGHT LIGHT.
LIKE: WE SPEND OUR WHOLE LIVES AFRAID OF IT. THIS BIG BUNDLE OF FEARS 'N' MYSTERIES, Y'KNOW? AS IF IT'S...AS IF IT'S THE THING ITSELF FOLKS SHOULD FEAR.
ARE YOU SURE ABOUT THIS?
SHH.
BUT IT'S NOT, IS IT?
(BEING SENTENCED TO EXECUTION BY A BUNCH OF BLOODY SPACEBASTARDS'LL PUT THAT SORTA THING IN PERSPECTIVE.)
LISTEN: IF YOU TAKE THE PROCESS PART OUT OF THE EQUATION... IF YOU IGNORE THE PAIN AND THE CREEPING FADEOUT-HEAT OF DEOXYGENATION, AND ALL THE TAWDRY PHYSICAL £$%& THAT GOES WITH IT--
--WHICH I CONCEDE IS A TALL ORDER--
--THEN THE SIMPLE TRUTH IS THIS: PEOPLE AREN'T REALLY AFRAID OF DEATH AT ALL.
AAAA! D-DAVID!
PEOPLE ARE AFRAID OF BEING DEAD.
AND THAT'S A WEE BIT BLOODY RIDICULOUS, WHEN YOU THINK ABOUT IT.
'COS WHATEVER FIDDLY BELIEFS YOU MIGHT HAVE ABOUT... ABOUT THE GREAT HEREAFTER--OR LACK THEREOF--

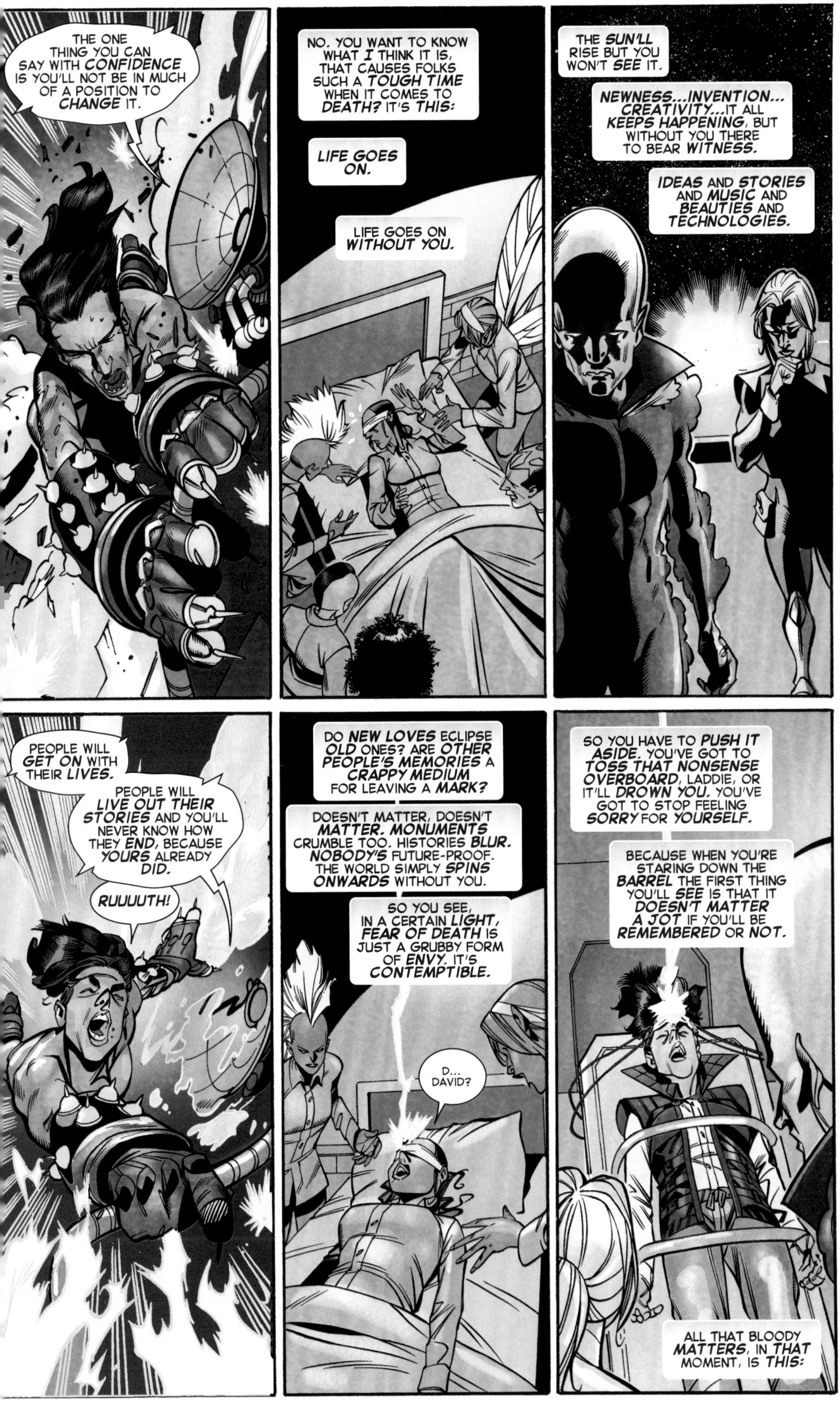
THE ONE THING YOU CAN SAY WITH CONFIDENCE IS YOU'LL NOT BE IN MUCH OF A POSITION TO CHANGE IT.
NO. YOU WANT TO KNOW WHAT I THINK IT IS, THAT CAUSES FOLKS SUCH A TOUGH TIME WHEN IT COMES TO DEATH? IT'S THIS:
LIFE GOES ON.
LIFE GOES ON WITHOUT YOU.
THE SUN'LL RISE BUT YOU WON'T SEE IT.
NEWNESS...INVENTION... CREATIVITY...IT ALL KEEPS HAPPENING, BUT WITHOUT YOU THERE TO BEAR WITNESS.
IDEAS AND STORIES AND MUSIC AND BEAUTIES AND TECHNOLOGIES.
PEOPLE WILL GET ON WITH THEIR LIVES.
PEOPLE WILL LIVE OUT THEIR STORIES AND YOU'LL NEVER KNOW HOW THEY END, BECAUSE YOURS ALREADY DID.
RUUUUTH!
DO NEW LOVES ECLIPSE OLD ONES? ARE OTHER PEOPLE'S MEMORIES A CRAPPY MEDIUM FOR LEAVING A MARK?
DOESN'T MATTER, DOESN'T MATTER. MONUMENTS CRUMBLE TOO. HISTORIES BLUR. NOBODY'S FUTURE-PROOF. THE WORLD SIMPLY SPINS ONWARDS WITHOUT YOU.
SO YOU SEE, IN A CERTAIN LIGHT, FEAR OF DEATH IS JUST A GRUBBY FORM OF ENVY. IT'S CONTEMPTIBLE.
D... DAVID?
SO YOU HAVE TO PUSH IT ASIDE. YOU'VE GOT TO TOSS THAT NONSENSE OVERBOARD, LADDIE, OR IT'LL DROWN YOU. YOU'VE GOT TO STOP FEELING SORRY FOR YOURSELF.
BECAUSE WHEN YOU'RE STARING DOWN THE BARREL THE FIRST THING YOU'LL SEE IS THAT IT DOESN'T MATTER A JOT IF YOU'LL BE REMEMBERED OR NOT.
ALL THAT BLOODY MATTERS, IN THAT MOMENT, IS THIS:

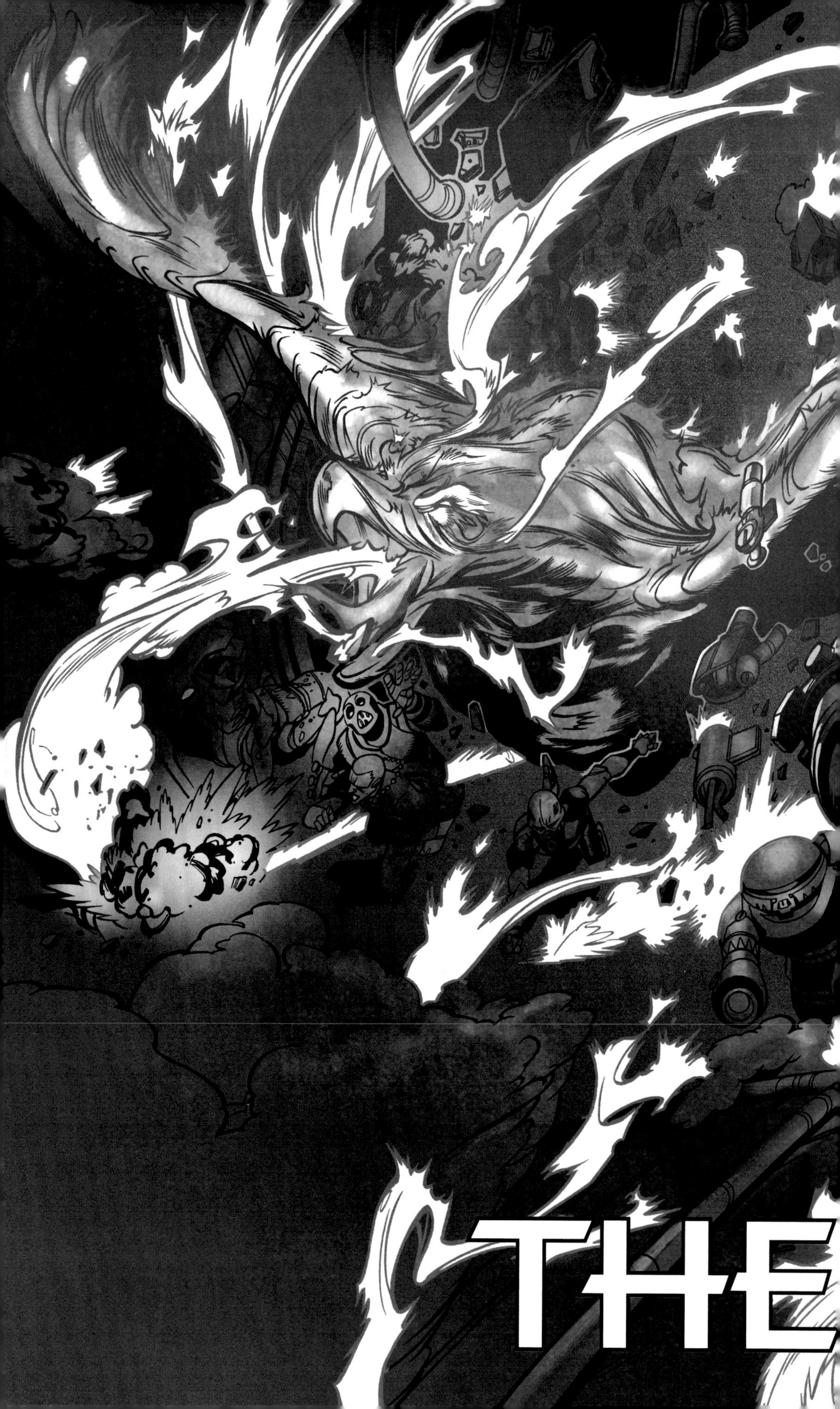
THE

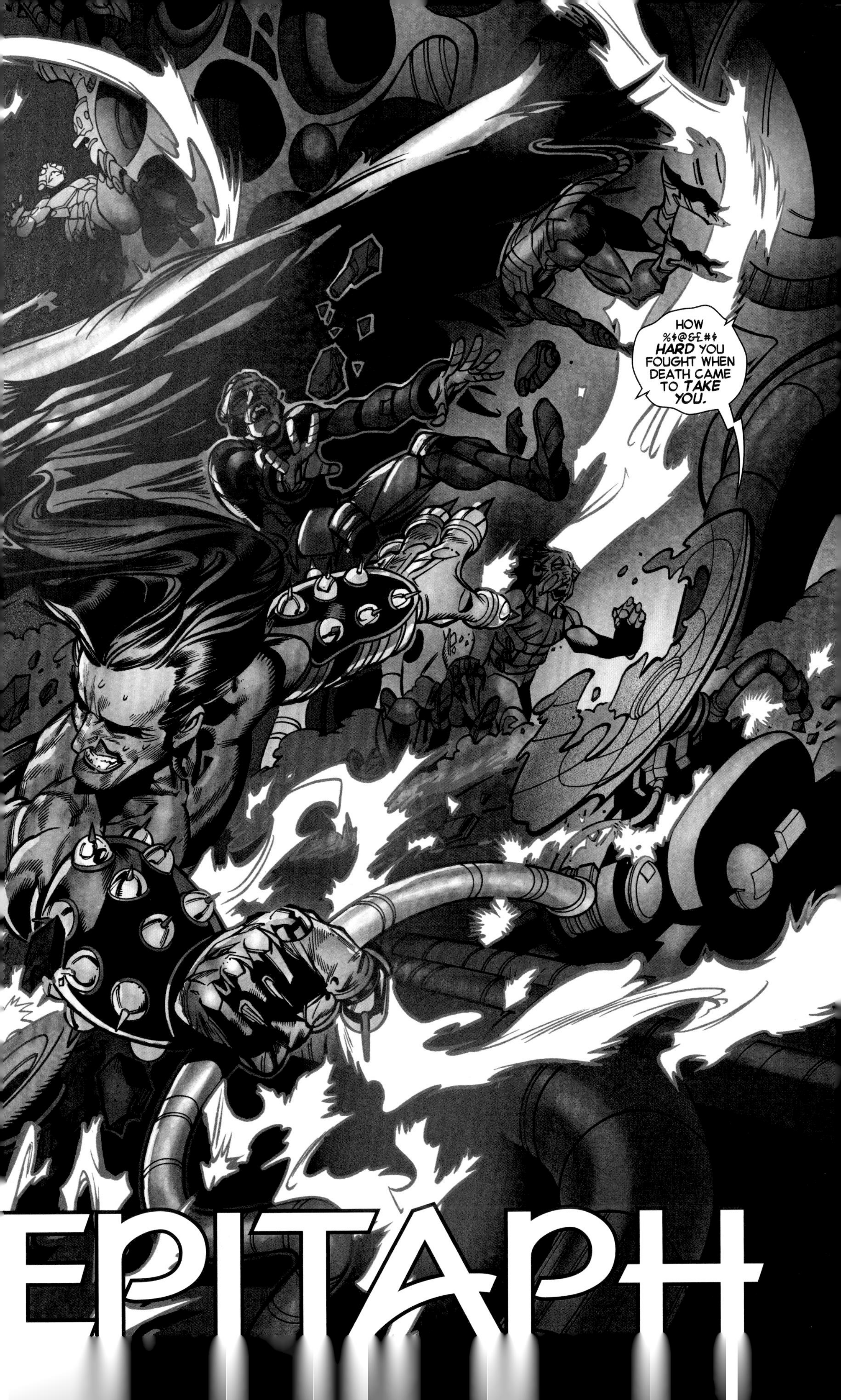
HOW %$@&£#$ HARD YOU FOUGHT WHEN DEATH CAME TO TAKE YOU.
EPITAPH

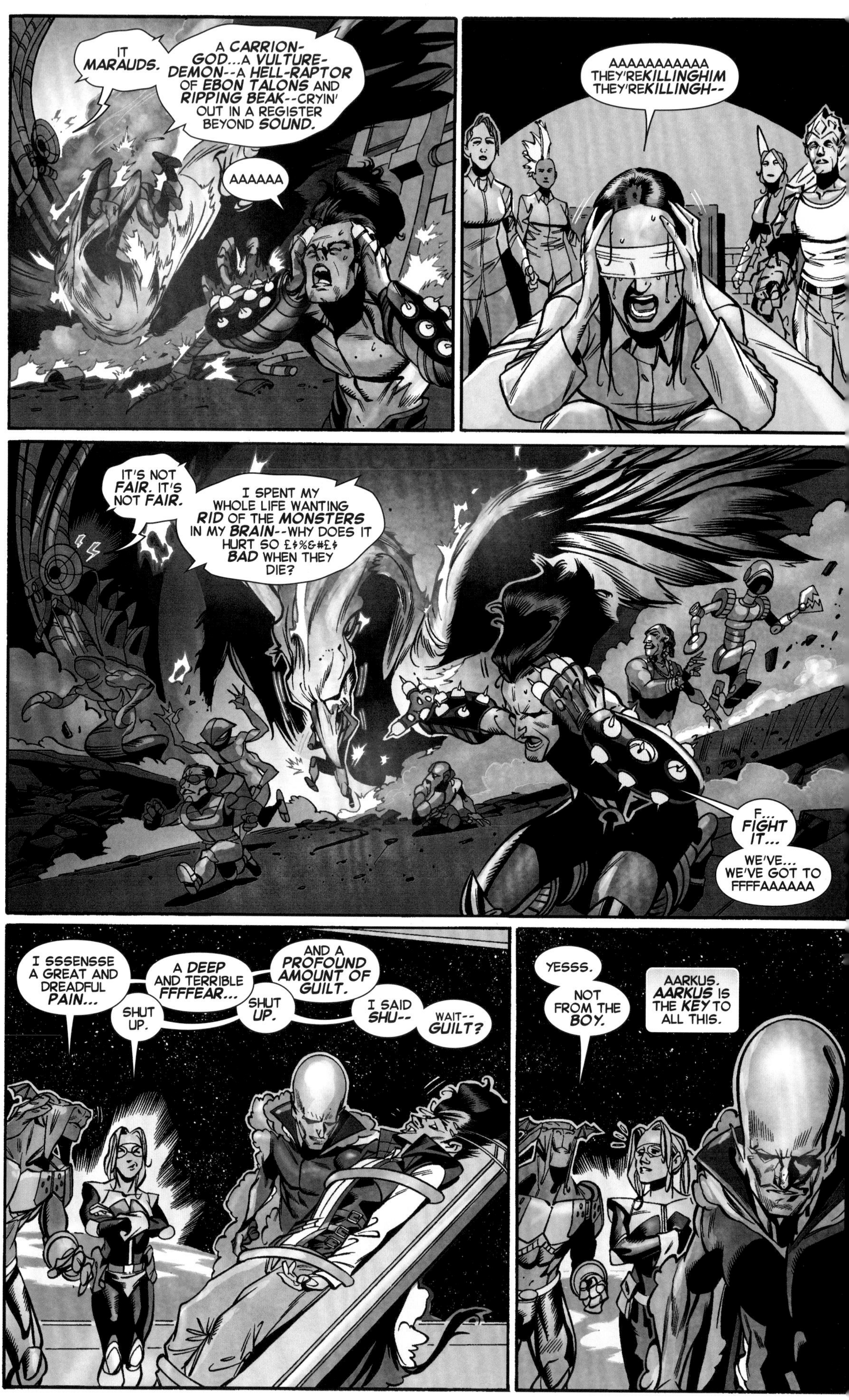
IT MARAUDS.
A CARRION-GOD...A VULTURE-DEMON--A HELL-RAPTOR OF EBON TALONS AND RIPPING BEAK--CRYIN' OUT IN A REGISTER BEYOND SOUND.
AAAAAA
AAAAAAAAAAA THEY'REKILLINGHIM THEY'REKILLINGH--
IT'S NOT FAIR. IT'S NOT FAIR.
I SPENT MY WHOLE LIFE WANTING RID OF THE MONSTERS IN MY BRAIN--WHY DOES IT HURT SO £$%&#£$ BAD WHEN THEY DIE?
F... FIGHT IT...
WE'VE... WE'VE GOT TO FFFFAAAAAAA
I SSSENSSE A GREAT AND DREADFUL PAIN...
SHUT UP.
A DEEP AND TERRIBLE FFFFEAR...
SHUT UP.
AND A PROFOUND AMOUNT OF GUILT.
I SAID SHU--
WAIT--GUILT?
YESSS.
NOT FROM THE BOY.
AARKUS. AARKUS IS THE KEY TO ALL THIS.

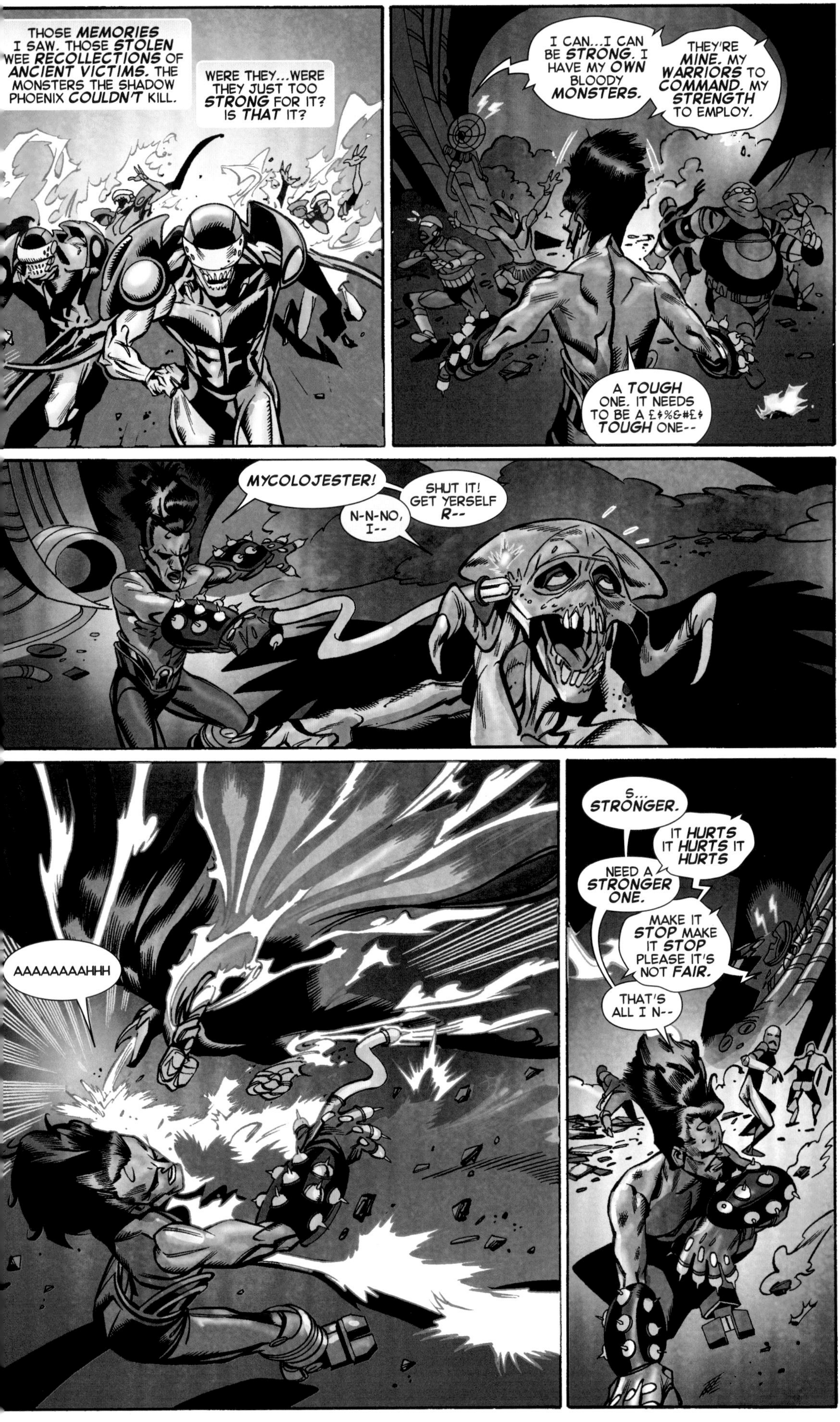
THOSE MEMORIES I SAW. THOSE STOLEN WEE RECOLLECTIONS OF ANCIENT VICTIMS. THE MONSTERS THE SHADOW PHOENIX COULDN'T KILL.
WERE THEY...WERE THEY JUST TOO STRONG FOR IT? IS THAT IT?
I CAN...I CAN BE STRONG. I HAVE MY OWN BLOODY MONSTERS.
THEY'RE MINE. MY WARRIORS TO COMMAND. MY STRENGTH TO EMPLOY.
A TOUGH ONE. IT NEEDS TO BE A £$%&#£$ TOUGH ONE--
MYCOLOJESTER!
N-N-NO, I--
SHUT IT! GET YERSELF R--
AAAAAAAAHHH
S... STRONGER.
IT HURTS IT HURTS IT HURTS
NEED A STRONGER ONE.
MAKE IT STOP MAKE IT STOP PLEASE IT'S NOT FAIR.
THAT'S ALL I N--

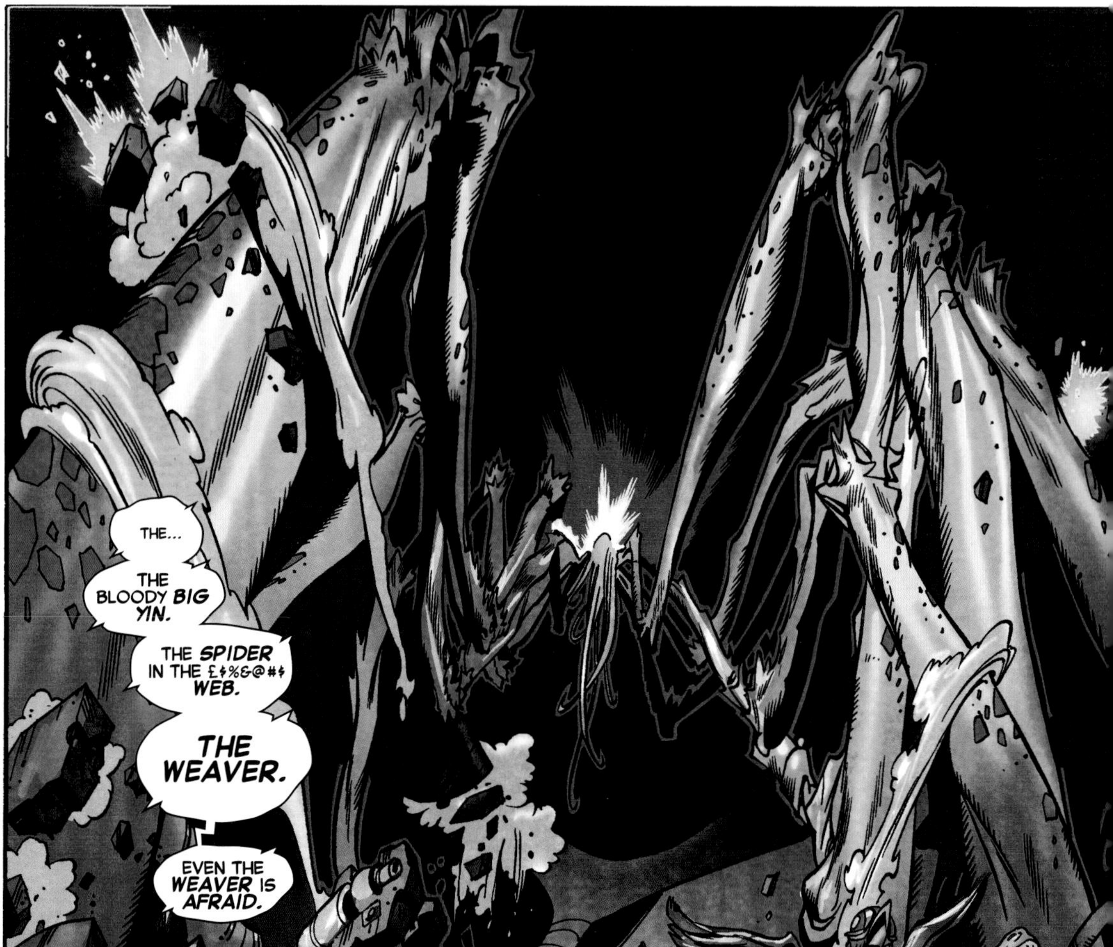
THE...
THE BLOODY BIG YIN.
THE SPIDER IN THE £$%&@#$ WEB.
THE WEAVER.
EVEN THE WEAVER IS AFRAID.
...
N...NO TIME FOR BLOODY HALF MEASURES.

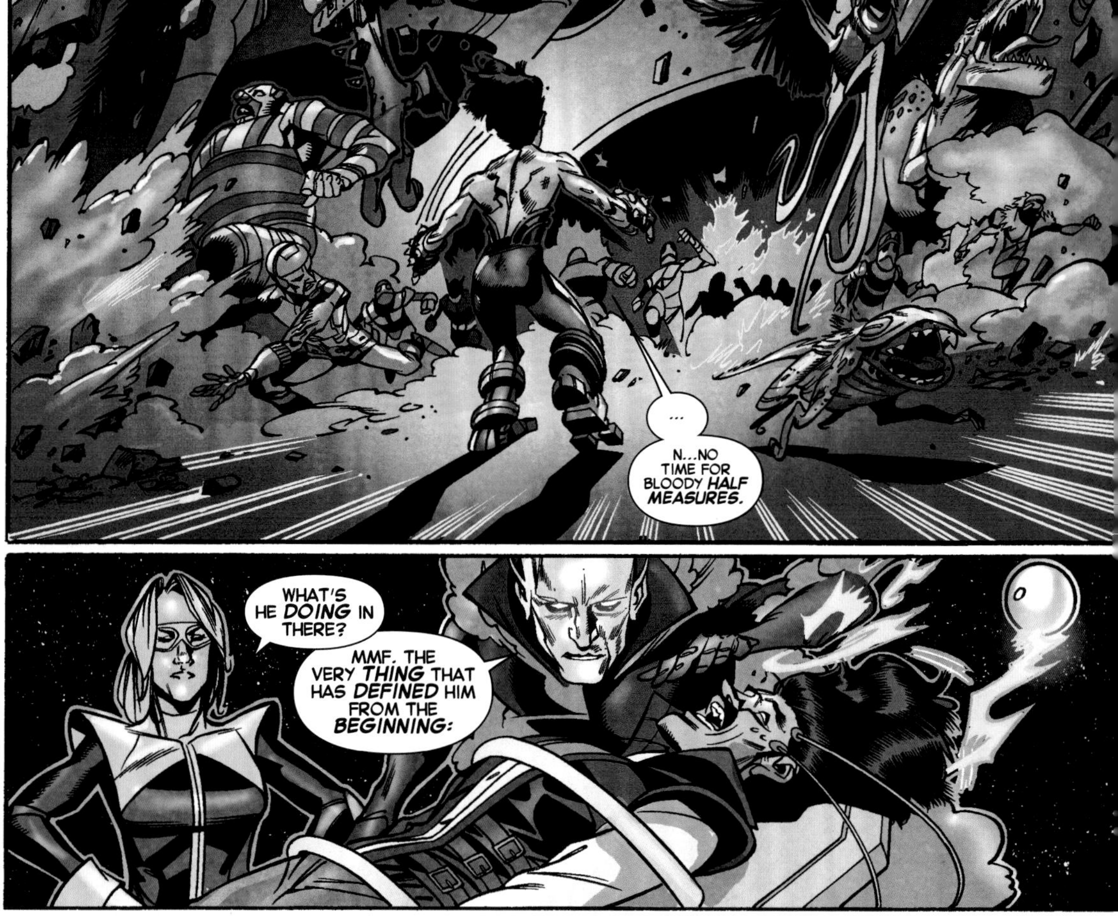
WHAT'S HE DOING IN THERE?
MMF. THE VERY THING THAT HAS DEFINED HIM FROM THE BEGINNING:

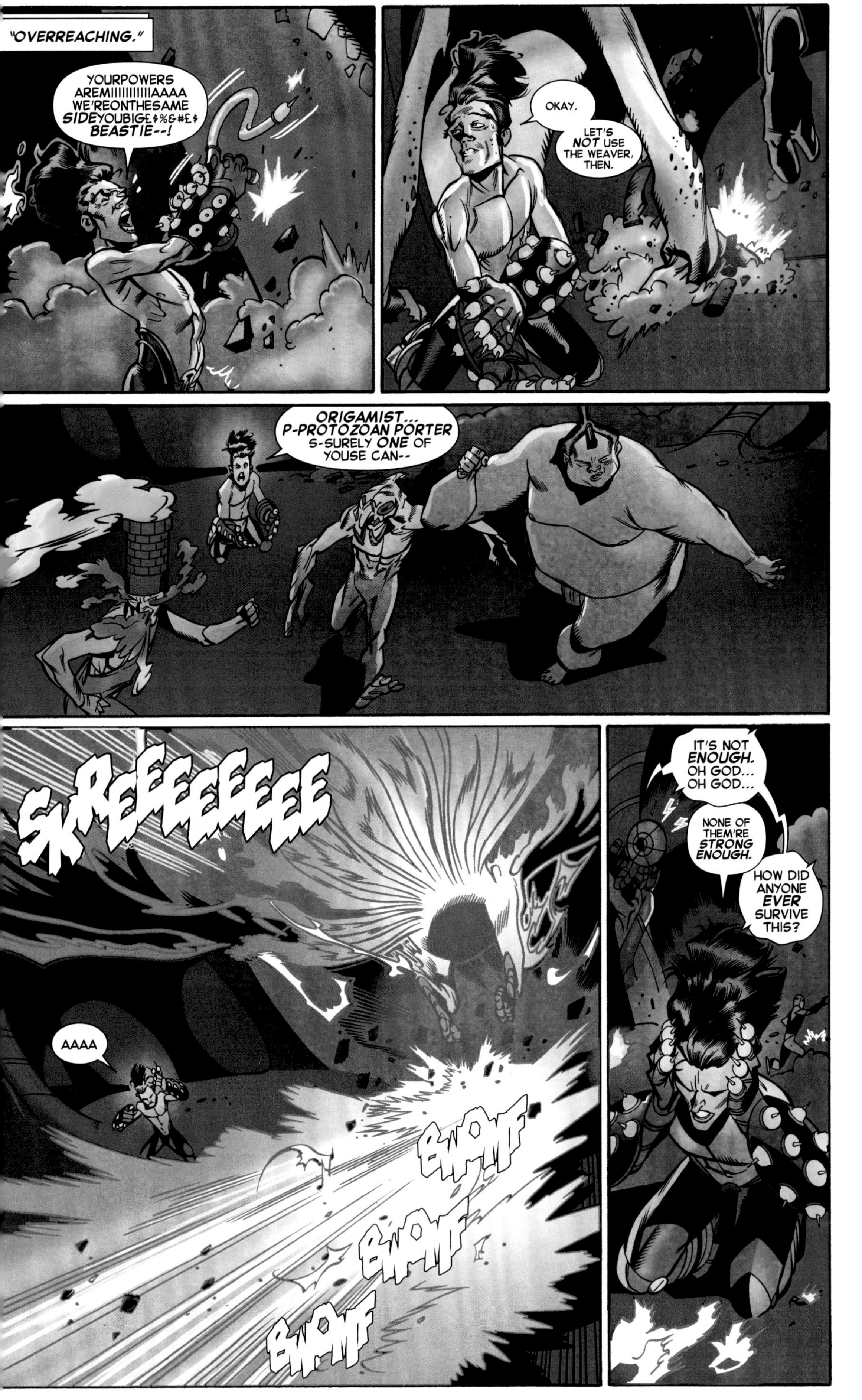
"OVERREACHING."
YOURPOWERS AREMIIIIIIIIIIIIAAAA WE'REONTHESAME SIDEYOUBIG$%&#£$ BEASTIE--!
OKAY.
LET'S NOT USE THE WEAVER, THEN.
ORIGAMIST... P-PROTOZOAN PORTER S-SURELY ONE OF YOUSE CAN--
SKREEEEEEEEE
AAAA
BWOMF
BWOMF
BWOMF
IT'S NOT ENOUGH. OH GOD... OH GOD...
NONE OF THEM'RE STRONG ENOUGH.
HOW DID ANYONE EVER SURVIVE THIS?

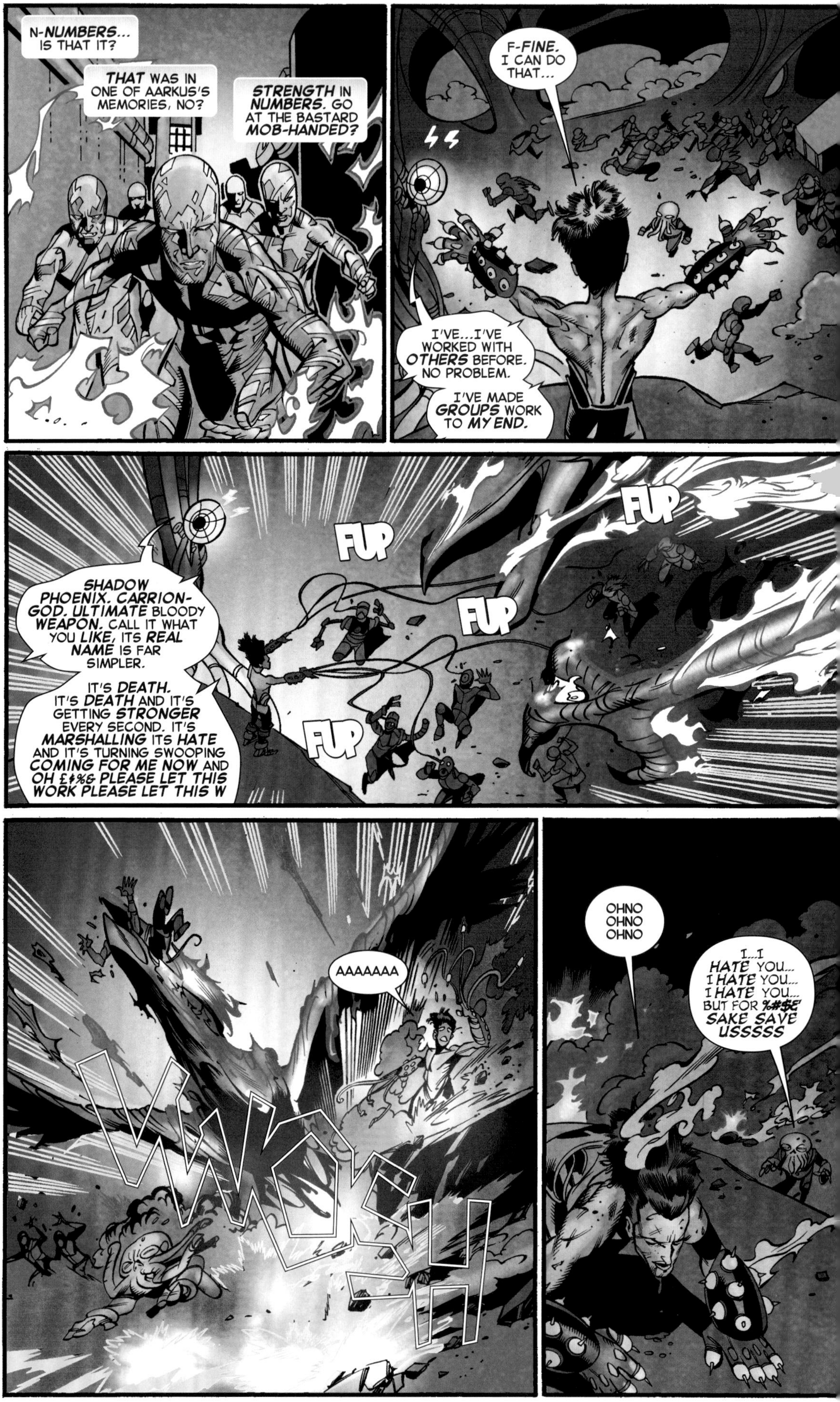

N-NUMBERS... IS THAT IT?
THAT WAS IN ONE OF AARKUS'S MEMORIES, NO?
STRENGTH IN NUMBERS. GO AT THE BASTARD MOB-HANDED?
F-FINE. I CAN DO THAT...
I'VE...I'VE WORKED WITH OTHERS BEFORE. NO PROBLEM.
I'VE MADE GROUPS WORK TO MY END.
SHADOW PHOENIX. CARRION-GOD. ULTIMATE BLOODY WEAPON. CALL IT WHAT YOU LIKE, ITS REAL NAME IS FAR SIMPLER.
IT'S DEATH. IT'S DEATH AND IT'S GETTING STRONGER EVERY SECOND. IT'S MARSHALLING ITS HATE AND IT'S TURNING SWOOPING COMING FOR ME NOW AND OH £$%& PLEASE LET THIS WORK PLEASE LET THIS W
FUP
FUP
FUP
FUP
AAAAAAA
WOOSH
OHNO OHNO OHNO
I...I HATE YOU... I HATE YOU... I HATE YOU... BUT FOR %#$£' SAKE SAVE USSSSS

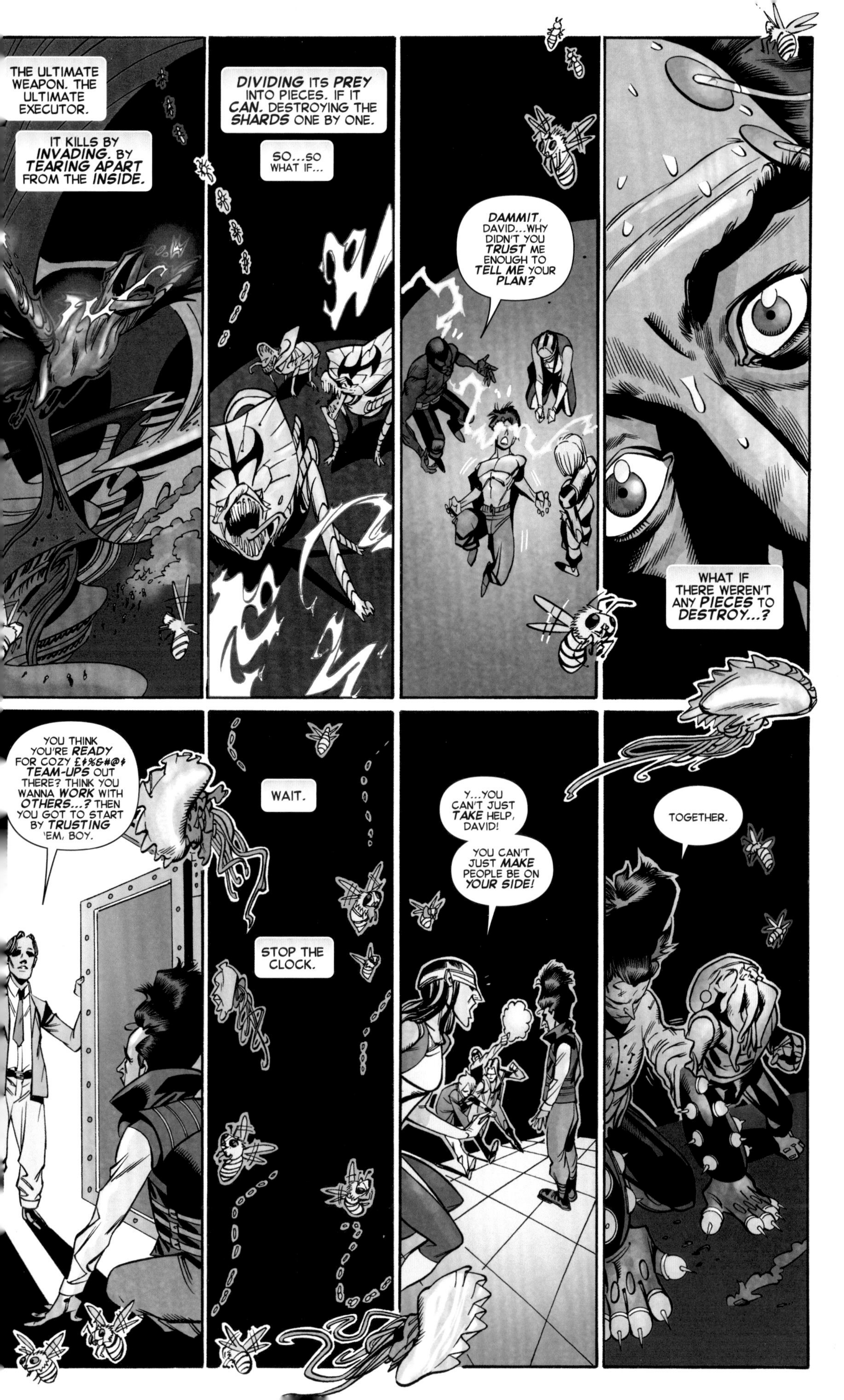
THE ULTIMATE WEAPON. THE ULTIMATE EXECUTOR.
IT KILLS BY INVADING. BY TEARING APART FROM THE INSIDE.
DIVIDING ITS PREY INTO PIECES. IF IT CAN. DESTROYING THE SHARDS ONE BY ONE.
SO...SO WHAT IF...
DAMMIT, DAVID...WHY DIDN'T YOU TRUST ME ENOUGH TO TELL ME YOUR PLAN?
WHAT IF THERE WEREN'T ANY PIECES TO DESTROY...?
YOU THINK YOU'RE READY FOR COZY £$%&#@$ TEAM-UPS OUT THERE? THINK YOU WANNA WORK WITH OTHERS...? THEN YOU GOT TO START BY TRUSTING 'EM, BOY.
WAIT.
STOP THE CLOCK.
Y...YOU CAN'T JUST TAKE HELP, DAVID!
YOU CAN'T JUST MAKE PEOPLE BE ON YOUR SIDE!
TOGETHER.

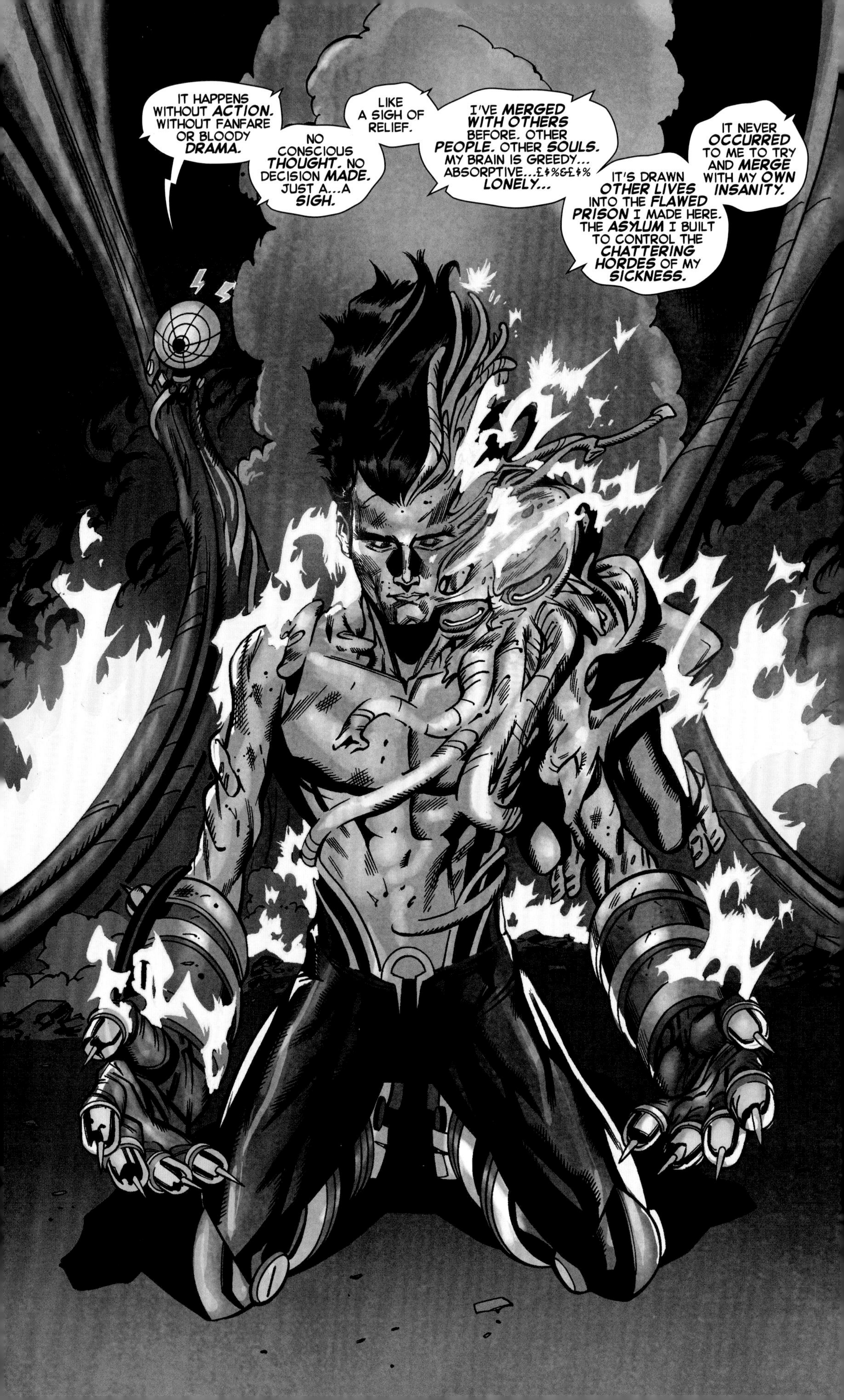
IT HAPPENS WITHOUT ACTION. WITHOUT FANFARE OR BLOODY DRAMA.
NO CONSCIOUS THOUGHT. NO DECISION MADE. JUST A...A SIGH.
LIKE A SIGH OF RELIEF.
I'VE MERGED WITH OTHERS BEFORE. OTHER PEOPLE. OTHER SOULS. MY BRAIN IS GREEDY... ABSORPTIVE...£$%&£$% LONELY...
IT'S DRAWN OTHER LIVES INTO THE FLAWED PRISON I MADE HERE. THE ASYLUM I BUILT TO CONTROL THE CHATTERING HORDES OF MY SICKNESS.
IT NEVER OCCURRED TO ME TO TRY AND MERGE WITH MY OWN INSANITY.

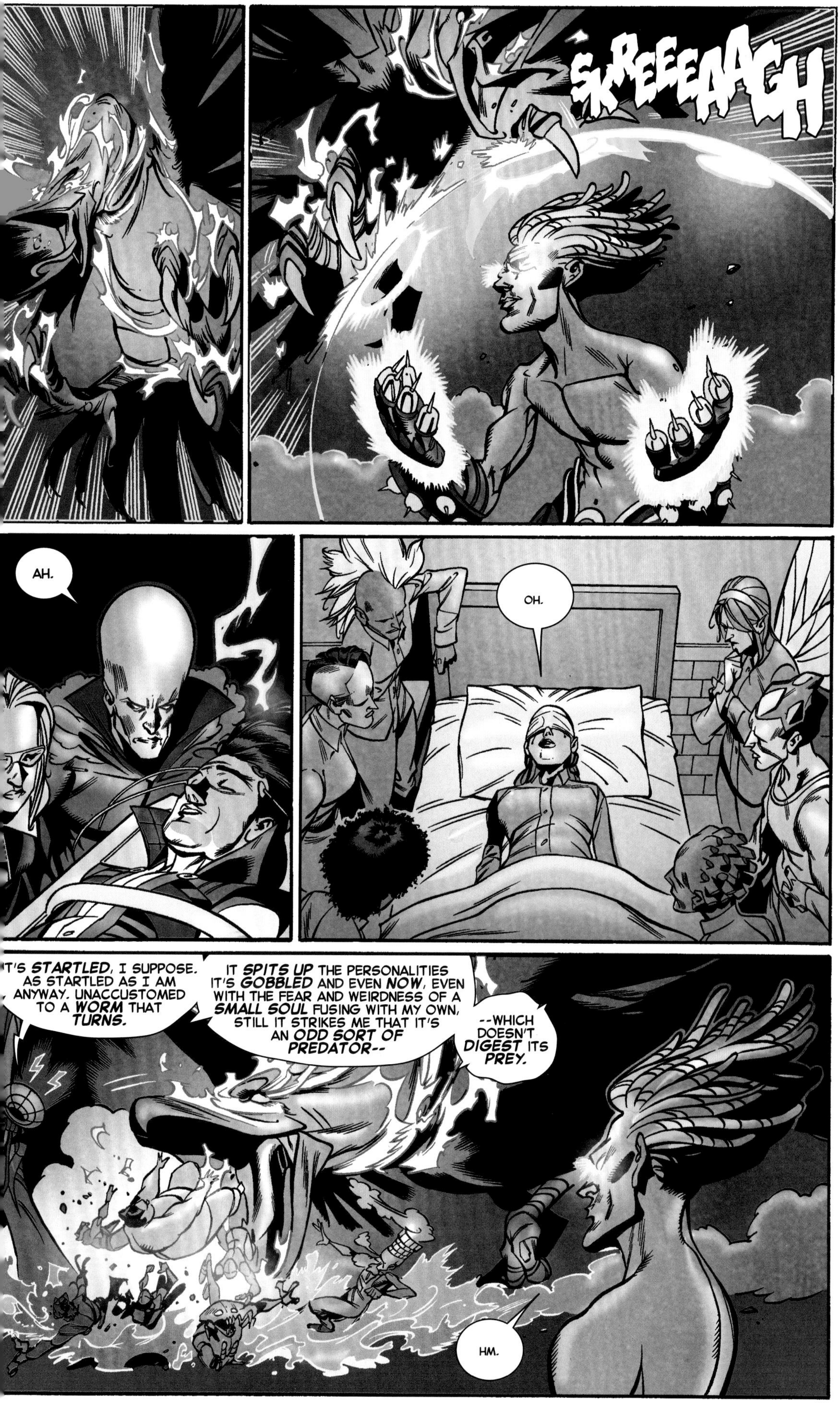

SKREEEAAAGH
AH.
OH.
IT'S STARTLED, I SUPPOSE. AS STARTLED AS I AM ANYWAY. UNACCUSTOMED TO A WORM THAT TURNS.
IT SPITS UP THE PERSONALITIES IT'S GOBBLED AND EVEN NOW, EVEN WITH THE FEAR AND WEIRDNESS OF A SMALL SOUL FUSING WITH MY OWN, STILL IT STRIKES ME THAT IT'S AN ODD SORT OF PREDATOR--
--WHICH DOESN'T DIGEST ITS PREY.
HM.

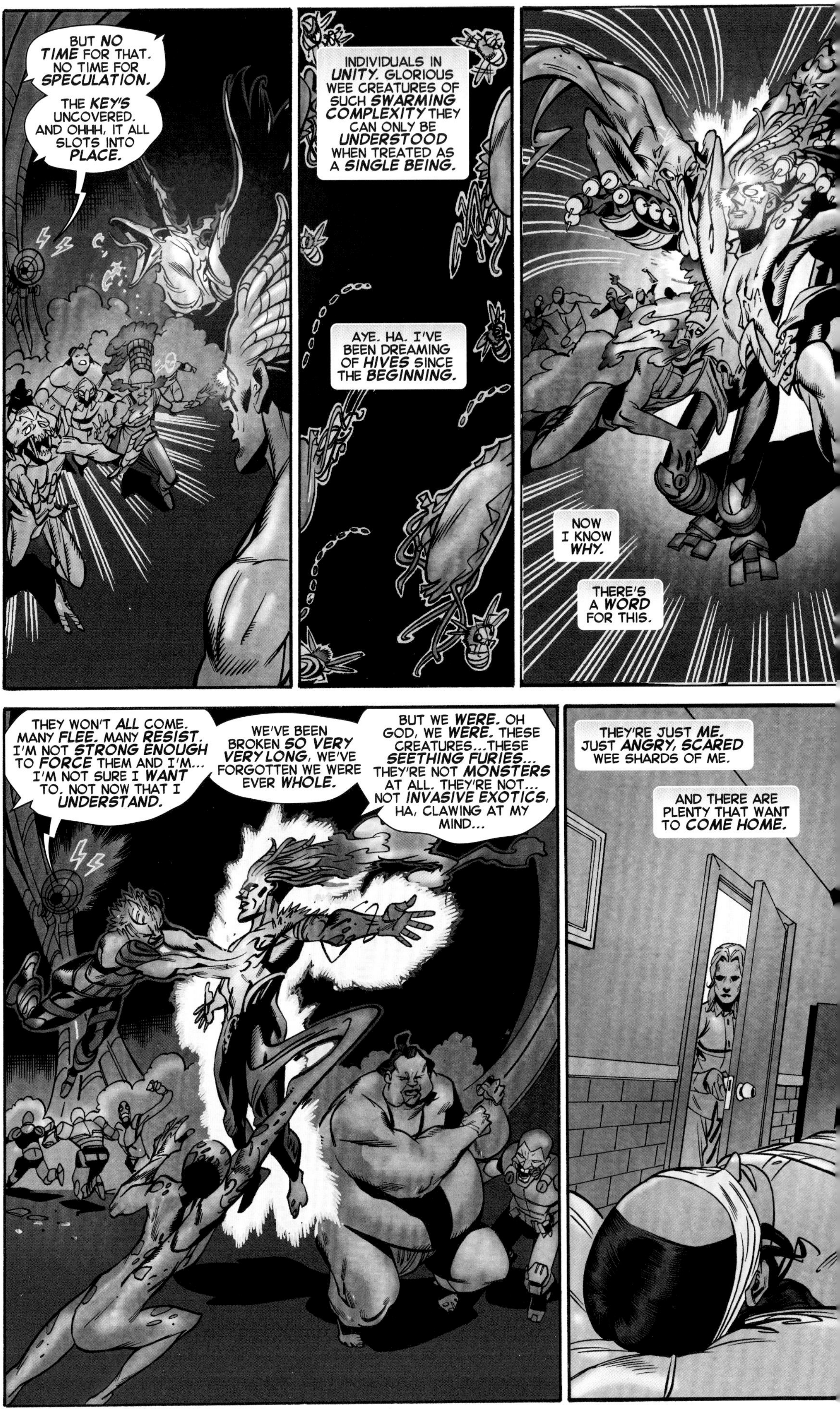
BUT NO TIME FOR THAT. NO TIME FOR SPECULATION.
THE KEY'S UNCOVERED. AND OHHH, IT ALL SLOTS INTO PLACE.
INDIVIDUALS IN UNITY. GLORIOUS WEE CREATURES OF SUCH SWARMING COMPLEXITY THEY CAN ONLY BE UNDERSTOOD WHEN TREATED AS A SINGLE BEING.
AYE. HA. I'VE BEEN DREAMING OF HIVES SINCE THE BEGINNING.
NOW I KNOW WHY.
THERE'S A WORD FOR THIS.
THEY WON'T ALL COME. MANY FLEE. MANY RESIST. I'M NOT STRONG ENOUGH TO FORCE THEM AND I'M... I'M NOT SURE I WANT TO. NOT NOW THAT I UNDERSTAND.
WE'VE BEEN BROKEN SO VERY VERY LONG, WE'VE FORGOTTEN WE WERE EVER WHOLE.
BUT WE WERE. OH GOD, WE WERE. THESE CREATURES...THESE SEETHING FURIES... THEY'RE NOT MONSTERS AT ALL. THEY'RE NOT... NOT INVASIVE EXOTICS, HA, CLAWING AT MY MIND...
THEY'RE JUST ME. JUST ANGRY, SCARED WEE SHARDS OF ME.
AND THERE ARE PLENTY THAT WANT TO COME HOME.

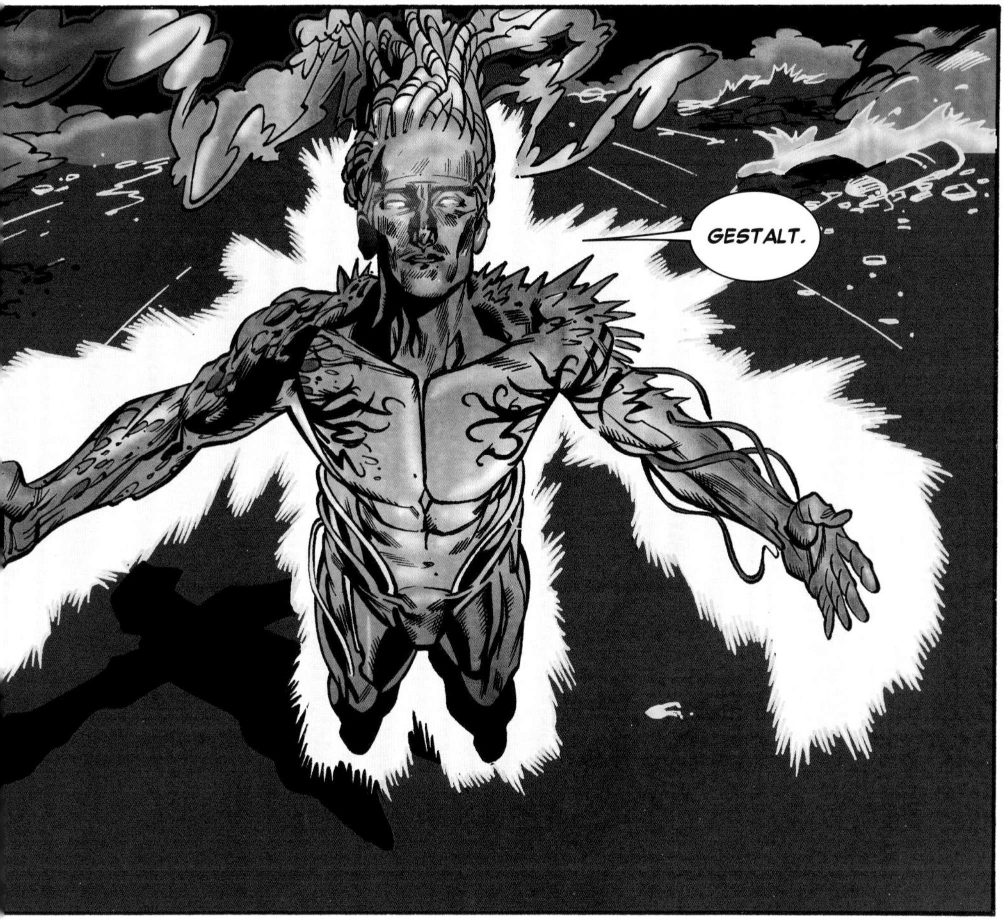
GESTALT.

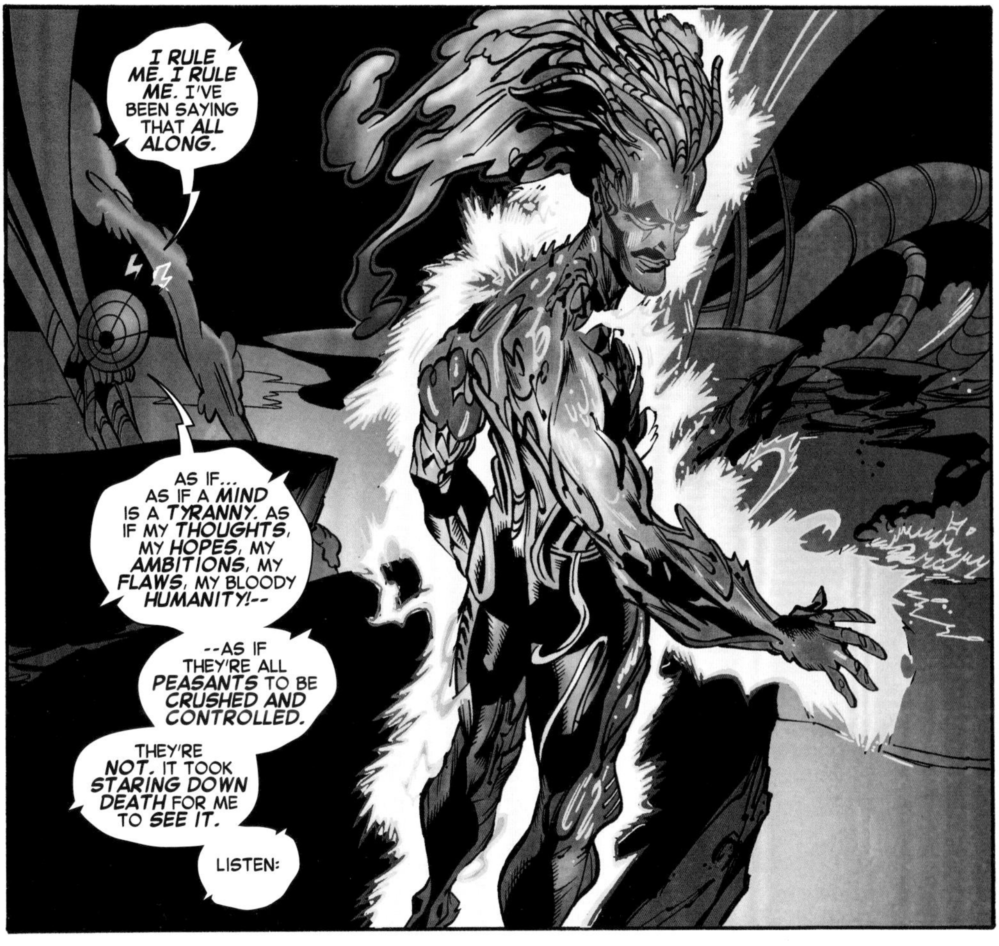
I RULE ME. I RULE ME. I'VE BEEN SAYING THAT ALL ALONG.
AS IF... AS IF A MIND IS A TYRANNY. AS IF MY THOUGHTS, MY HOPES, MY AMBITIONS, MY FLAWS, MY BLOODY HUMANITY!--
--AS IF THEY'RE ALL PEASANTS TO BE CRUSHED AND CONTROLLED.
THEY'RE NOT. IT TOOK STARING DOWN DEATH FOR ME TO SEE IT.
LISTEN:

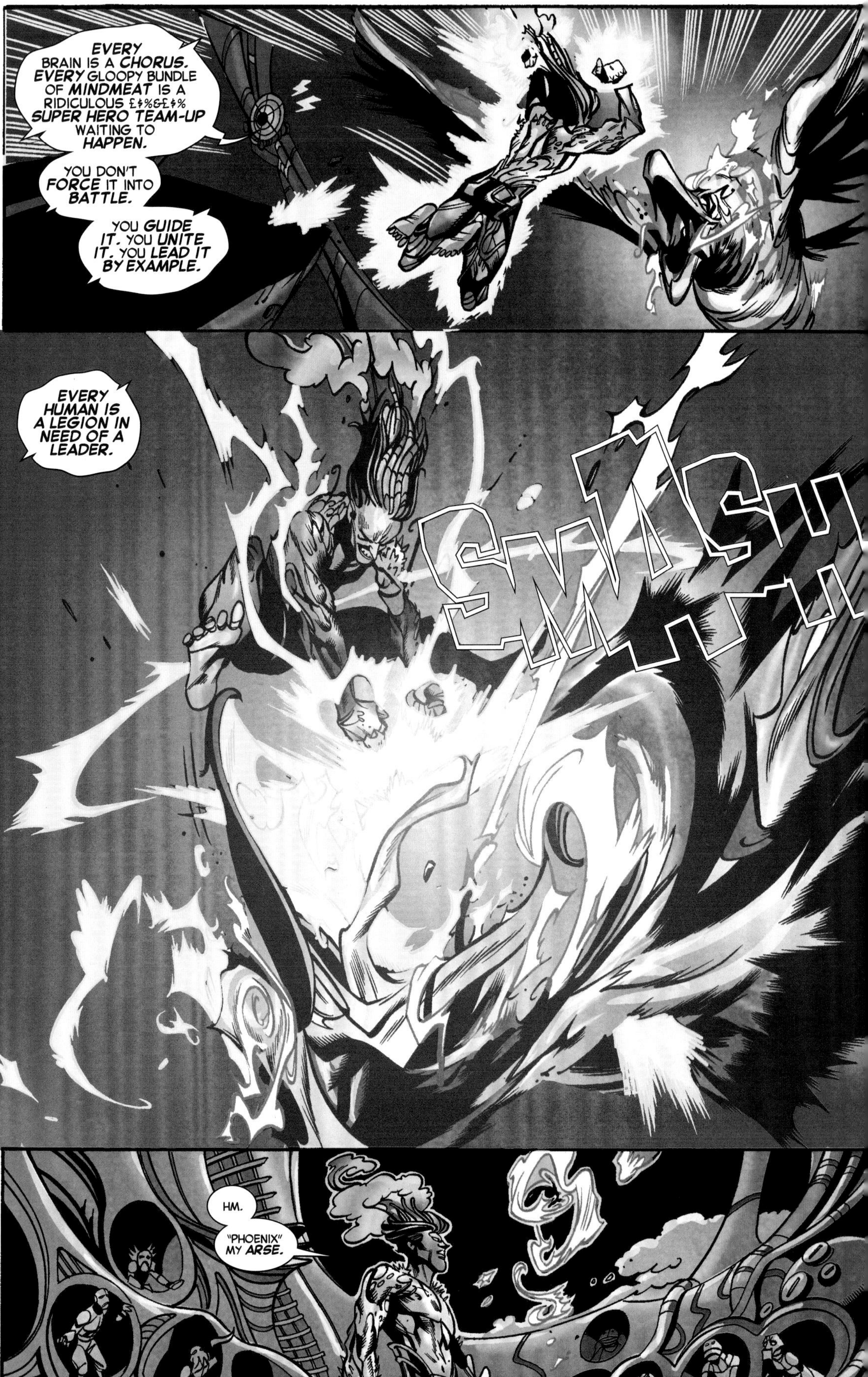
EVERY BRAIN IS A CHORUS. EVERY GLOOPY BUNDLE OF MINDMEAT IS A RIDICULOUS £$%&£$% SUPER HERO TEAM-UP WAITING TO HAPPEN.
YOU DON'T FORCE IT INTO BATTLE.
YOU GUIDE IT. YOU UNITE IT. YOU LEAD IT BY EXAMPLE.
EVERY HUMAN IS A LEGION IN NEED OF A LEADER.
SMASH
HM.
"PHOENIX" MY ARSE.

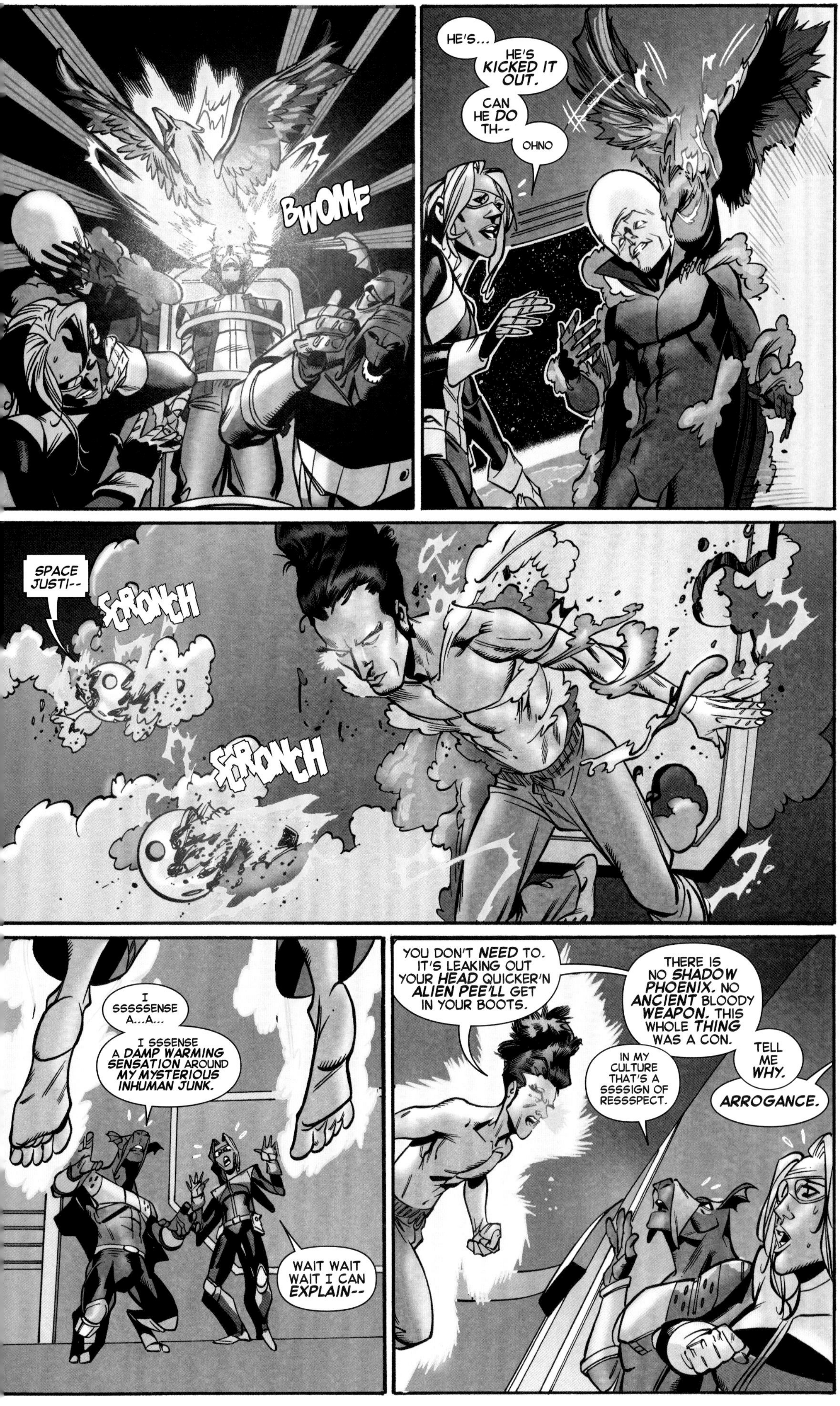
BWOMF
HE'S...
HE'S KICKED IT OUT.
CAN HE DO TH--
OHNO
SPACE JUSTI--
SCRONCH
SCRONCH
I SSSSSENSE A...A...
I SSSENSE A DAMP WARMING SENSATION AROUND MY MYSTERIOUS INHUMAN JUNK.
WAIT WAIT WAIT I CAN EXPLAIN--
YOU DON'T NEED TO. IT'S LEAKING OUT YOUR HEAD QUICKER'N ALIEN PEE'LL GET IN YOUR BOOTS.
THERE IS NO SHADOW PHOENIX. NO ANCIENT BLOODY WEAPON. THIS WHOLE THING WAS A CON.
IN MY CULTURE THAT'S A SSSSIGN OF RESSSPECT.
TELL ME WHY.
ARROGANCE.

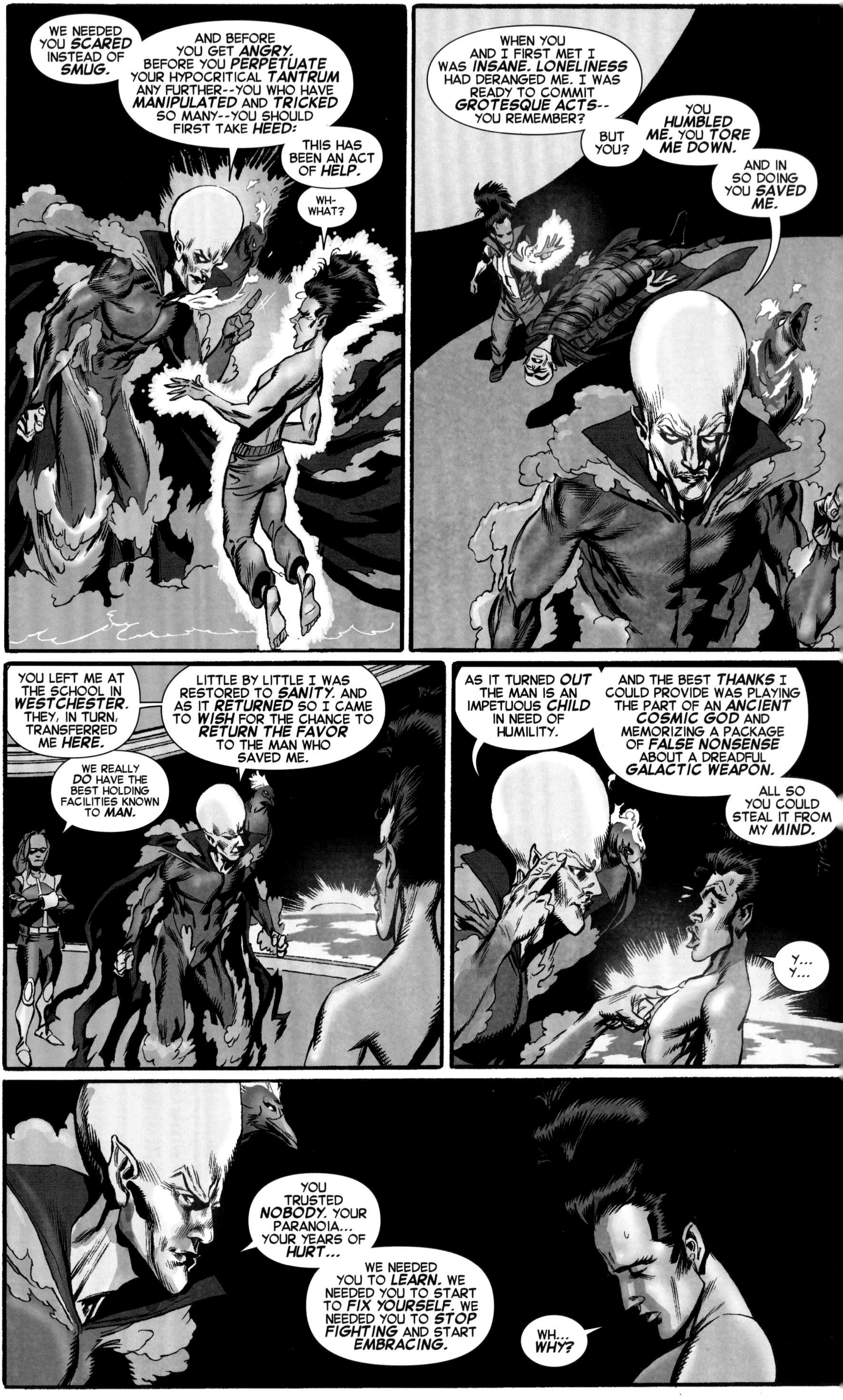
WE NEEDED YOU SCARED INSTEAD OF SMUG.
AND BEFORE YOU GET ANGRY. BEFORE YOU PERPETUATE YOUR HYPOCRITICAL TANTRUM ANY FURTHER--YOU WHO HAVE MANIPULATED AND TRICKED SO MANY--YOU SHOULD FIRST TAKE HEED:
THIS HAS BEEN AN ACT OF HELP.
WH- WHAT?
WHEN YOU AND I FIRST MET I WAS INSANE. LONELINESS HAD DERANGED ME. I WAS READY TO COMMIT GROTESQUE ACTS-- YOU REMEMBER?
BUT YOU?
YOU HUMBLED ME. YOU TORE ME DOWN.
AND IN SO DOING YOU SAVED ME.
YOU LEFT ME AT THE SCHOOL IN WESTCHESTER. THEY, IN TURN, TRANSFERRED ME HERE.
LITTLE BY LITTLE I WAS RESTORED TO SANITY. AND AS IT RETURNED SO I CAME TO WISH FOR THE CHANCE TO RETURN THE FAVOR TO THE MAN WHO SAVED ME.
WE REALLY DO HAVE THE BEST HOLDING FACILITIES KNOWN TO MAN.
AS IT TURNED OUT THE MAN IS AN IMPETUOUS CHILD IN NEED OF HUMILITY.
AND THE BEST THANKS I COULD PROVIDE WAS PLAYING THE PART OF AN ANCIENT COSMIC GOD AND MEMORIZING A PACKAGE OF FALSE NONSENSE ABOUT A DREADFUL GALACTIC WEAPON.
ALL SO YOU COULD STEAL IT FROM MY MIND.
Y... Y...
YOU TRUSTED NOBODY. YOUR PARANOIA... YOUR YEARS OF HURT...
WE NEEDED YOU TO LEARN. WE NEEDED YOU TO START TO FIX YOURSELF. WE NEEDED YOU TO STOP FIGHTING AND START EMBRACING.
WH... WHY?

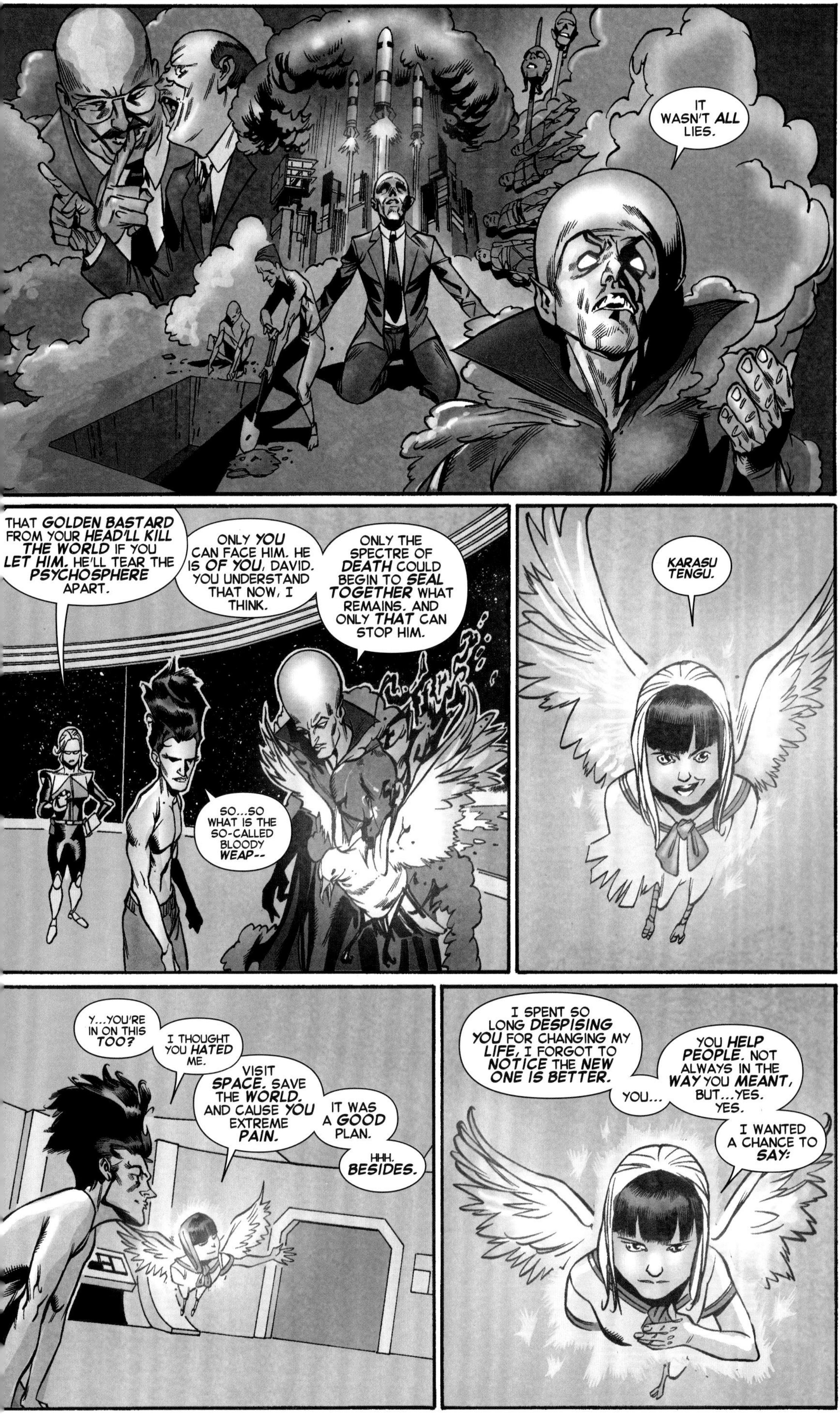
IT WASN'T ALL LIES.
THAT GOLDEN BASTARD FROM YOUR HEAD'LL KILL THE WORLD IF YOU LET HIM. HE'LL TEAR THE PSYCHOSPHERE APART.
ONLY YOU CAN FACE HIM. HE IS OF YOU, DAVID. YOU UNDERSTAND THAT NOW, I THINK.
ONLY THE SPECTRE OF DEATH COULD BEGIN TO SEAL TOGETHER WHAT REMAINS. AND ONLY THAT CAN STOP HIM.
SO...SO WHAT IS THE SO-CALLED BLOODY WEAP--
KARASU TENGU.
Y...YOU'RE IN ON THIS TOO?
I THOUGHT YOU HATED ME.
VISIT SPACE. SAVE THE WORLD. AND CAUSE YOU EXTREME PAIN.
IT WAS A GOOD PLAN.
HHH. BESIDES.
I SPENT SO LONG DESPISING YOU FOR CHANGING MY LIFE, I FORGOT TO NOTICE THE NEW ONE IS BETTER.
YOU...
YOU HELP PEOPLE. NOT ALWAYS IN THE WAY YOU MEANT, BUT...YES. YES.
I WANTED A CHANCE TO SAY:

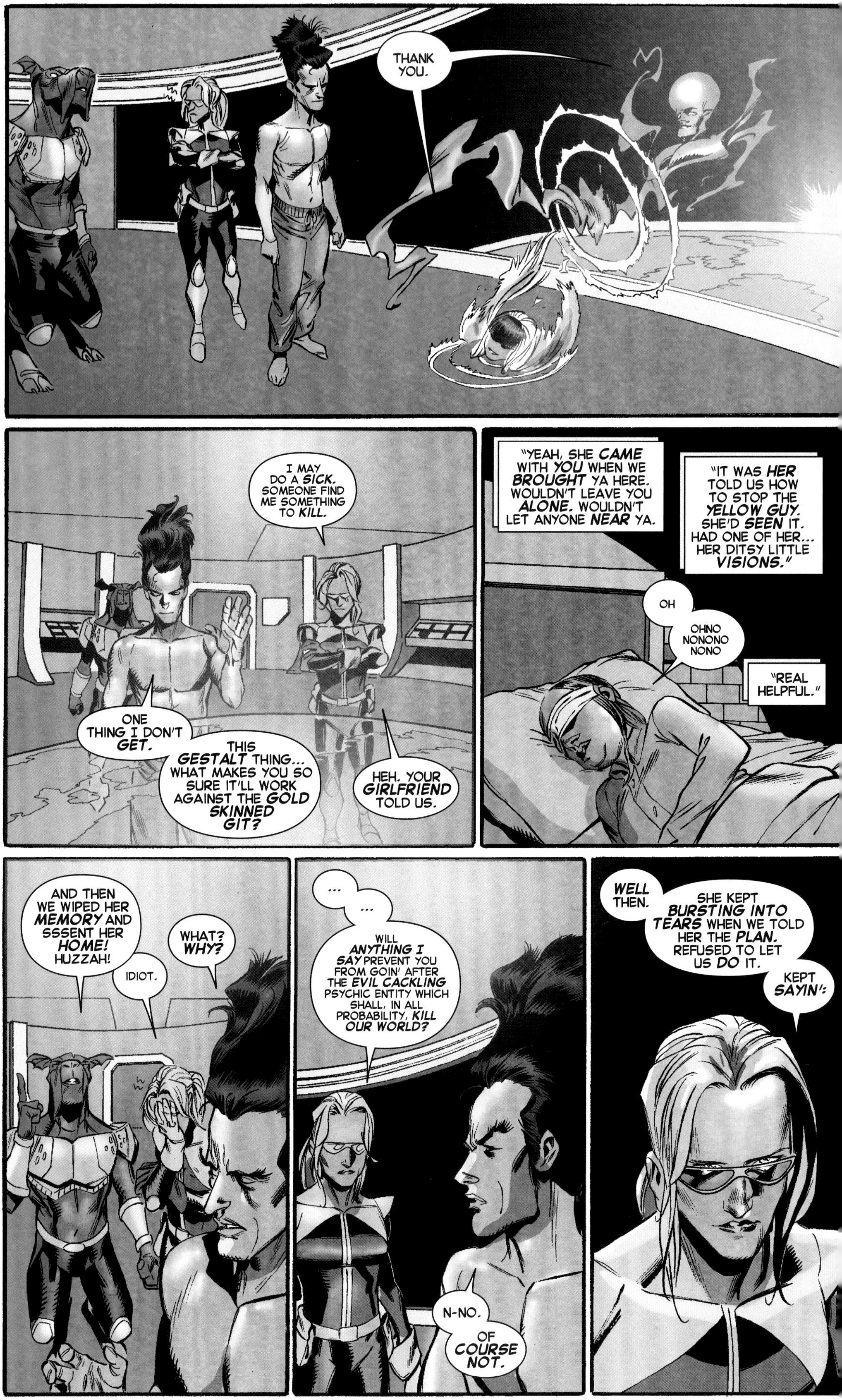
THANK YOU.
I MAY DO A SICK. SOMEONE FIND ME SOMETHING TO KILL.
ONE THING I DON'T GET.
THIS GESTALT THING... WHAT MAKES YOU SO SURE IT'LL WORK AGAINST THE GOLD SKINNED GIT?
HEH. YOUR GIRLFRIEND TOLD US.
"YEAH, SHE CAME WITH YOU WHEN WE BROUGHT YA HERE. WOULDN'T LEAVE YOU ALONE. WOULDN'T LET ANYONE NEAR YA.
"IT WAS HER TOLD US HOW TO STOP THE YELLOW GUY. SHE'D SEEN IT. HAD ONE OF HER... HER DITSY LITTLE VISIONS."
OH
OHNO NONONO NONO
"REAL HELPFUL."
AND THEN WE WIPED HER MEMORY AND SSSENT HER HOME! HUZZAH!
IDIOT.
WHAT? WHY?
...
...
WILL ANYTHING I SAY PREVENT YOU FROM GOIN' AFTER THE EVIL CACKLING PSYCHIC ENTITY WHICH SHALL, IN ALL PROBABILITY, KILL OUR WORLD?
N-NO.
OF COURSE NOT.
WELL THEN.
SHE KEPT BURSTING INTO TEARS WHEN WE TOLD HER THE PLAN. REFUSED TO LET US DO IT.
KEPT SAYIN':

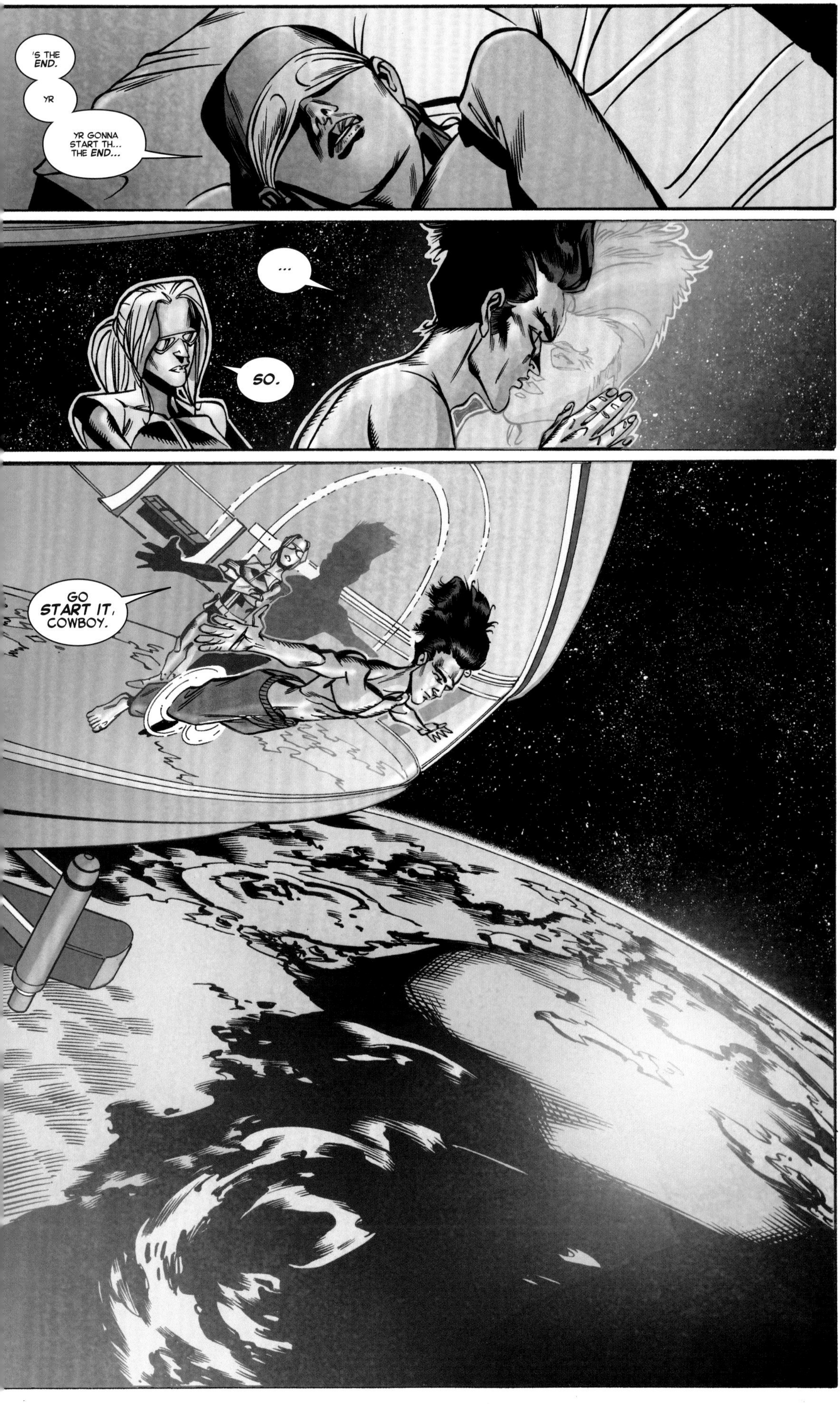
'S THE END.
YR
YR GONNA START TH... THE END...
...
SO.
GO START IT, COWBOY.

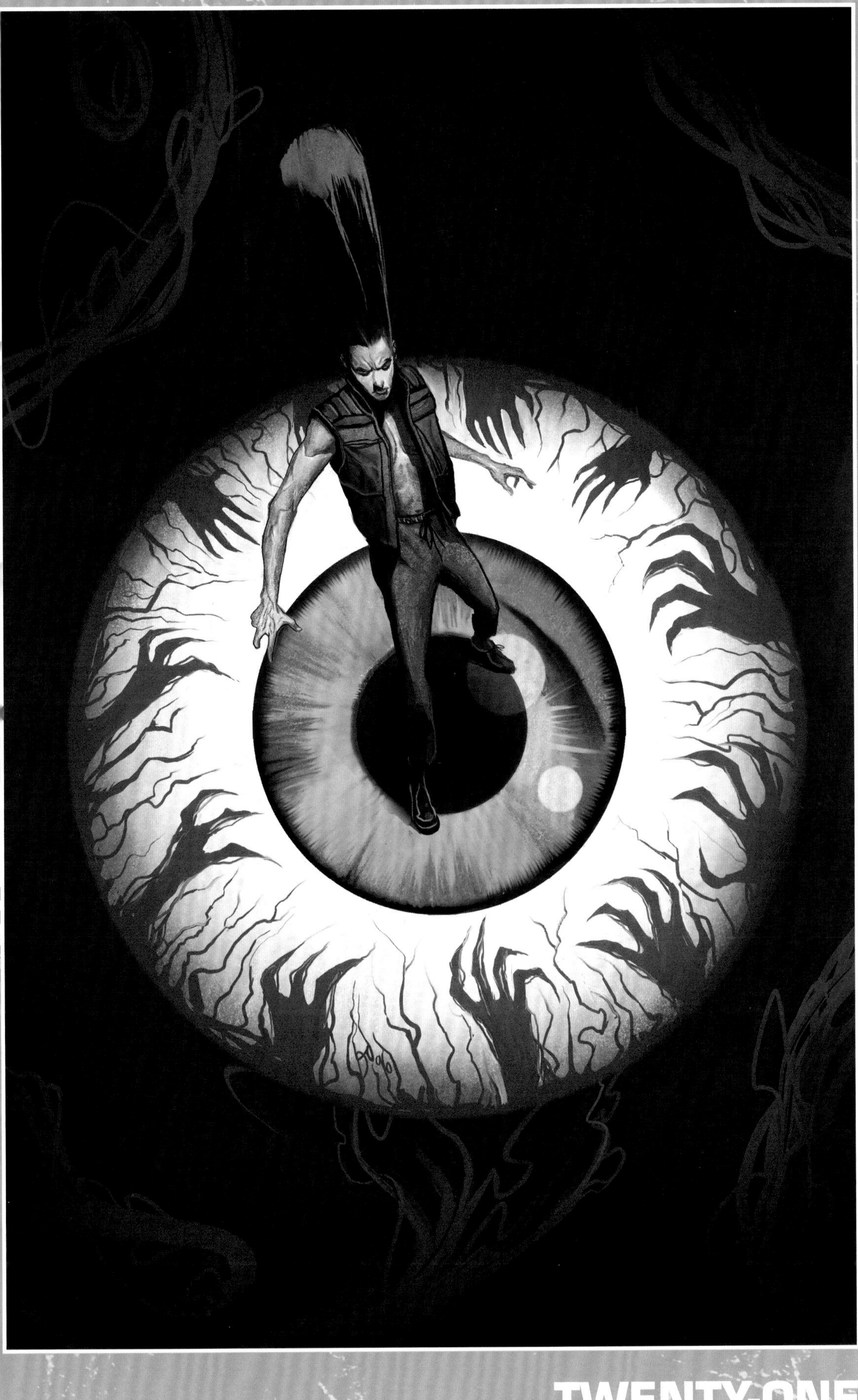

TWENTY-ONE

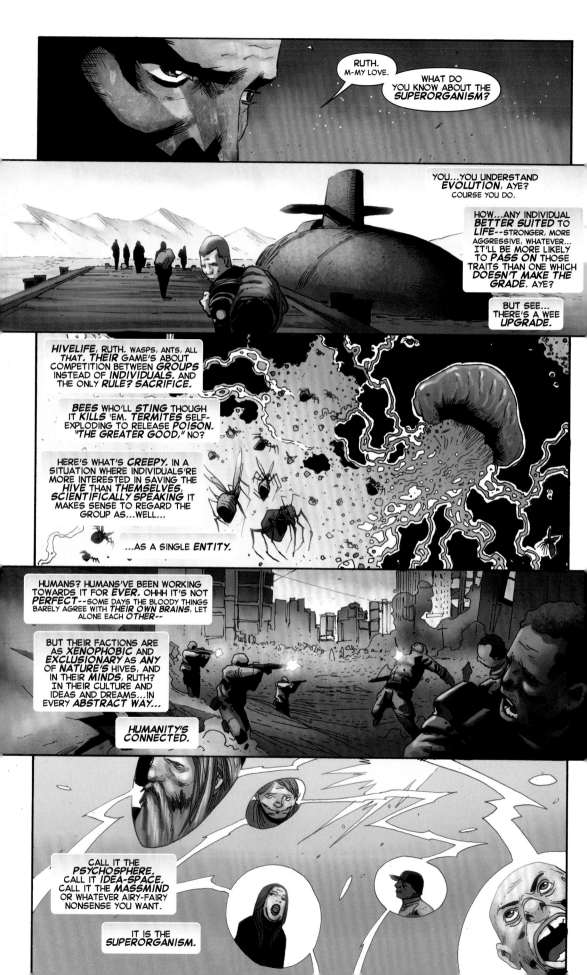

RUTH. M-MY LOVE.

WHAT DO YOU KNOW ABOUT THE *SUPERORGANISM?*

YOU...YOU UNDERSTAND *EVOLUTION*, AYE? COURSE YOU DO.

HOW...ANY INDIVIDUAL *BETTER SUITED* TO *LIFE*--STRONGER, MORE AGGRESSIVE, WHATEVER... IT'LL BE MORE LIKELY TO *PASS ON* THOSE TRAITS THAN ONE WHICH *DOESN'T MAKE THE GRADE.* AYE?

BUT SEE... THERE'S A WEE *UPGRADE.*

HIVELIFE, RUTH. WASPS, ANTS, ALL *THAT. THEIR* GAME'S ABOUT COMPETITION BETWEEN *GROUPS* INSTEAD OF *INDIVIDUALS.* AND THE ONLY *RULE? SACRIFICE.*

BEES WHO'LL *STING* THOUGH IT *KILLS* 'EM. *TERMITES* SELF-EXPLODING TO RELEASE *POISON.* *"THE GREATER GOOD,"* NO?

HERE'S WHAT'S *CREEPY.* IN A SITUATION WHERE INDIVIDUALS'RE MORE INTERESTED IN SAVING THE *HIVE* THAN *THEMSELVES, SCIENTIFICALLY SPEAKING* IT MAKES SENSE TO REGARD THE GROUP AS...WELL...

...AS A SINGLE *ENTITY.*

HUMANS? HUMANS'VE BEEN WORKING TOWARDS IT FOR *EVER.* OHHH IT'S NOT *PERFECT*--SOME DAYS THE BLOODY THINGS BARELY AGREE WITH *THEIR OWN BRAINS,* LET ALONE EACH *OTHER*--

BUT THEIR FACTIONS ARE AS *XENOPHOBIC* AND *EXCLUSIONARY* AS *ANY* OF *NATURE'S* HIVES, AND IN THEIR *MINDS,* RUTH? IN THEIR CULTURE AND IDEAS AND DREAMS...IN EVERY *ABSTRACT WAY...*

HUMANITY'S CONNECTED.

CALL IT THE *PSYCHOSPHERE.* CALL IT *IDEA-SPACE.* CALL IT THE *MASSMIND* OR WHATEVER AIRY-FAIRY NONSENSE YOU WANT.

IT IS THE *SUPERORGANISM.*

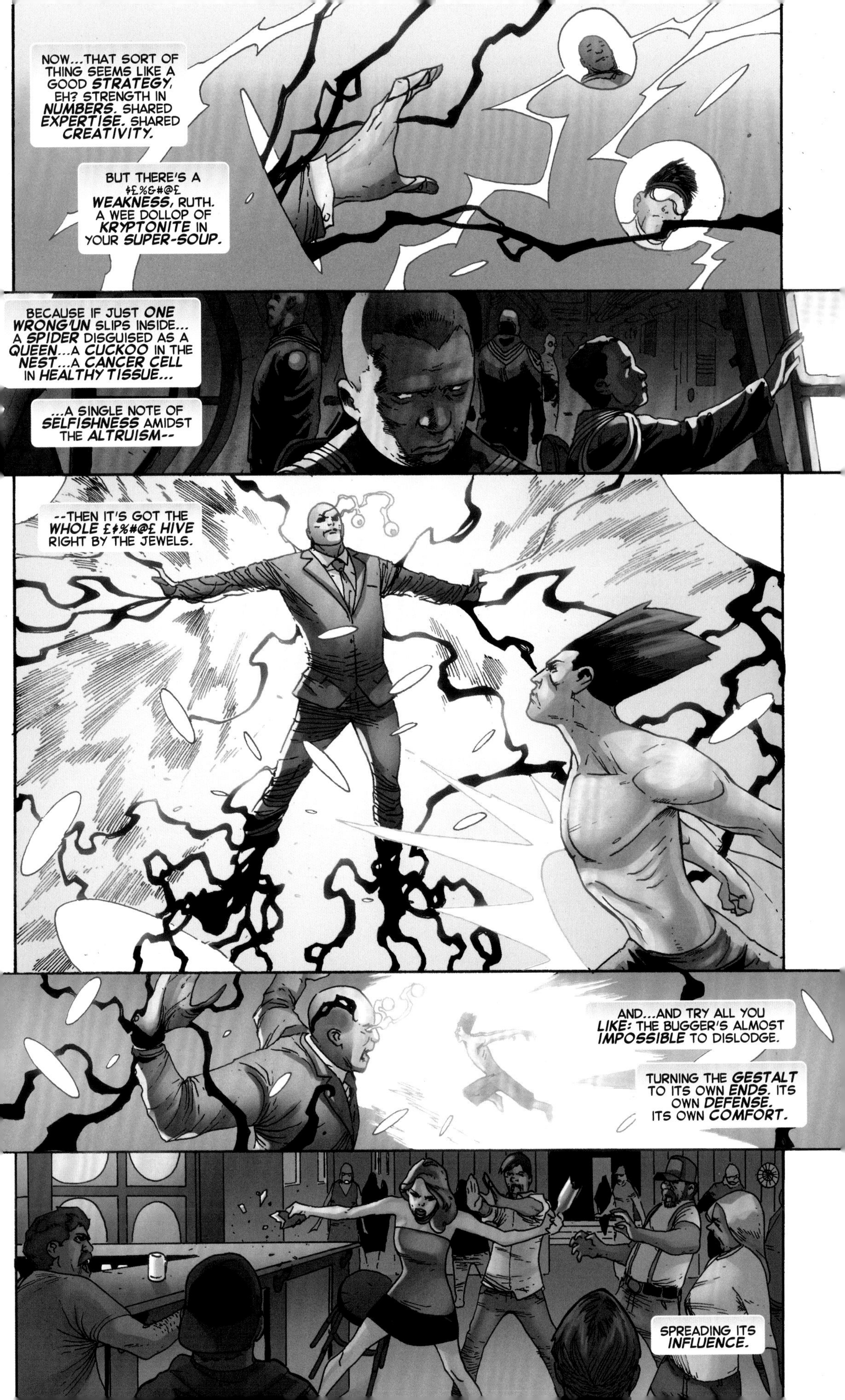
NOW...THAT SORT OF THING SEEMS LIKE A GOOD STRATEGY, EH? STRENGTH IN NUMBERS. SHARED EXPERTISE. SHARED CREATIVITY.
BUT THERE'S A $£%&#@£ WEAKNESS, RUTH. A WEE DOLLOP OF KRYPTONITE IN YOUR SUPER-SOUP.
BECAUSE IF JUST ONE WRONG'UN SLIPS INSIDE... A SPIDER DISGUISED AS A QUEEN...A CUCKOO IN THE NEST...A CANCER CELL IN HEALTHY TISSUE...
...A SINGLE NOTE OF SELFISHNESS AMIDST THE ALTRUISM--
--THEN IT'S GOT THE WHOLE £$%#@£ HIVE RIGHT BY THE JEWELS.
AND...AND TRY ALL YOU LIKE: THE BUGGER'S ALMOST IMPOSSIBLE TO DISLODGE.
TURNING THE GESTALT TO ITS OWN ENDS. ITS OWN DEFENSE. ITS OWN COMFORT.
SPREADING ITS INFLUENCE.

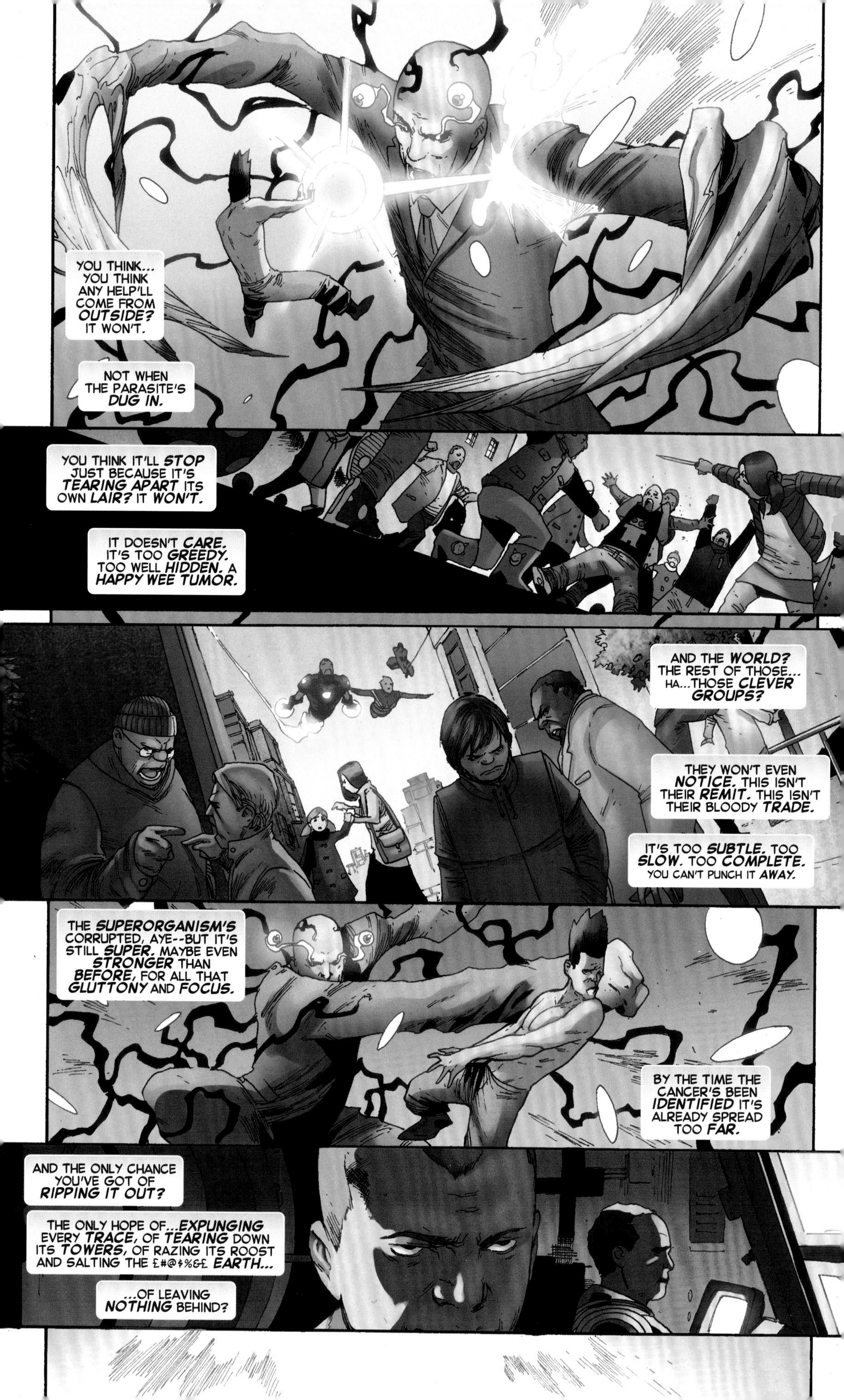
YOU THINK... YOU THINK ANY HELP'LL COME FROM OUTSIDE? IT WON'T.
NOT WHEN THE PARASITE'S DUG IN.
YOU THINK IT'LL STOP JUST BECAUSE IT'S TEARING APART ITS OWN LAIR? IT WON'T.
IT DOESN'T CARE. IT'S TOO GREEDY. TOO WELL HIDDEN. A HAPPY WEE TUMOR.
AND THE WORLD? THE REST OF THOSE... HA...THOSE CLEVER GROUPS?
THEY WON'T EVEN NOTICE. THIS ISN'T THEIR REMIT. THIS ISN'T THEIR BLOODY TRADE.
IT'S TOO SUBTLE. TOO SLOW. TOO COMPLETE. YOU CAN'T PUNCH IT AWAY.
THE SUPERORGANISM'S CORRUPTED, AYE--BUT IT'S STILL SUPER. MAYBE EVEN STRONGER THAN BEFORE, FOR ALL THAT GLUTTONY AND FOCUS.
BY THE TIME THE CANCER'S BEEN IDENTIFIED IT'S ALREADY SPREAD TOO FAR.
AND THE ONLY CHANCE YOU'VE GOT OF RIPPING IT OUT?
THE ONLY HOPE OF...EXPUNGING EVERY TRACE, OF TEARING DOWN ITS TOWERS, OF RAZING ITS ROOST AND SALTING THE £#@$%&£ EARTH...
...OF LEAVING NOTHING BEHIND?

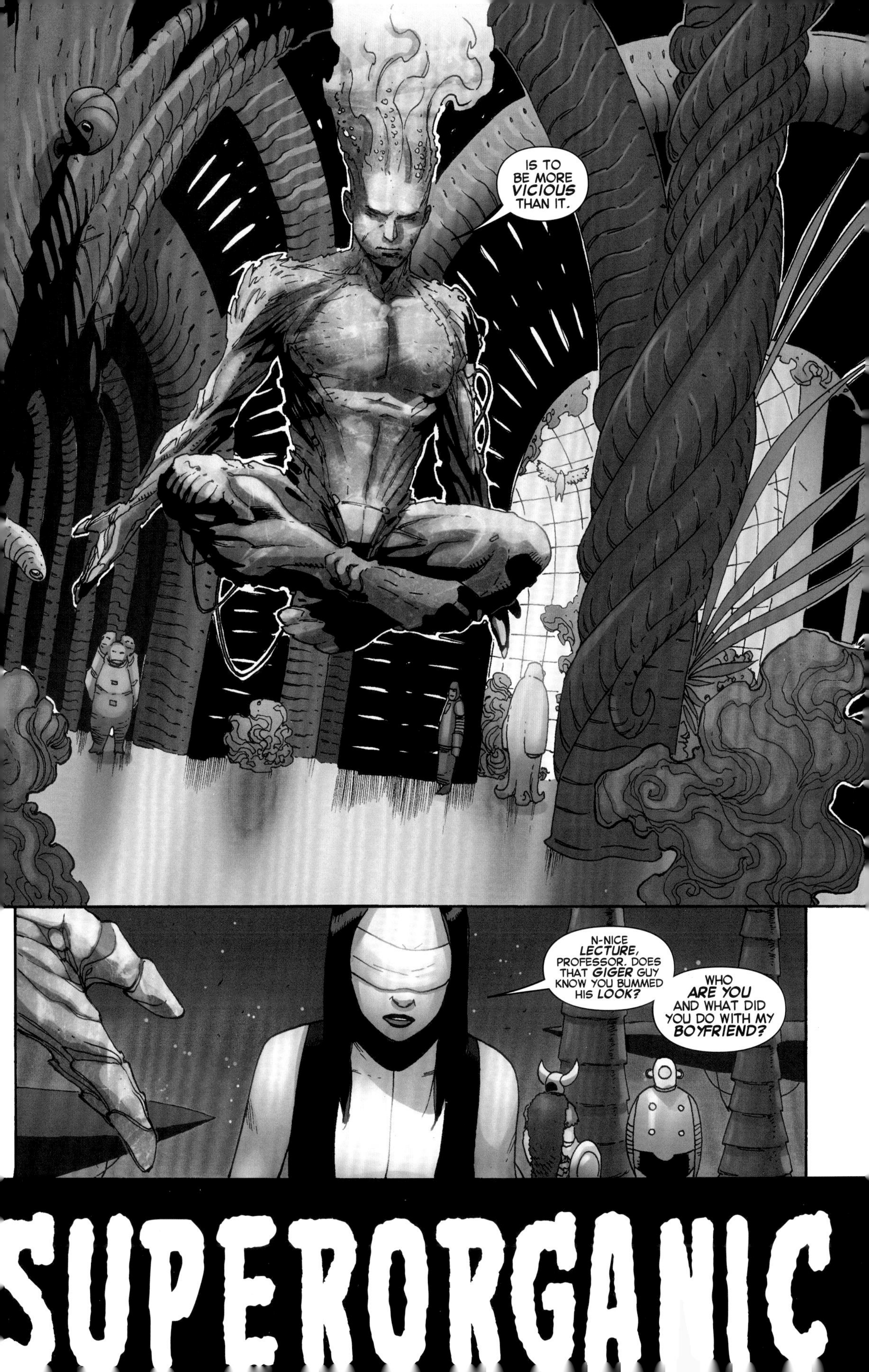
IS TO BE MORE VICIOUS THAN IT.
N-NICE LECTURE, PROFESSOR. DOES THAT GIGER GUY KNOW YOU BUMMED HIS LOOK?
WHO ARE YOU AND WHAT DID YOU DO WITH MY BOYFRIEND?
SUPERORGANIC

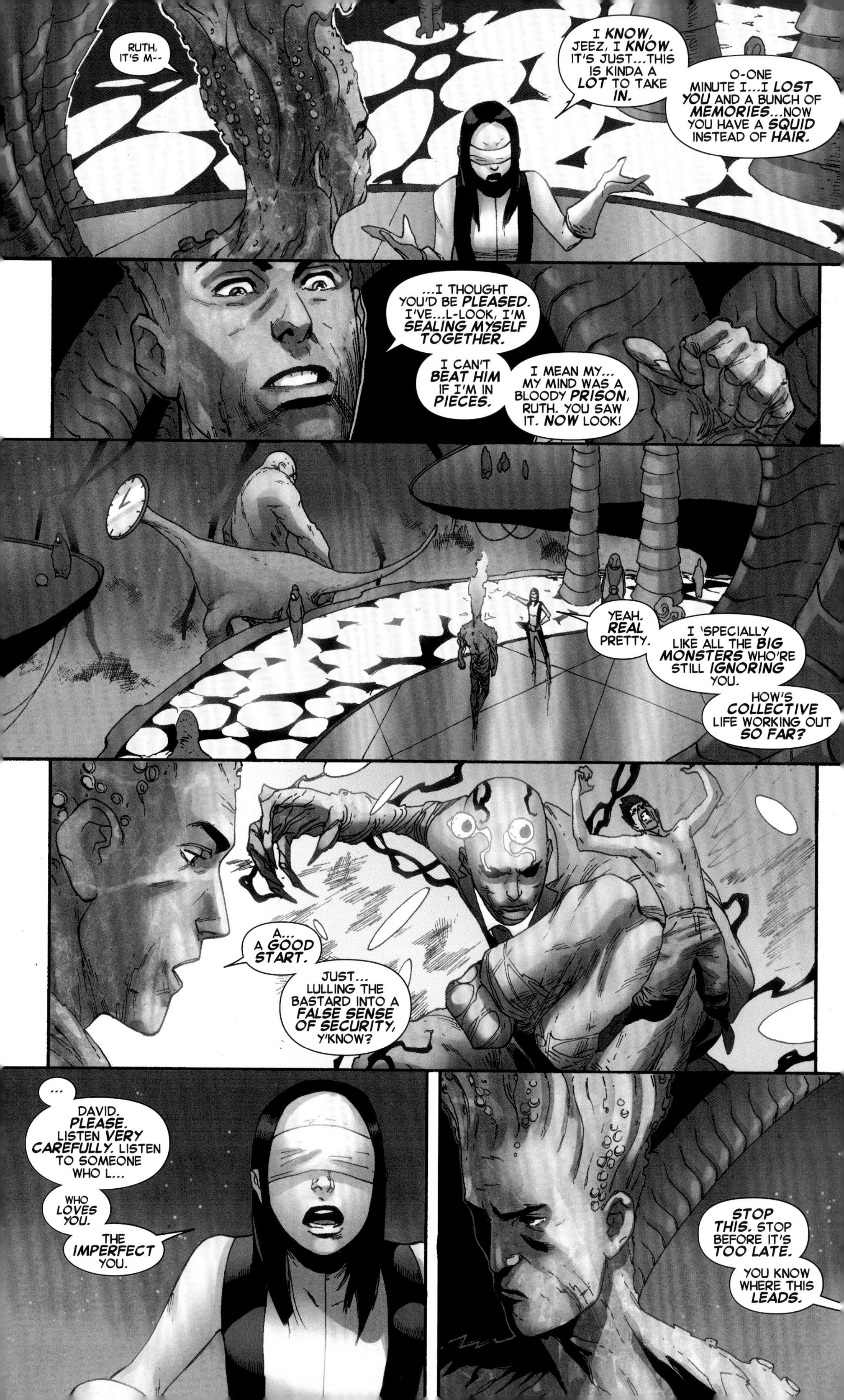
RUTH, IT'S M--
I KNOW, JEEZ, I KNOW. IT'S JUST...THIS IS KINDA A LOT TO TAKE IN.
O-ONE MINUTE I...I LOST YOU AND A BUNCH OF MEMORIES...NOW YOU HAVE A SQUID INSTEAD OF HAIR.
...I THOUGHT YOU'D BE PLEASED. I'VE...L-LOOK, I'M SEALING MYSELF TOGETHER.
I CAN'T BEAT HIM IF I'M IN PIECES.
I MEAN MY... MY MIND WAS A BLOODY PRISON, RUTH. YOU SAW IT. NOW LOOK!
YEAH. REAL PRETTY.
I 'SPECIALLY LIKE ALL THE BIG MONSTERS WHO'RE STILL IGNORING YOU.
HOW'S COLLECTIVE LIFE WORKING OUT SO FAR?
A... A GOOD START.
JUST... LULLING THE BASTARD INTO A FALSE SENSE OF SECURITY, Y'KNOW?
...
DAVID. PLEASE. LISTEN VERY CAREFULLY. LISTEN TO SOMEONE WHO L...
WHO LOVES YOU.
THE IMPERFECT YOU.
STOP THIS. STOP BEFORE IT'S TOO LATE.
YOU KNOW WHERE THIS LEADS.

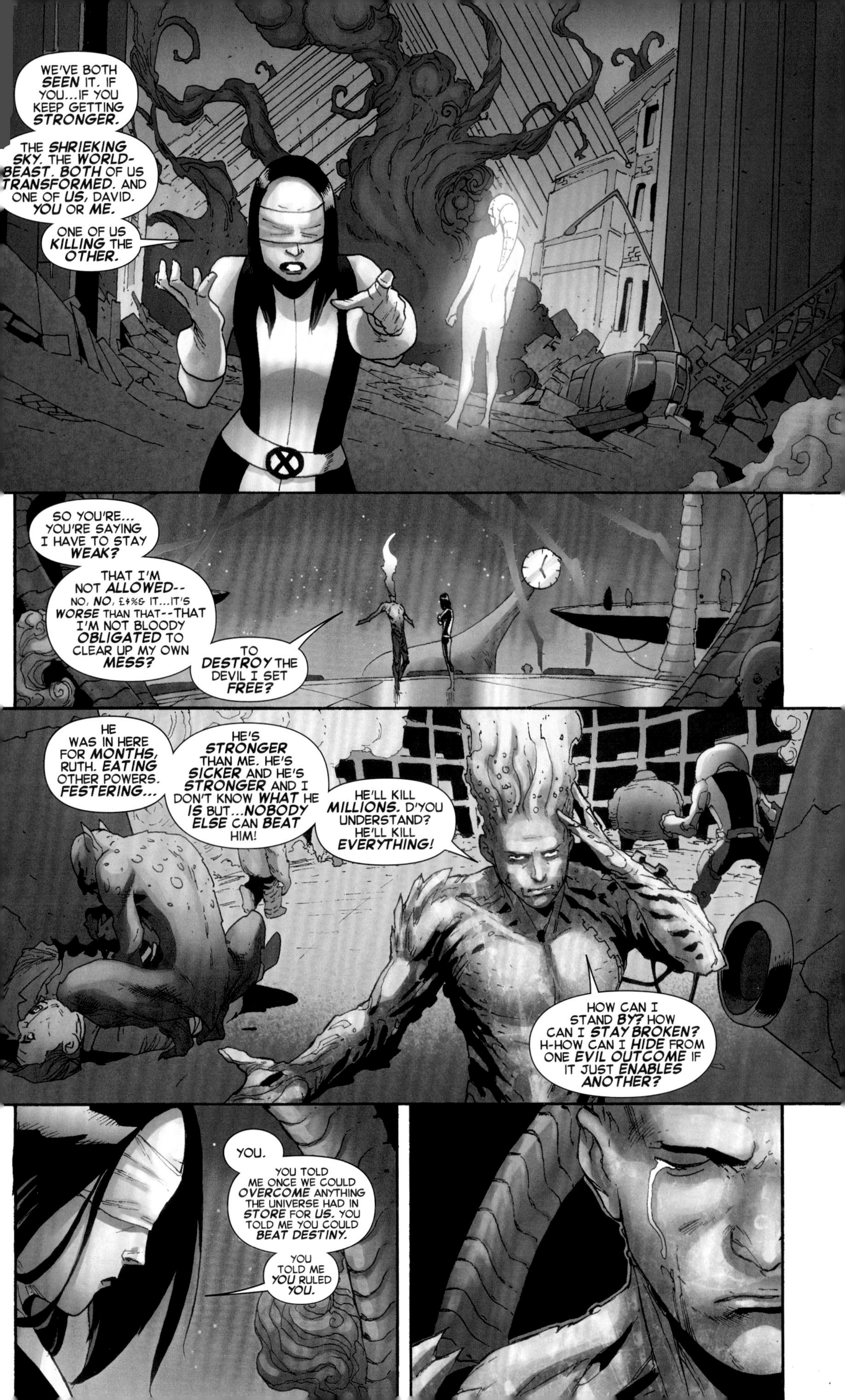
WE'VE BOTH SEEN IT. IF YOU...IF YOU KEEP GETTING STRONGER.
THE SHRIEKING SKY. THE WORLD-BEAST. BOTH OF US TRANSFORMED. AND ONE OF US, DAVID. YOU OR ME.
ONE OF US KILLING THE OTHER.
SO YOU'RE... YOU'RE SAYING I HAVE TO STAY WEAK?
THAT I'M NOT ALLOWED-- NO, NO, £$%& IT...IT'S WORSE THAN THAT--THAT I'M NOT BLOODY OBLIGATED TO CLEAR UP MY OWN MESS?
TO DESTROY THE DEVIL I SET FREE?
HE WAS IN HERE FOR MONTHS, RUTH. EATING OTHER POWERS. FESTERING...
HE'S STRONGER THAN ME. HE'S SICKER AND HE'S STRONGER AND I DON'T KNOW WHAT HE IS BUT...NOBODY ELSE CAN BEAT HIM!
HE'LL KILL MILLIONS. D'YOU UNDERSTAND? HE'LL KILL EVERYTHING!
HOW CAN I STAND BY? HOW CAN I STAY BROKEN? H-HOW CAN I HIDE FROM ONE EVIL OUTCOME IF IT JUST ENABLES ANOTHER?
YOU.
YOU TOLD ME ONCE WE COULD OVERCOME ANYTHING THE UNIVERSE HAD IN STORE FOR US. YOU TOLD ME YOU COULD BEAT DESTINY.
YOU TOLD ME YOU RULED YOU.

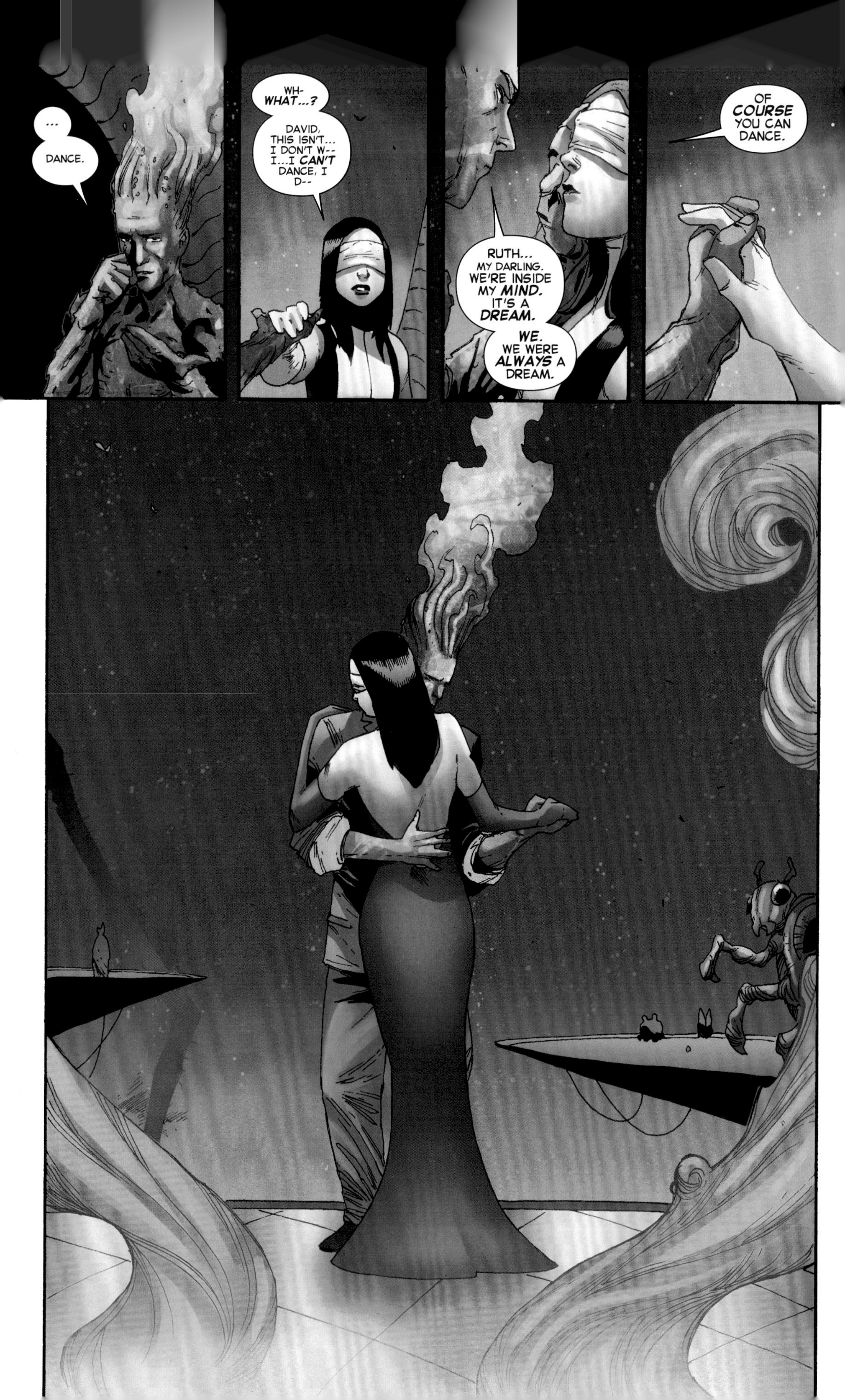
...
DANCE.
WH- WHAT...?
DAVID, THIS ISN'T... I DON'T W-- I...I CAN'T DANCE, I D--
RUTH... MY DARLING. WE'RE INSIDE MY MIND. IT'S A DREAM.
WE. WE WERE ALWAYS A DREAM.
OF COURSE YOU CAN DANCE.

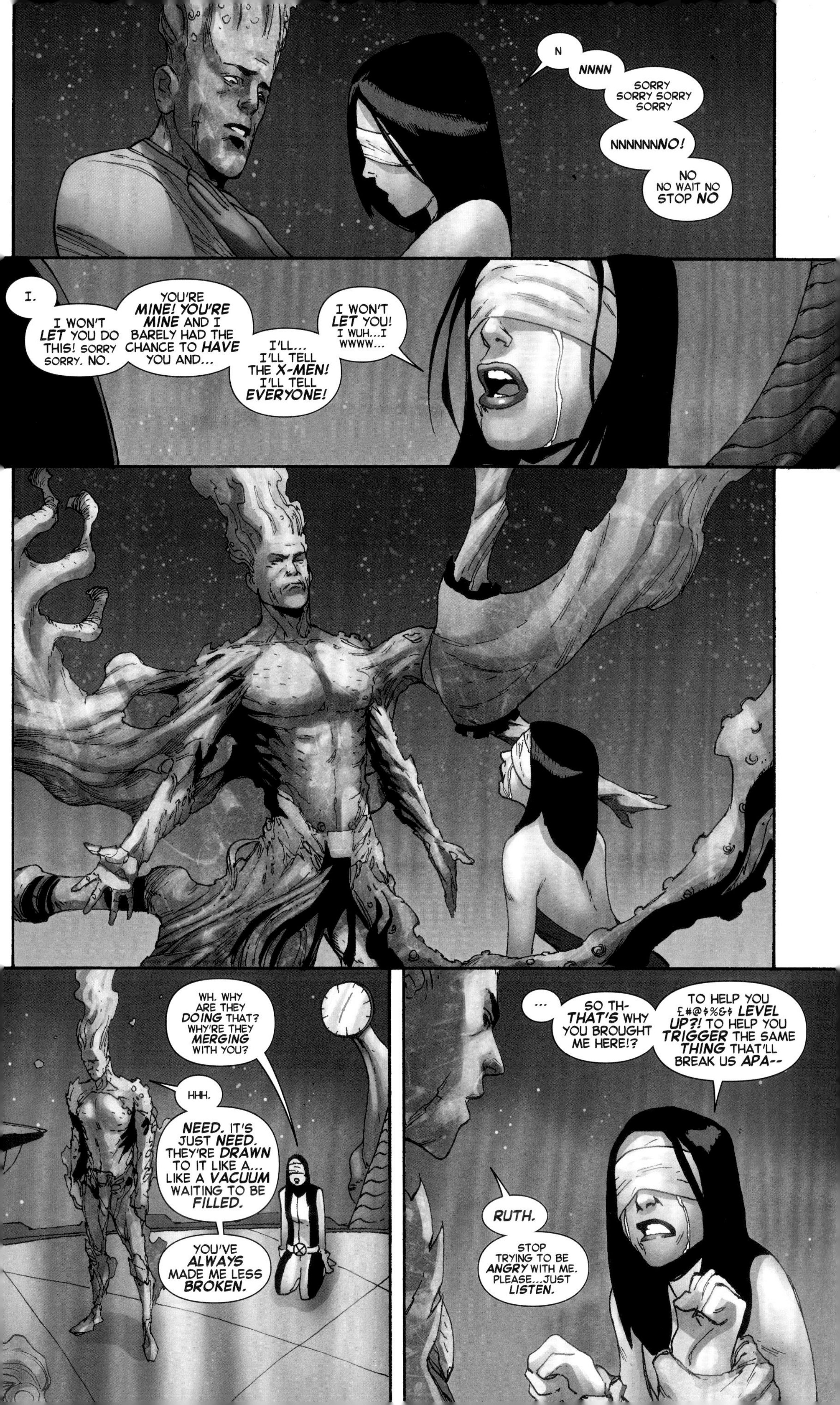
N
NNNN
SORRY SORRY SORRY SORRY
NNNNNNNO!
NO NO WAIT NO STOP NO
I.
I WON'T LET YOU DO THIS! SORRY SORRY. NO.
YOU'RE MINE! YOU'RE MINE AND I BARELY HAD THE CHANCE TO HAVE YOU AND...
I'LL... I'LL TELL THE X-MEN! I'LL TELL EVERYONE!
I WON'T LET YOU! I WUH...I WWWW...
WH. WHY ARE THEY DOING THAT? WHY'RE THEY MERGING WITH YOU?
HHH.
NEED. IT'S JUST NEED. THEY'RE DRAWN TO IT LIKE A... LIKE A VACUUM WAITING TO BE FILLED.
YOU'VE ALWAYS MADE ME LESS BROKEN.
...
SO TH- THAT'S WHY YOU BROUGHT ME HERE!?
TO HELP YOU £#@$%&$ LEVEL UP?! TO HELP YOU TRIGGER THE SAME THING THAT'LL BREAK US APA--
RUTH.
STOP TRYING TO BE ANGRY WITH ME. PLEASE...JUST LISTEN.

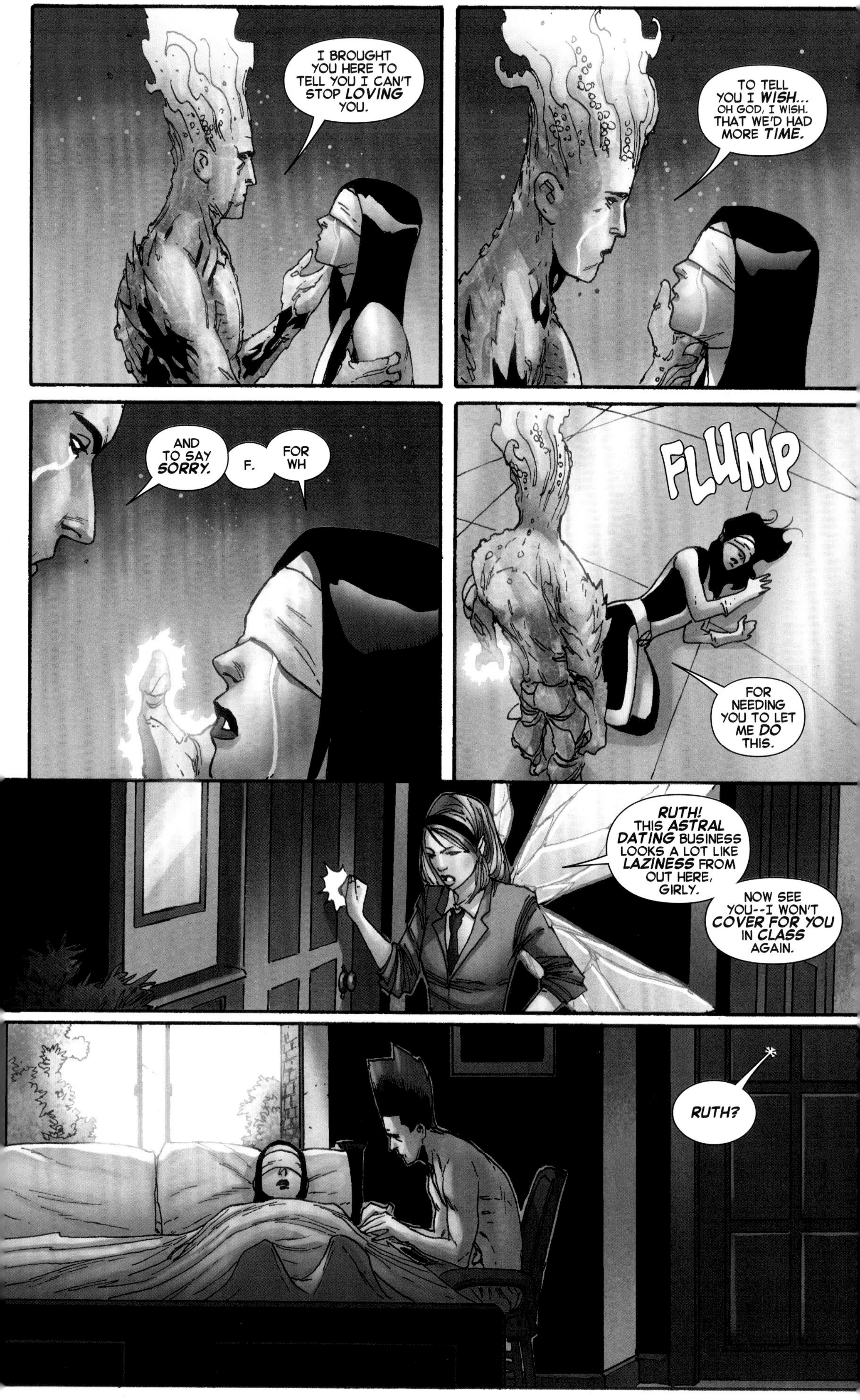

I BROUGHT YOU HERE TO TELL YOU I CAN'T STOP LOVING YOU.
TO TELL YOU I WISH... OH GOD, I WISH. THAT WE'D HAD MORE TIME.
AND TO SAY SORRY.
F.
FOR WH
FLUMP
FOR NEEDING YOU TO LET ME DO THIS.
RUTH! THIS ASTRAL DATING BUSINESS LOOKS A LOT LIKE LAZINESS FROM OUT HERE, GIRLY.
NOW SEE YOU--I WON'T COVER FOR YOU IN CLASS AGAIN.
RUTH?

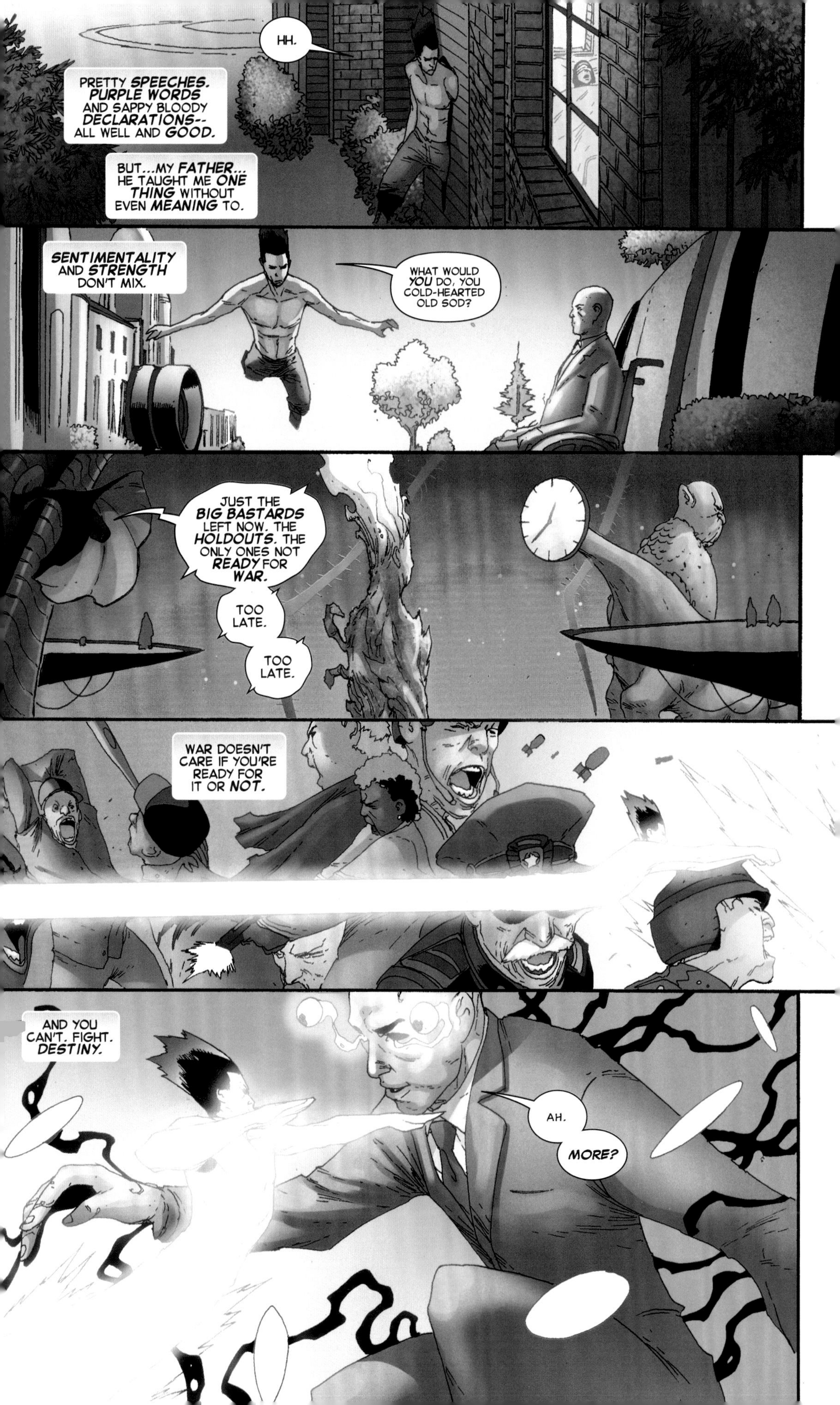
HH.
PRETTY SPEECHES. PURPLE WORDS AND SAPPY BLOODY DECLARATIONS-- ALL WELL AND GOOD.
BUT...MY FATHER... HE TAUGHT ME ONE THING WITHOUT EVEN MEANING TO.
SENTIMENTALITY AND STRENGTH DON'T MIX.
WHAT WOULD YOU DO, YOU COLD-HEARTED OLD SOD?
JUST THE BIG BASTARDS LEFT NOW. THE HOLDOUTS. THE ONLY ONES NOT READY FOR WAR.
TOO LATE.
TOO LATE.
WAR DOESN'T CARE IF YOU'RE READY FOR IT OR NOT.
AND YOU CAN'T. FIGHT. DESTINY.
AH.
MORE?

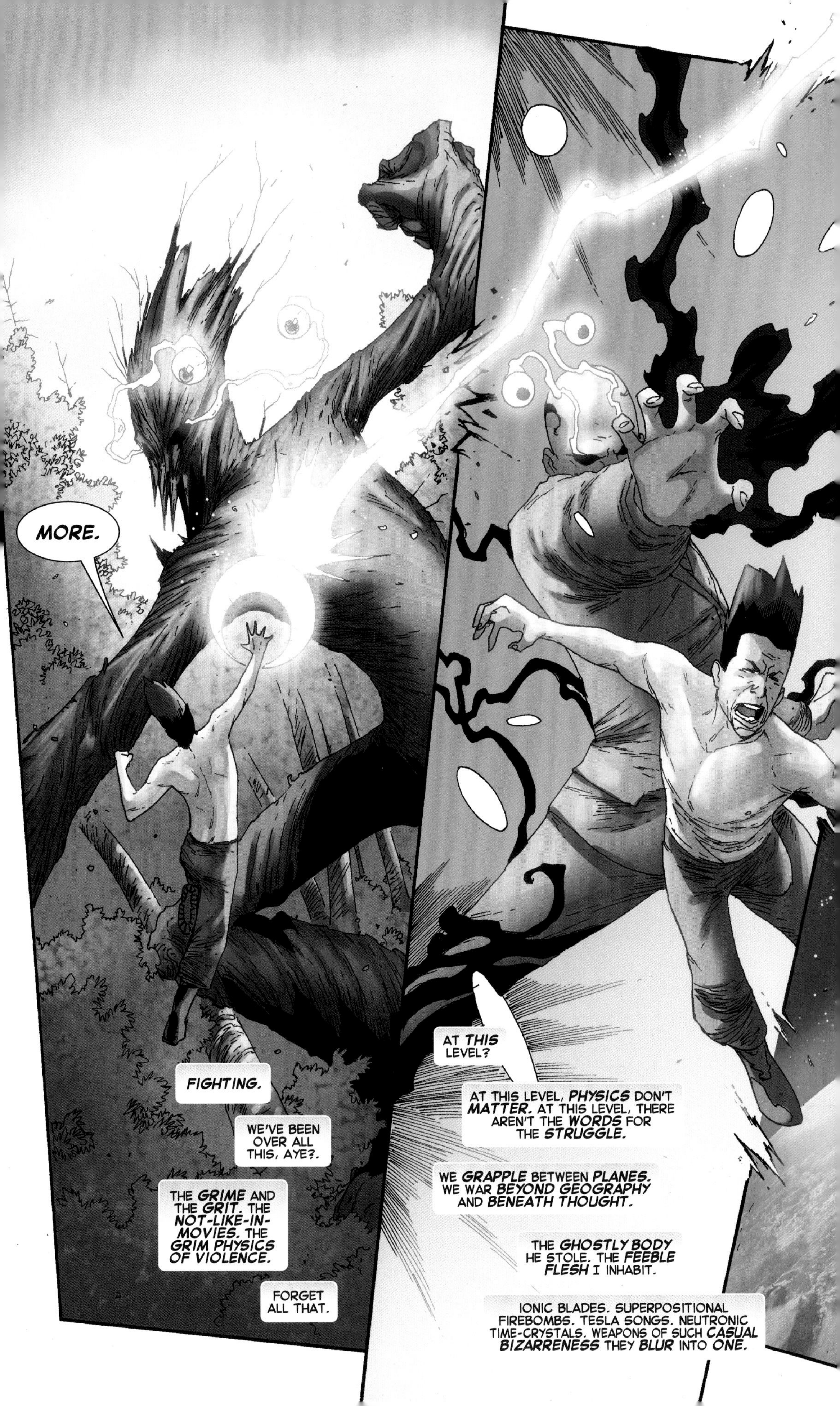

MORE.
FIGHTING.
WE'VE BEEN OVER ALL THIS, AYE?.
THE GRIME AND THE GRIT. THE NOT-LIKE-IN-MOVIES. THE GRIM PHYSICS OF VIOLENCE.
FORGET ALL THAT.
AT THIS LEVEL?
AT THIS LEVEL, PHYSICS DON'T MATTER. AT THIS LEVEL, THERE AREN'T THE WORDS FOR THE STRUGGLE.
WE GRAPPLE BETWEEN PLANES. WE WAR BEYOND GEOGRAPHY AND BENEATH THOUGHT.
THE GHOSTLY BODY HE STOLE. THE FEEBLE FLESH I INHABIT.
IONIC BLADES. SUPERPOSITIONAL FIREBOMBS. TESLA SONGS. NEUTRONIC TIME-CRYSTALS. WEAPONS OF SUCH CASUAL BIZARRENESS THEY BLUR INTO ONE.

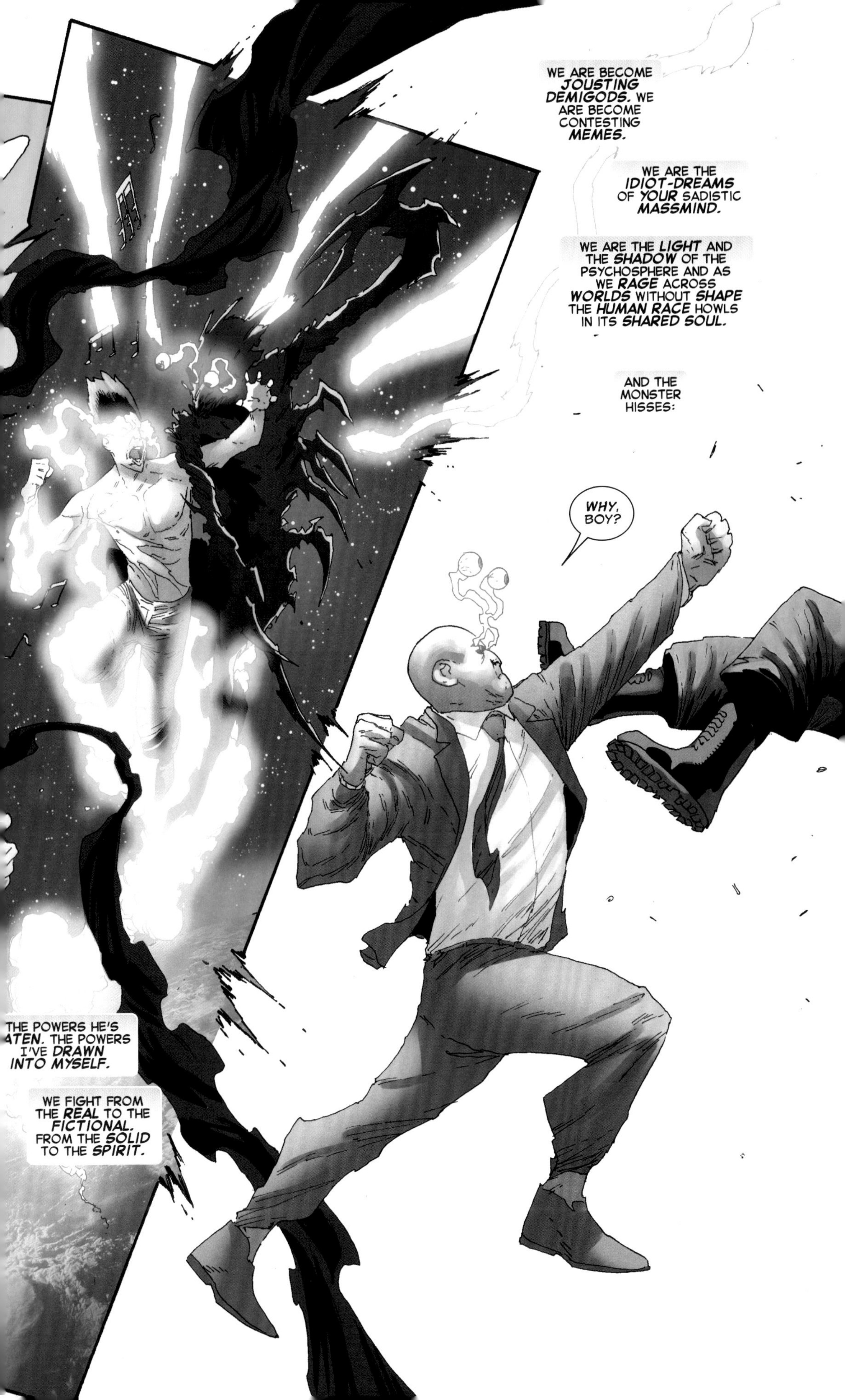

WE ARE BECOME JOUSTING DEMIGODS. WE ARE BECOME CONTESTING MEMES.
WE ARE THE IDIOT-DREAMS OF YOUR SADISTIC MASSMIND.
WE ARE THE LIGHT AND THE SHADOW OF THE PSYCHOSPHERE AND AS WE RAGE ACROSS WORLDS WITHOUT SHAPE THE HUMAN RACE HOWLS IN ITS SHARED SOUL.
AND THE MONSTER HISSES:
WHY, BOY?
THE POWERS HE'S ATEN. THE POWERS I'VE DRAWN INTO MYSELF.
WE FIGHT FROM THE REAL TO THE FICTIONAL. FROM THE SOLID TO THE SPIRIT.

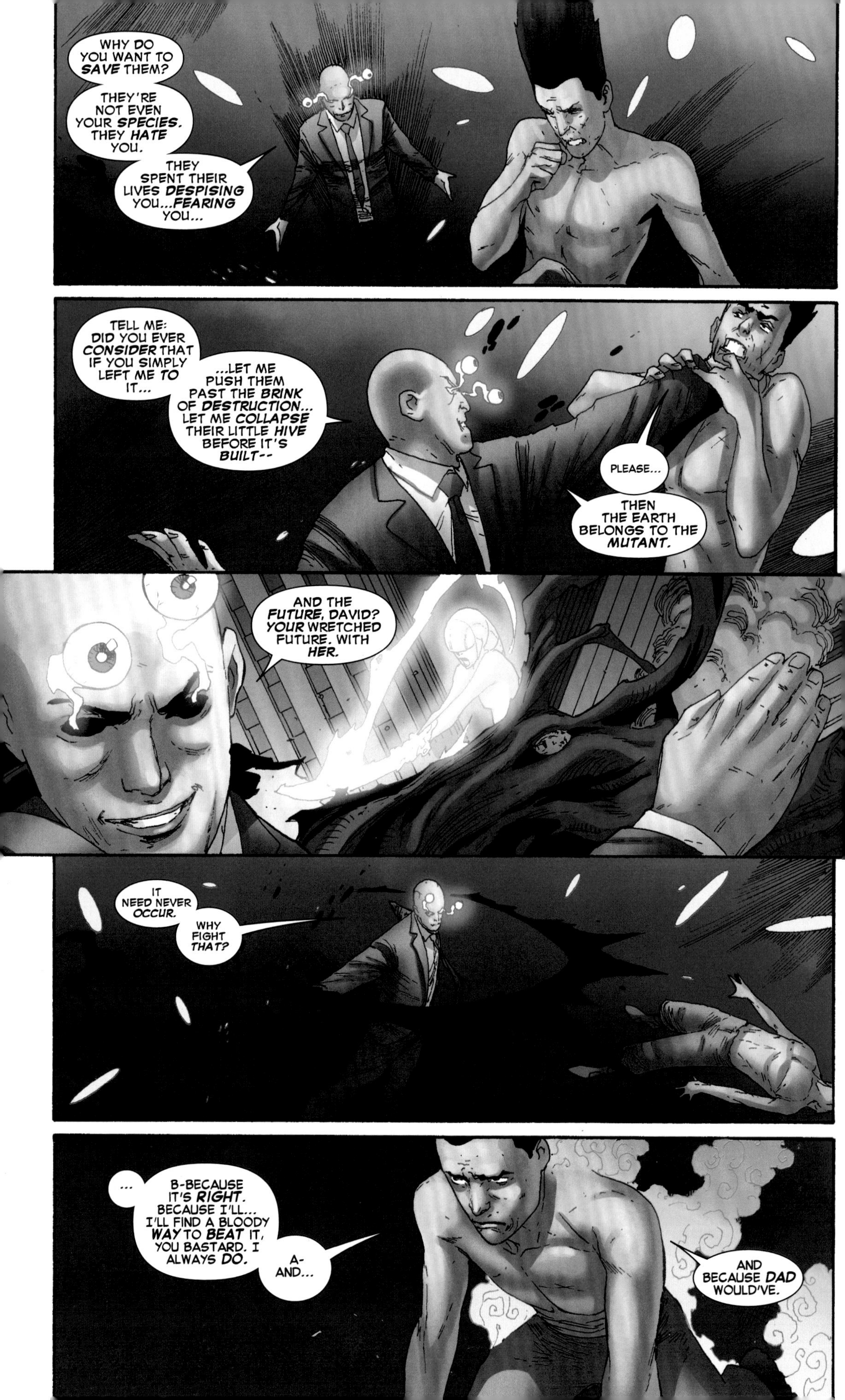
WHY DO YOU WANT TO SAVE THEM?
THEY'RE NOT EVEN YOUR SPECIES. THEY HATE YOU.
THEY SPENT THEIR LIVES DESPISING YOU...FEARING YOU...
TELL ME: DID YOU EVER CONSIDER THAT IF YOU SIMPLY LEFT ME TO IT...
...LET ME PUSH THEM PAST THE BRINK OF DESTRUCTION... LET ME COLLAPSE THEIR LITTLE HIVE BEFORE IT'S BUILT--
PLEASE...
THEN THE EARTH BELONGS TO THE MUTANT.
AND THE FUTURE, DAVID? YOUR WRETCHED FUTURE. WITH HER.
IT NEED NEVER OCCUR.
WHY FIGHT THAT?
...
B-BECAUSE IT'S RIGHT. BECAUSE I'LL... I'LL FIND A BLOODY WAY TO BEAT IT, YOU BASTARD. I ALWAYS DO.
A- AND...
AND BECAUSE DAD WOULD'VE.

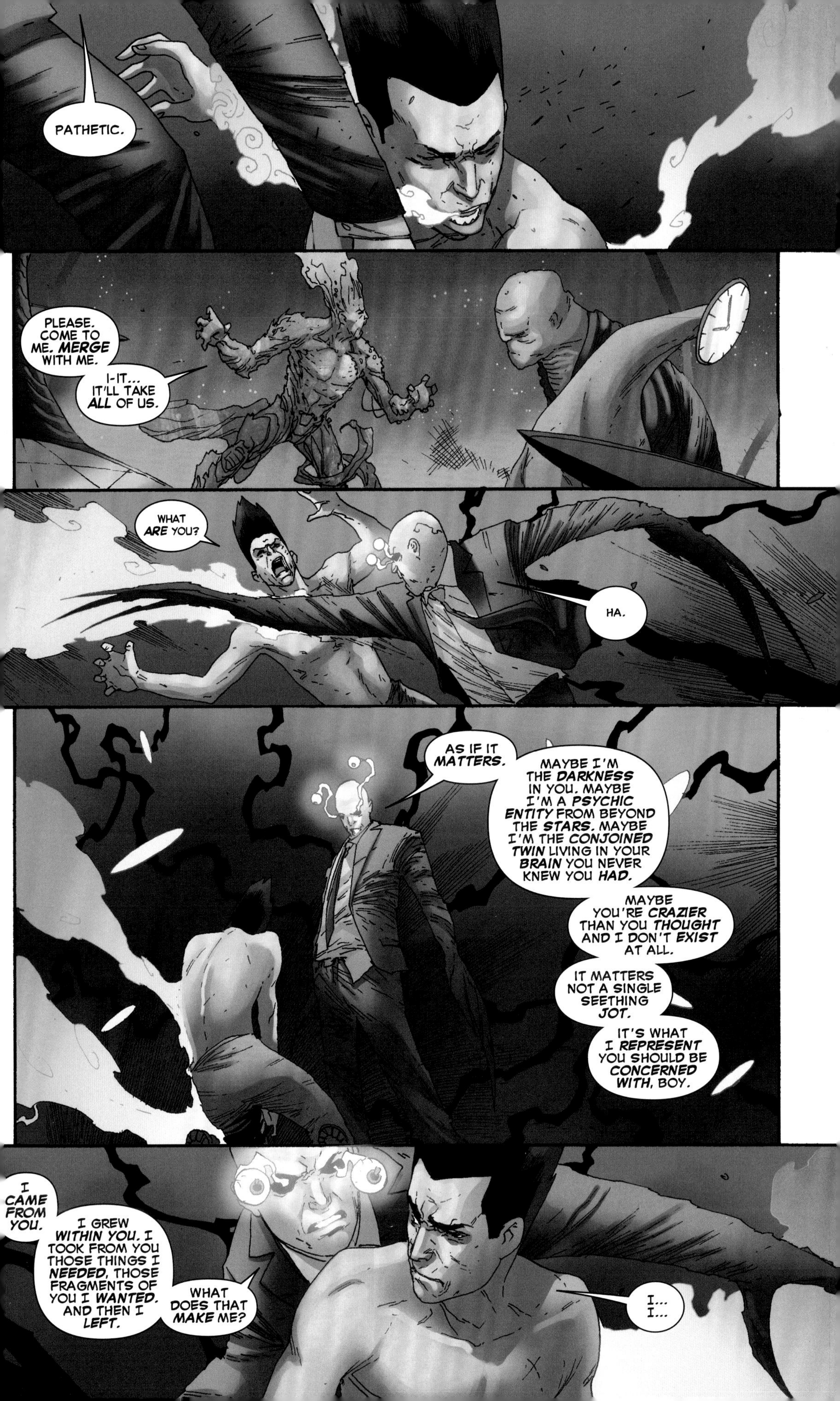

PATHETIC.
PLEASE. COME TO ME. MERGE WITH ME.
I-IT... IT'LL TAKE ALL OF US.
WHAT ARE YOU?
HA.
AS IF IT MATTERS.
MAYBE I'M THE DARKNESS IN YOU. MAYBE I'M A PSYCHIC ENTITY FROM BEYOND THE STARS. MAYBE I'M THE CONJOINED TWIN LIVING IN YOUR BRAIN YOU NEVER KNEW YOU HAD.
MAYBE YOU'RE CRAZIER THAN YOU THOUGHT AND I DON'T EXIST AT ALL.
IT MATTERS NOT A SINGLE SEETHING JOT.
IT'S WHAT I REPRESENT YOU SHOULD BE CONCERNED WITH, BOY.
I CAME FROM YOU.
I GREW WITHIN YOU. I TOOK FROM YOU THOSE THINGS I NEEDED, THOSE FRAGMENTS OF YOU I WANTED. AND THEN I LEFT.
WHAT DOES THAT MAKE ME?
I... I...

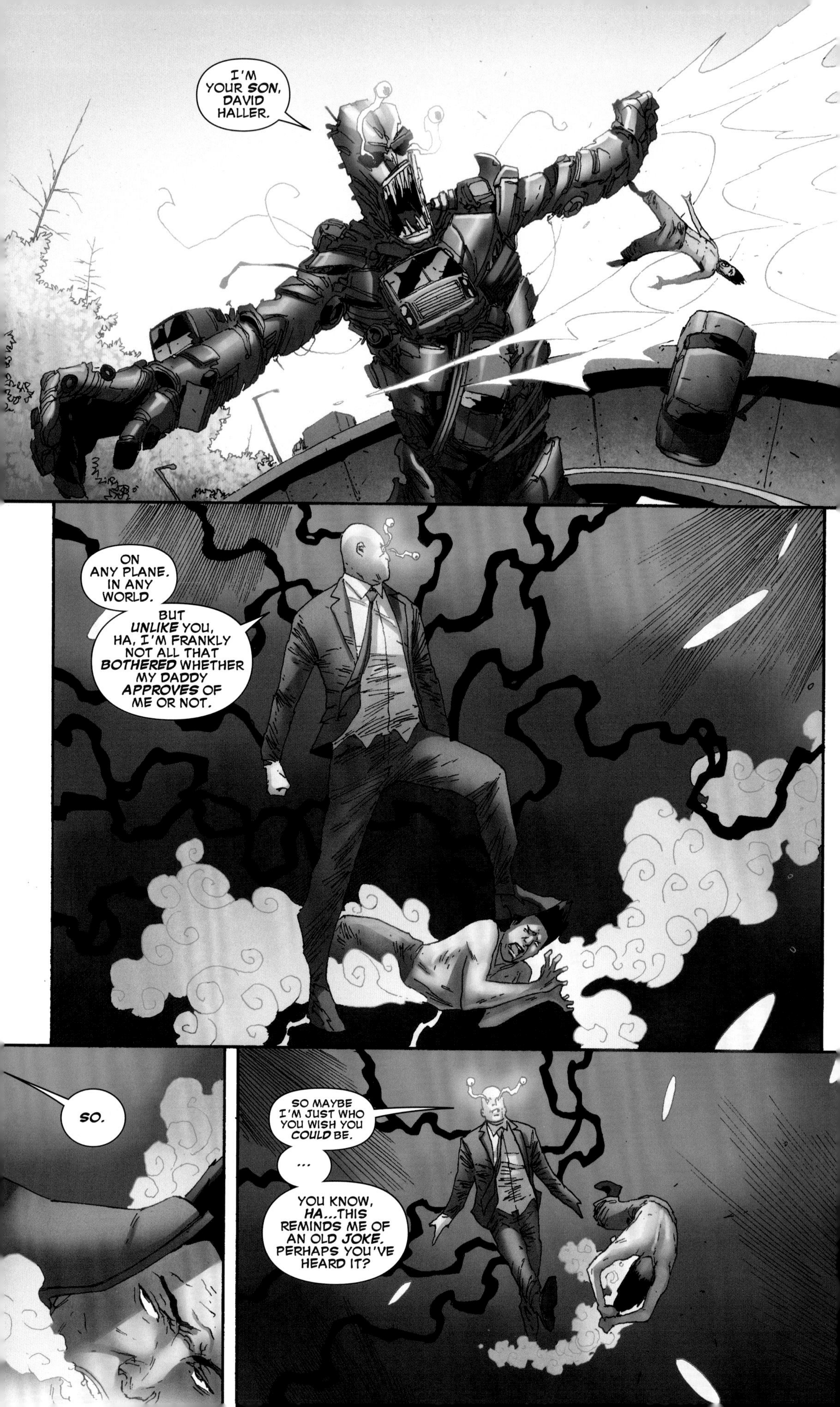
I'M YOUR SON, DAVID HALLER.
ON ANY PLANE. IN ANY WORLD.
BUT UNLIKE YOU, HA, I'M FRANKLY NOT ALL THAT BOTHERED WHETHER MY DADDY APPROVES OF ME OR NOT.
SO.
SO MAYBE I'M JUST WHO YOU WISH YOU COULD BE.
...
YOU KNOW, HA...THIS REMINDS ME OF AN OLD JOKE. PERHAPS YOU'VE HEARD IT?

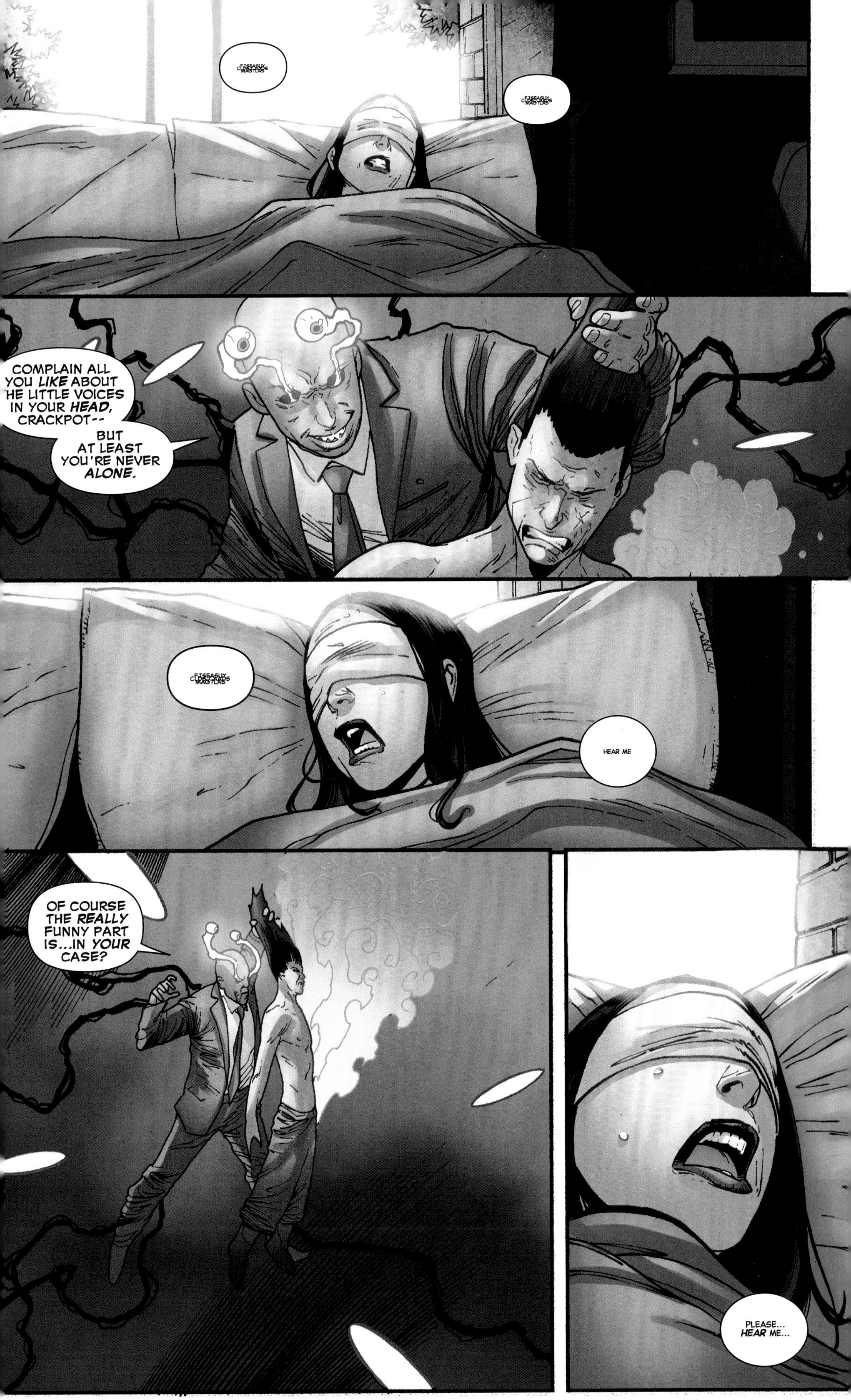

COMPLAIN ALL YOU LIKE ABOUT HE LITTLE VOICES IN YOUR HEAD, CRACKPOT--
BUT AT LEAST YOU'RE NEVER ALONE.
HEAR ME
OF COURSE THE REALLY FUNNY PART IS...IN YOUR CASE?
PLEASE... HEAR ME...

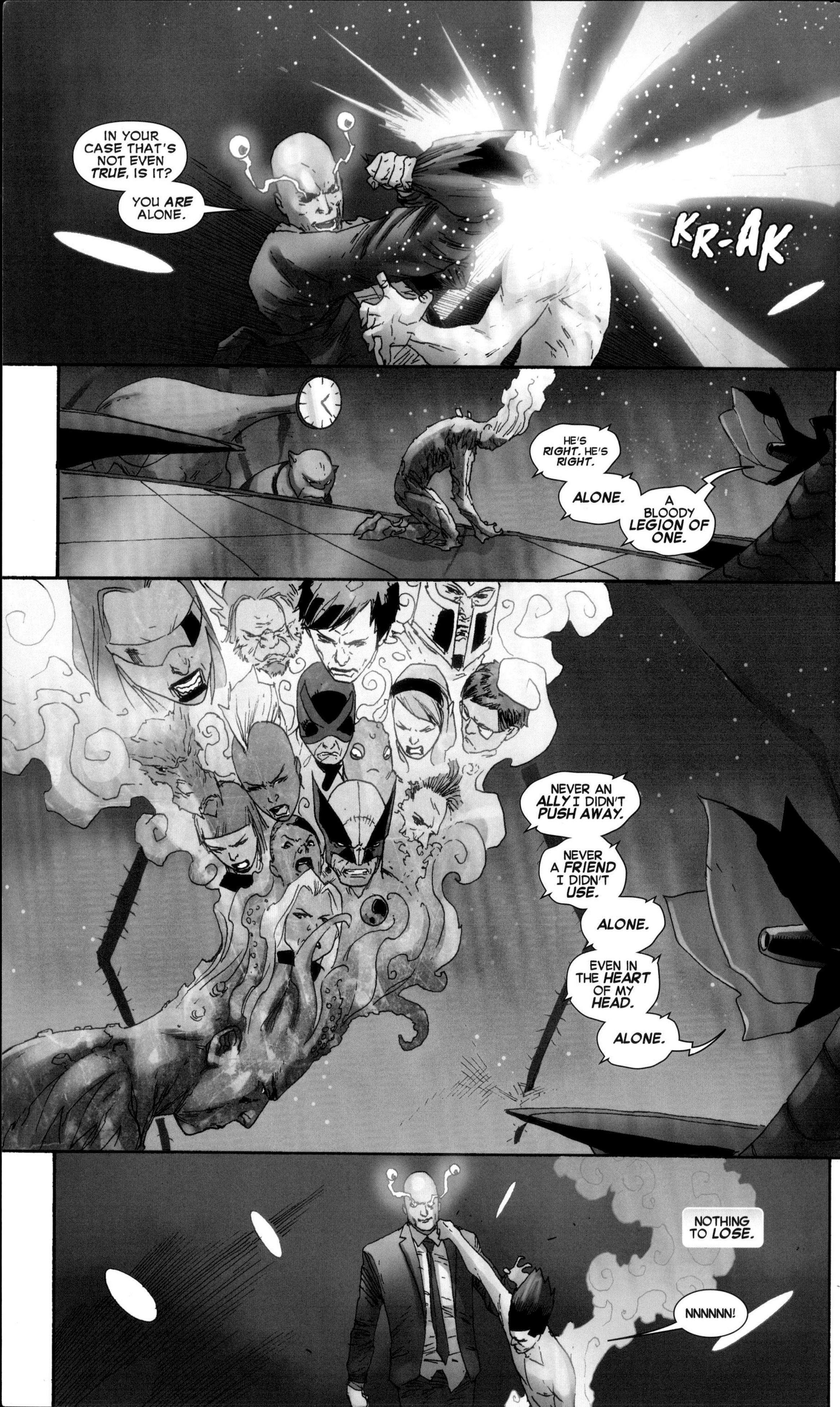
IN YOUR CASE THAT'S NOT EVEN TRUE, IS IT?
YOU ARE ALONE.
KR-AK
HE'S RIGHT. HE'S RIGHT.
ALONE.
A BLOODY LEGION OF ONE.
NEVER AN ALLY I DIDN'T PUSH AWAY.
NEVER A FRIEND I DIDN'T USE.
ALONE.
EVEN IN THE HEART OF MY HEAD.
ALONE.
NOTHING TO LOSE.
NNNNNN!

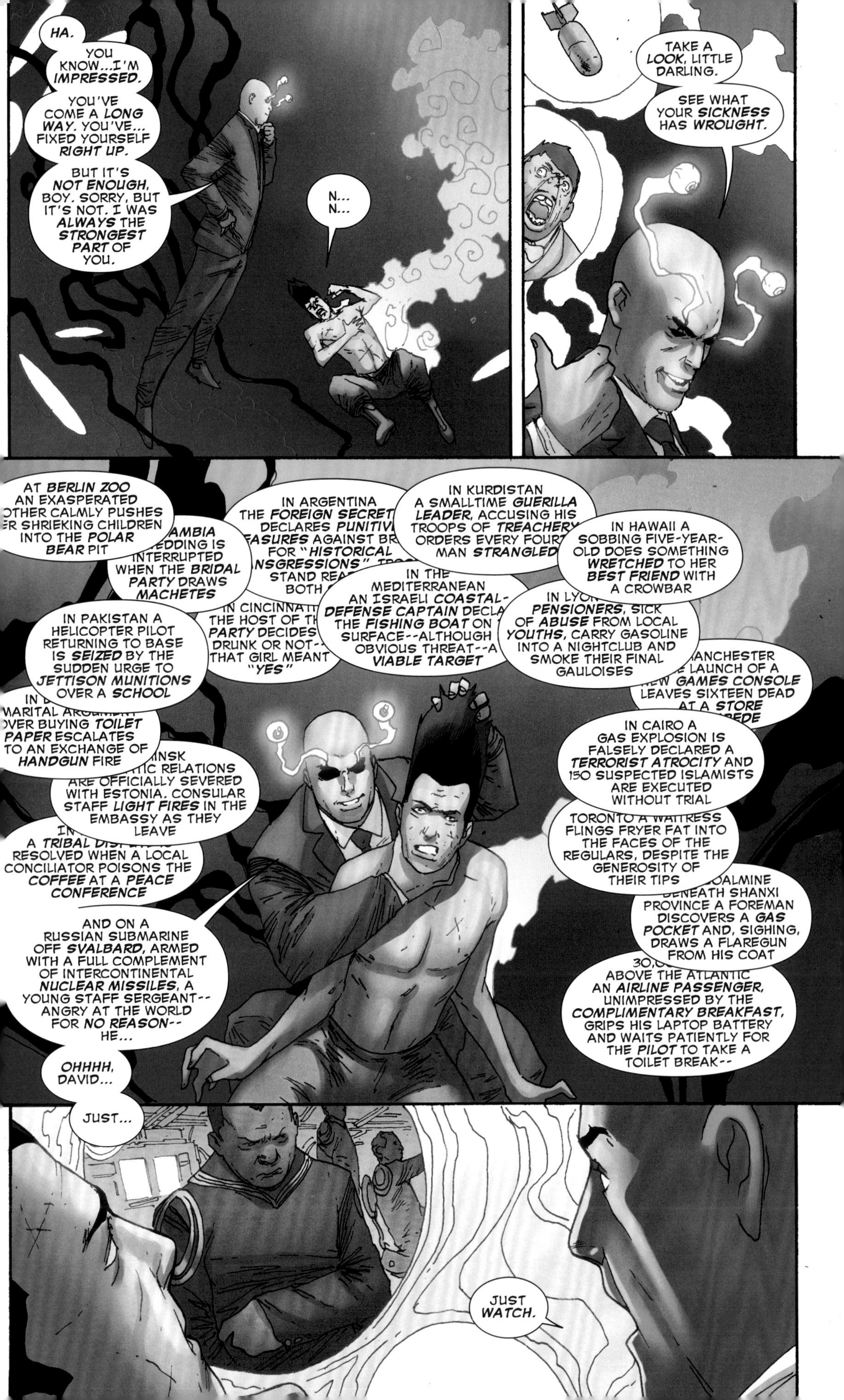
HA.
YOU KNOW...I'M IMPRESSED.
YOU'VE COME A LONG WAY. YOU'VE... FIXED YOURSELF RIGHT UP.
BUT IT'S NOT ENOUGH, BOY. SORRY, BUT IT'S NOT. I WAS ALWAYS THE STRONGEST PART OF YOU.
N... N...
TAKE A LOOK, LITTLE DARLING.
SEE WHAT YOUR SICKNESS HAS WROUGHT.
AT BERLIN ZOO AN EXASPERATED OTHER CALMLY PUSHES ER SHRIEKING CHILDREN INTO THE POLAR BEAR PIT
AMBIA EDDING IS INTERRUPTED WHEN THE BRIDAL PARTY DRAWS MACHETES
IN ARGENTINA THE FOREIGN SECRET DECLARES PUNITIV EASURES AGAINST BR FOR "HISTORICAL NSGRESSIONS". STAND REA BOTH
IN KURDISTAN A SMALLTIME GUERILLA LEADER, ACCUSING HIS TROOPS OF TREACHERY ORDERS EVERY FOURT MAN STRANGLED
IN HAWAII A SOBBING FIVE-YEAR-OLD DOES SOMETHING WRETCHED TO HER BEST FRIEND WITH A CROWBAR
IN THE MEDITERRANEAN AN ISRAELI COASTAL-DEFENSE CAPTAIN DECLA THE FISHING BOAT ON SURFACE--ALTHOUGH OBVIOUS THREAT--A VIABLE TARGET
IN CINCINNATI THE HOST OF TH PARTY DECIDES DRUNK OR NOT-- THAT GIRL MEANT "YES"
IN LYON PENSIONERS, SICK OF ABUSE FROM LOCAL YOUTHS, CARRY GASOLINE INTO A NIGHTCLUB AND SMOKE THEIR FINAL GAULOISES
IN PAKISTAN A HELICOPTER PILOT RETURNING TO BASE IS SEIZED BY THE SUDDEN URGE TO JETTISON MUNITIONS OVER A SCHOOL
MANCHESTER LAUNCH OF A NEW GAMES CONSOLE LEAVES SIXTEEN DEAD AT A STORE
MARITAL ARGUMENT OVER BUYING TOILET PAPER ESCALATES TO AN EXCHANGE OF HANDGUN FIRE
IN CAIRO A GAS EXPLOSION IS FALSELY DECLARED A TERRORIST ATROCITY AND 150 SUSPECTED ISLAMISTS ARE EXECUTED WITHOUT TRIAL
MINSK TIC RELATIONS ARE OFFICIALLY SEVERED WITH ESTONIA. CONSULAR STAFF LIGHT FIRES IN THE EMBASSY AS THEY LEAVE
TORONTO A WAITRESS FLINGS FRYER FAT INTO THE FACES OF THE REGULARS, DESPITE THE GENEROSITY OF THEIR TIPS
A TRIBAL DIS RESOLVED WHEN A LOCAL CONCILIATOR POISONS THE COFFEE AT A PEACE CONFERENCE
COALMINE BENEATH SHANXI PROVINCE A FOREMAN DISCOVERS A GAS POCKET AND, SIGHING, DRAWS A FLAREGUN FROM HIS COAT
AND ON A RUSSIAN SUBMARINE OFF SVALBARD, ARMED WITH A FULL COMPLEMENT OF INTERCONTINENTAL NUCLEAR MISSILES, A YOUNG STAFF SERGEANT-- ANGRY AT THE WORLD FOR NO REASON-- HE...
ABOVE THE ATLANTIC AN AIRLINE PASSENGER, UNIMPRESSED BY THE COMPLIMENTARY BREAKFAST, GRIPS HIS LAPTOP BATTERY AND WAITS PATIENTLY FOR THE PILOT TO TAKE A TOILET BREAK--
OHHHH, DAVID...
JUST...
JUST WATCH.

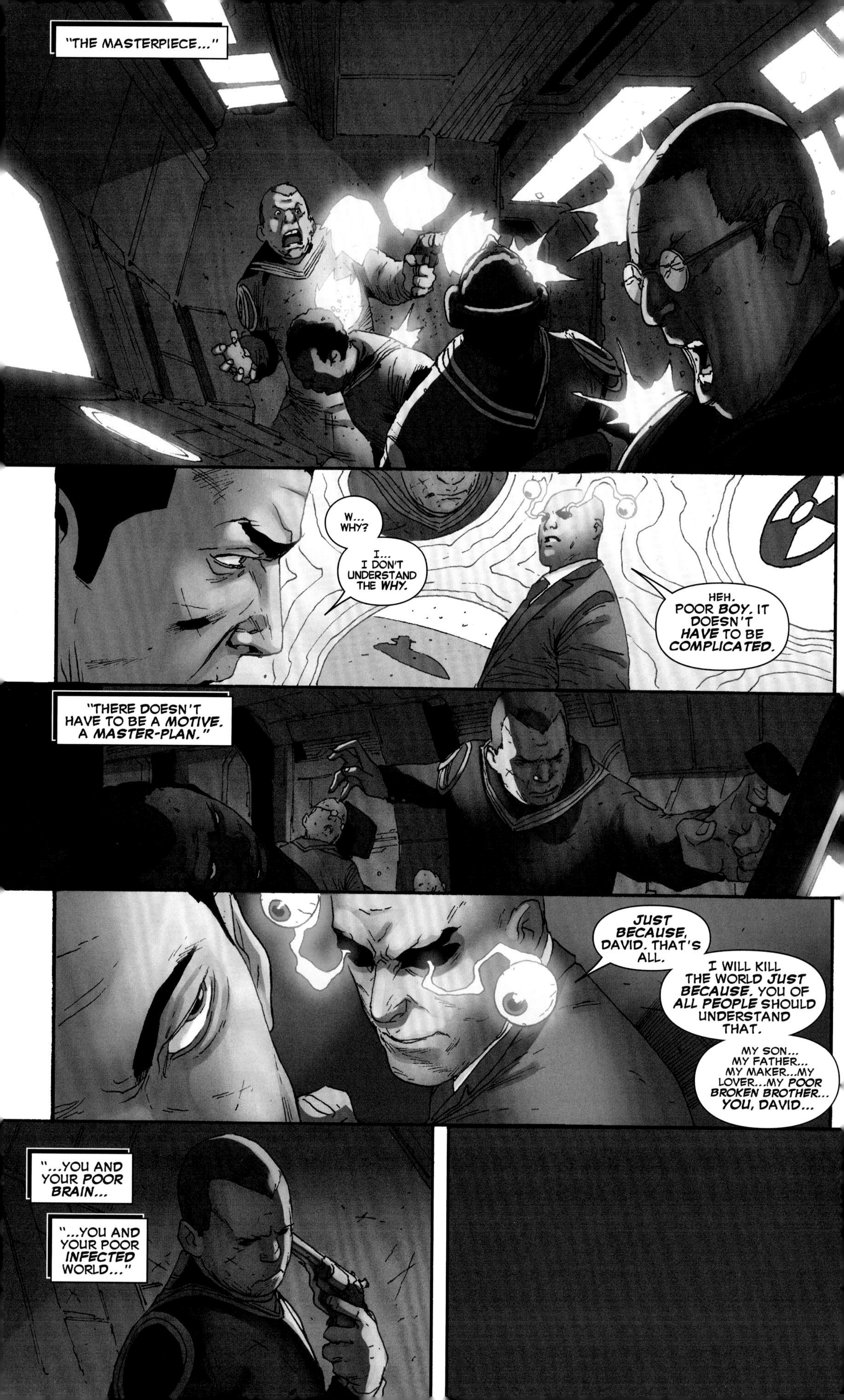
"THE MASTERPIECE..."
W... WHY?
I... I DON'T UNDERSTAND THE WHY.
HEH. POOR BOY. IT DOESN'T HAVE TO BE COMPLICATED.
"THERE DOESN'T HAVE TO BE A MOTIVE. A MASTER-PLAN."
JUST BECAUSE, DAVID. THAT'S ALL.
I WILL KILL THE WORLD JUST BECAUSE. YOU OF ALL PEOPLE SHOULD UNDERSTAND THAT.
MY SON... MY FATHER... MY MAKER... MY LOVER... MY POOR BROKEN BROTHER... YOU, DAVID...
"...YOU AND YOUR POOR BRAIN...
"...YOU AND YOUR POOR INFECTED WORLD..."

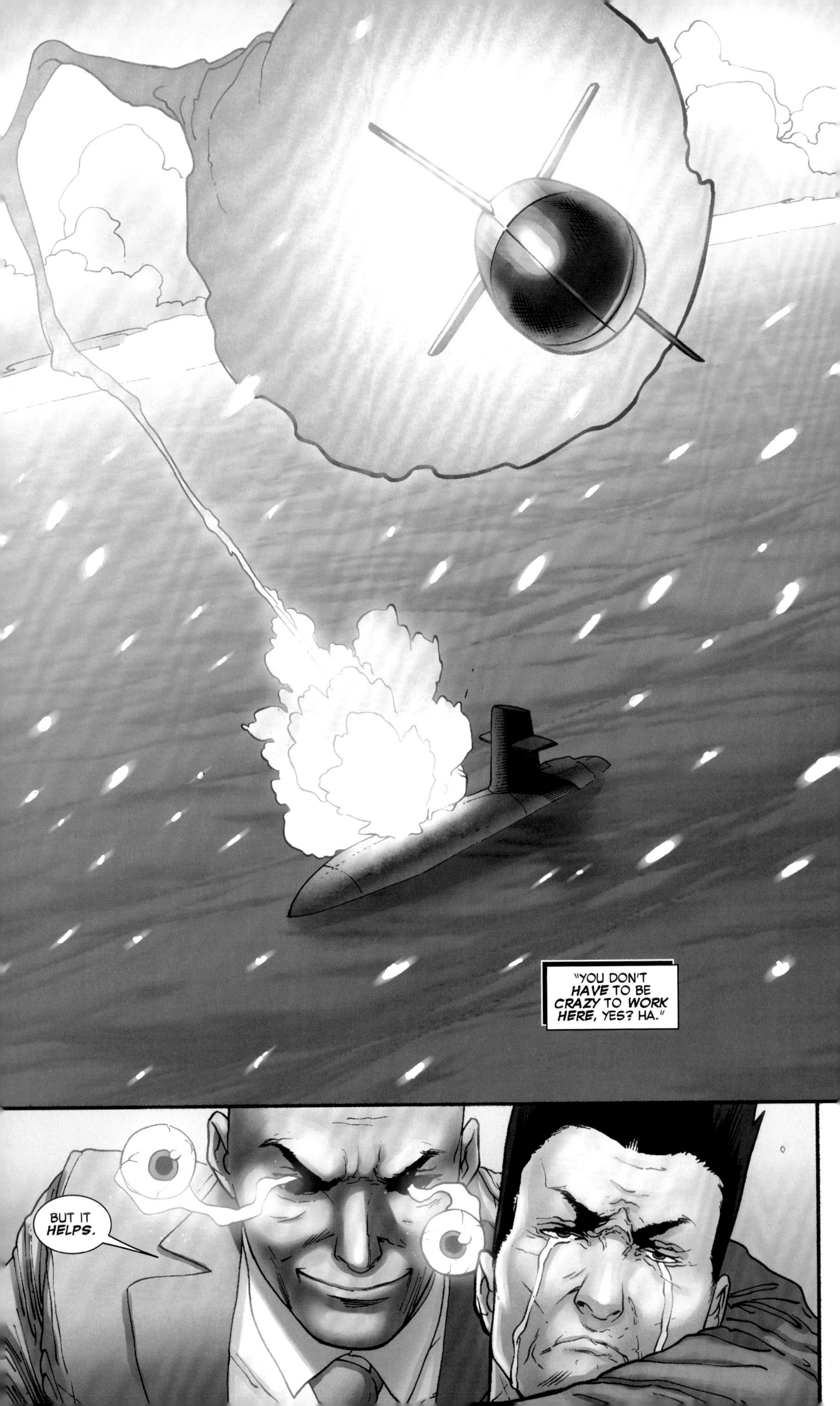
"YOU DON'T HAVE TO BE CRAZY TO WORK HERE, YES? HA."
BUT IT HELPS.

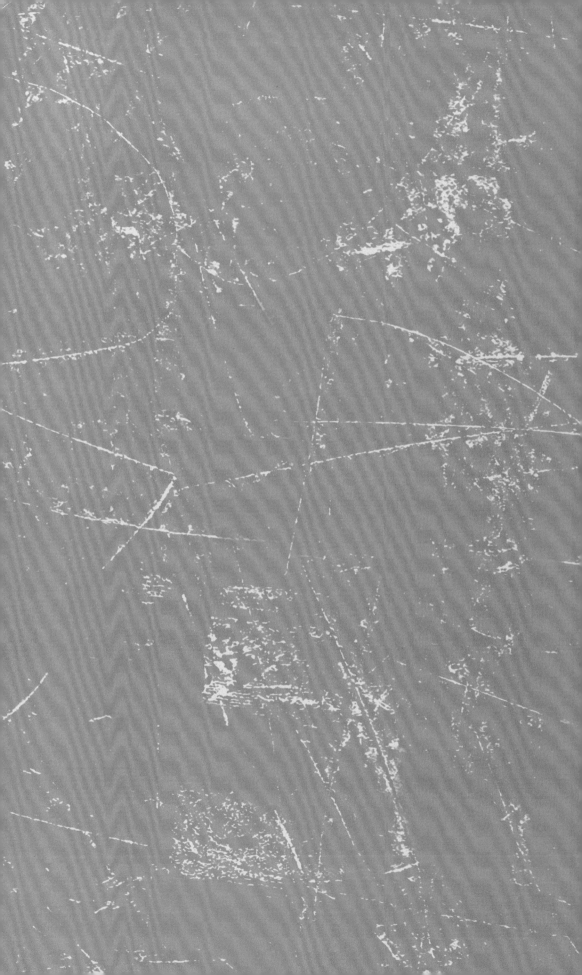

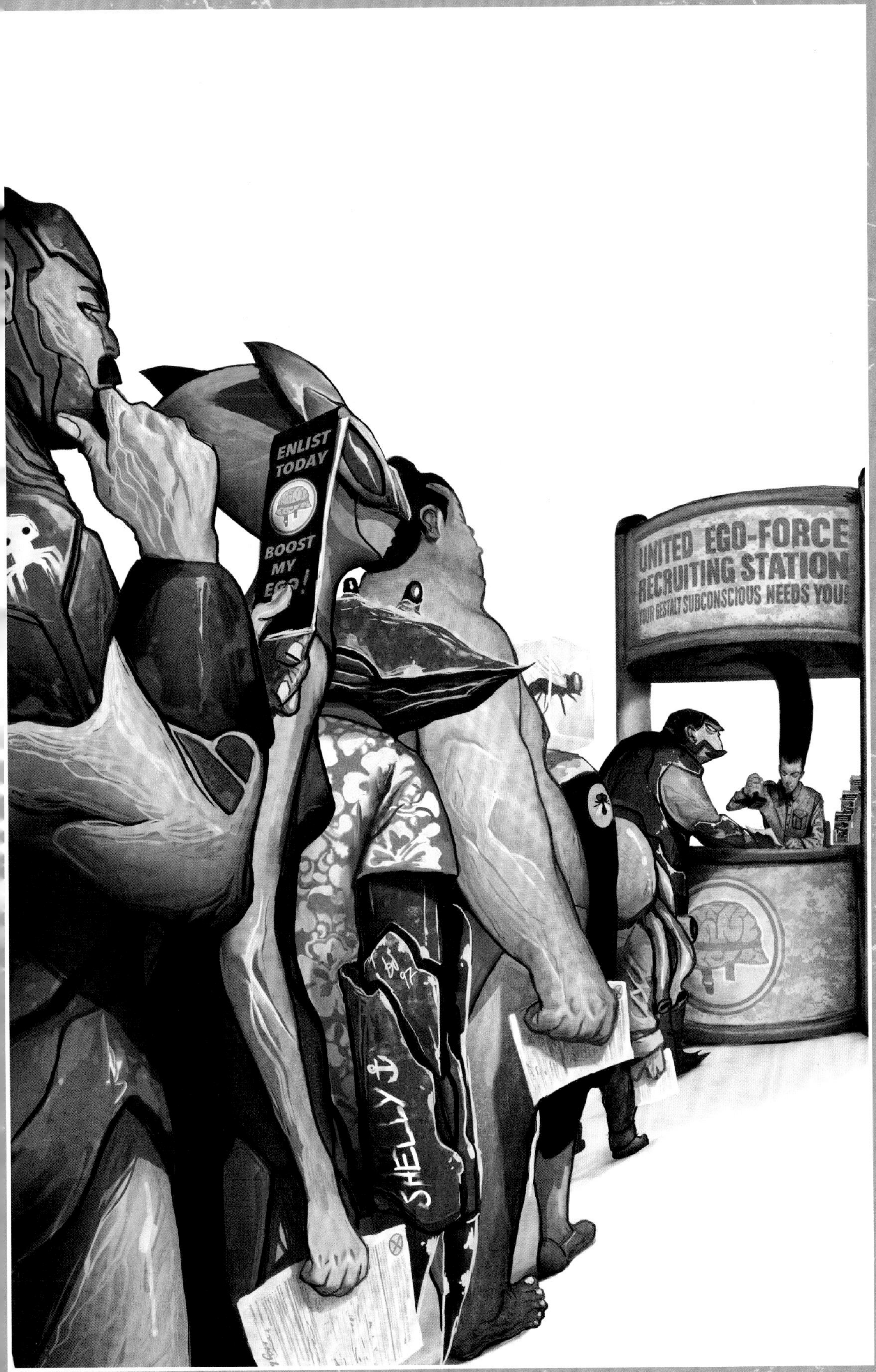
ENLIST TODAY
BOOST MY
UNITED EGO-FORCE
RECRUITING STATION
YOUR GESTALT SUBCONSCIOUS NEEDS YOU!
SHELLY

TWENTY-TWO

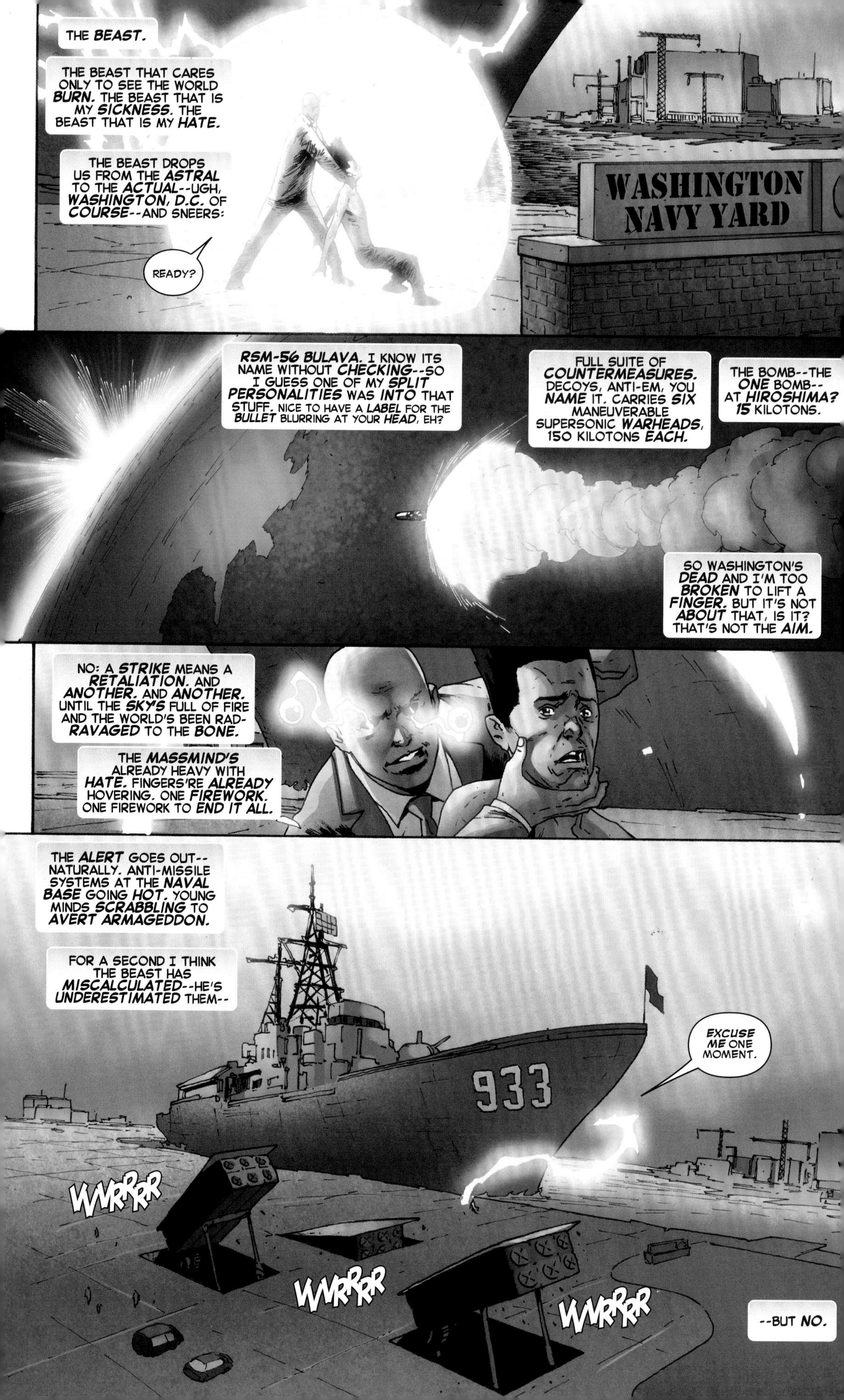
THE BEAST.
THE BEAST THAT CARES ONLY TO SEE THE WORLD BURN. THE BEAST THAT IS MY SICKNESS. THE BEAST THAT IS MY HATE.
THE BEAST DROPS US FROM THE ASTRAL TO THE ACTUAL--UGH, WASHINGTON, D.C. OF COURSE--AND SNEERS:
READY?
WASHINGTON NAVY YARD
RSM-56 BULAVA. I KNOW ITS NAME WITHOUT CHECKING--SO I GUESS ONE OF MY SPLIT PERSONALITIES WAS INTO THAT STUFF. NICE TO HAVE A LABEL FOR THE BULLET BLURRING AT YOUR HEAD, EH?
FULL SUITE OF COUNTERMEASURES. DECOYS, ANTI-EM, YOU NAME IT. CARRIES SIX MANEUVERABLE SUPERSONIC WARHEADS, 150 KILOTONS EACH.
THE BOMB--THE ONE BOMB--AT HIROSHIMA? 15 KILOTONS.
SO WASHINGTON'S DEAD AND I'M TOO BROKEN TO LIFT A FINGER. BUT IT'S NOT ABOUT THAT, IS IT? THAT'S NOT THE AIM.
NO: A STRIKE MEANS A RETALIATION. AND ANOTHER. AND ANOTHER. UNTIL THE SKY'S FULL OF FIRE AND THE WORLD'S BEEN RAD-RAVAGED TO THE BONE.
THE MASSMIND'S ALREADY HEAVY WITH HATE. FINGERS'RE ALREADY HOVERING. ONE FIREWORK. ONE FIREWORK TO END IT ALL.
THE ALERT GOES OUT--NATURALLY. ANTI-MISSILE SYSTEMS AT THE NAVAL BASE GOING HOT. YOUNG MINDS SCRABBLING TO AVERT ARMAGEDDON.
FOR A SECOND I THINK THE BEAST HAS MISCALCULATED--HE'S UNDERESTIMATED THEM--
EXCUSE ME ONE MOMENT.
933
WVRRRR
WVRRRR
WVRRRR
--BUT NO.

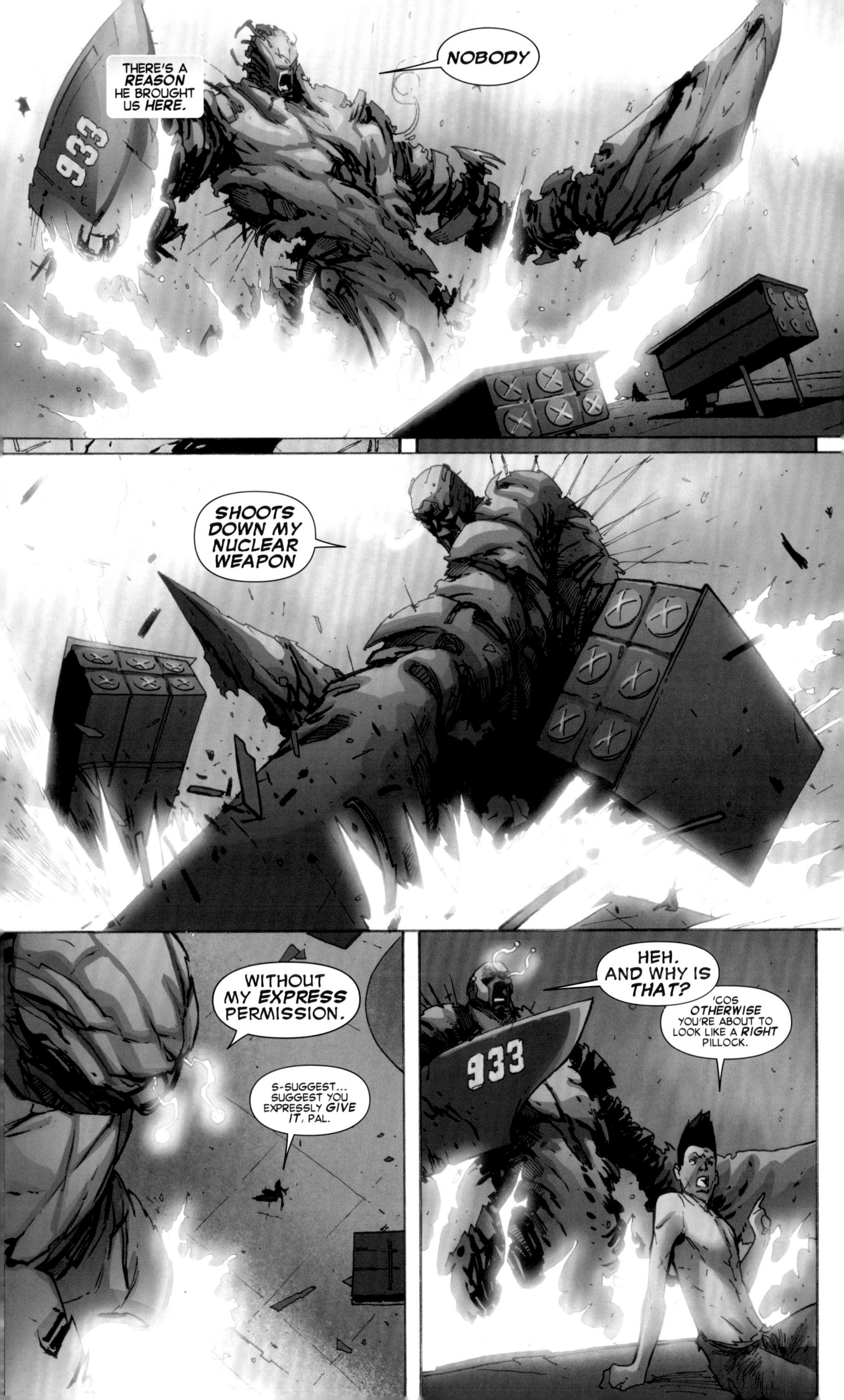
THERE'S A REASON HE BROUGHT US HERE.
NOBODY
SHOOTS DOWN MY NUCLEAR WEAPON
WITHOUT MY EXPRESS PERMISSION.
S-SUGGEST... SUGGEST YOU EXPRESSLY GIVE IT, PAL.
HEH. AND WHY IS THAT?
'COS OTHERWISE YOU'RE ABOUT TO LOOK LIKE A RIGHT PILLOCK.

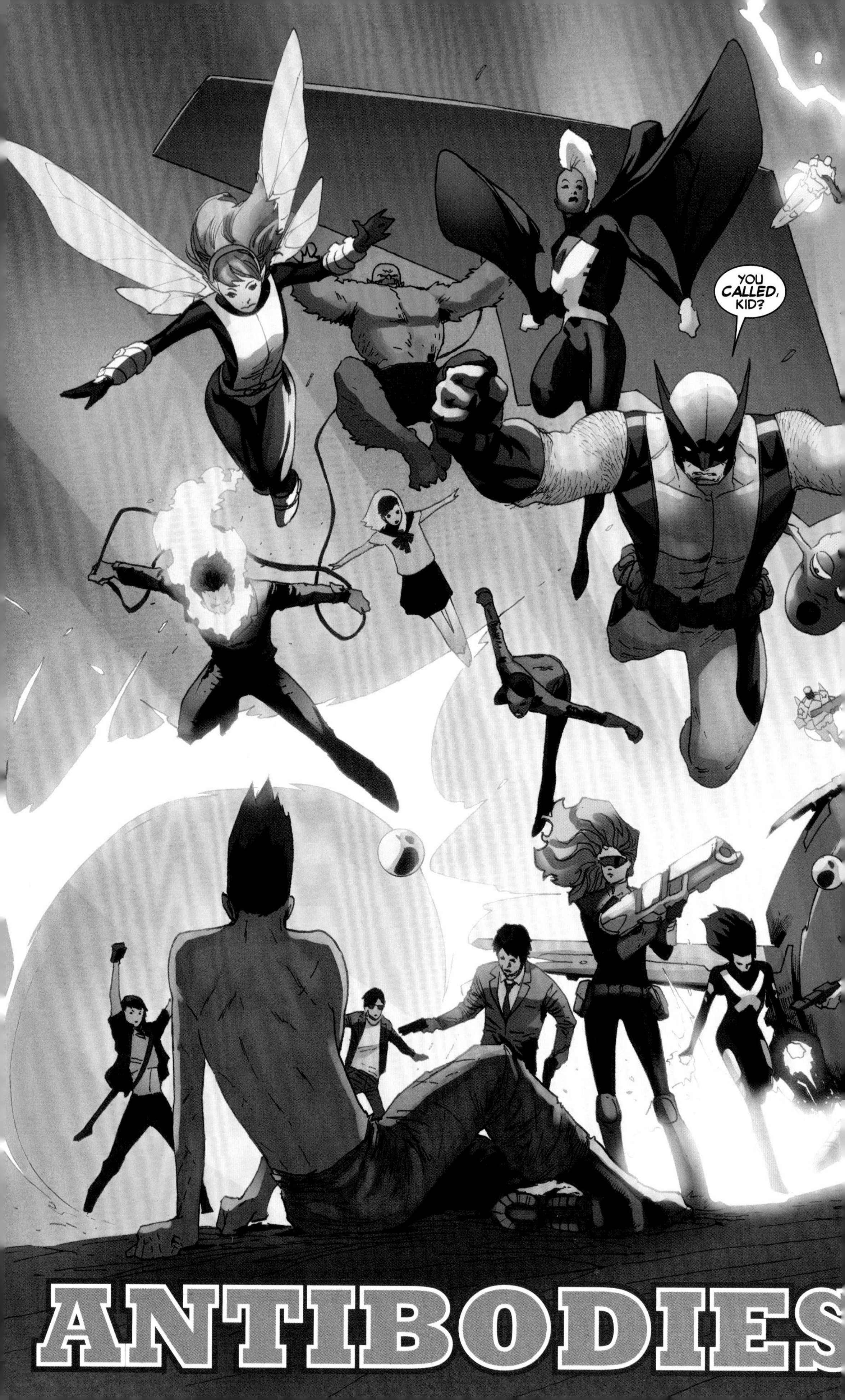
YOU CALLED, KID?
ANTIBODIES

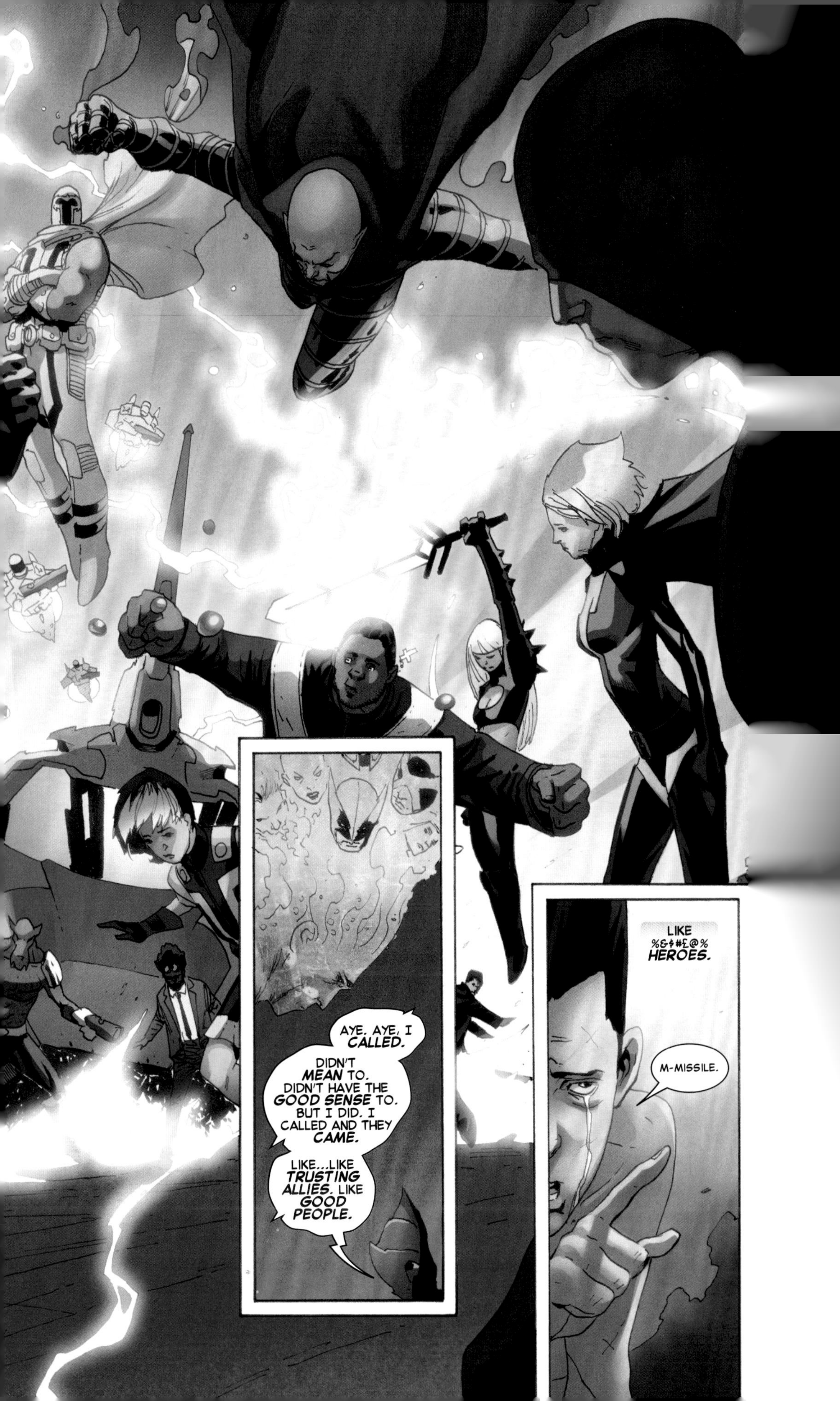
AYE. AYE, I CALLED.
DIDN'T MEAN TO. DIDN'T HAVE THE GOOD SENSE TO. BUT I DID. I CALLED AND THEY CAME.
LIKE...LIKE TRUSTING ALLIES. LIKE GOOD PEOPLE.
LIKE %&$#£@% HEROES.
M-MISSILE.

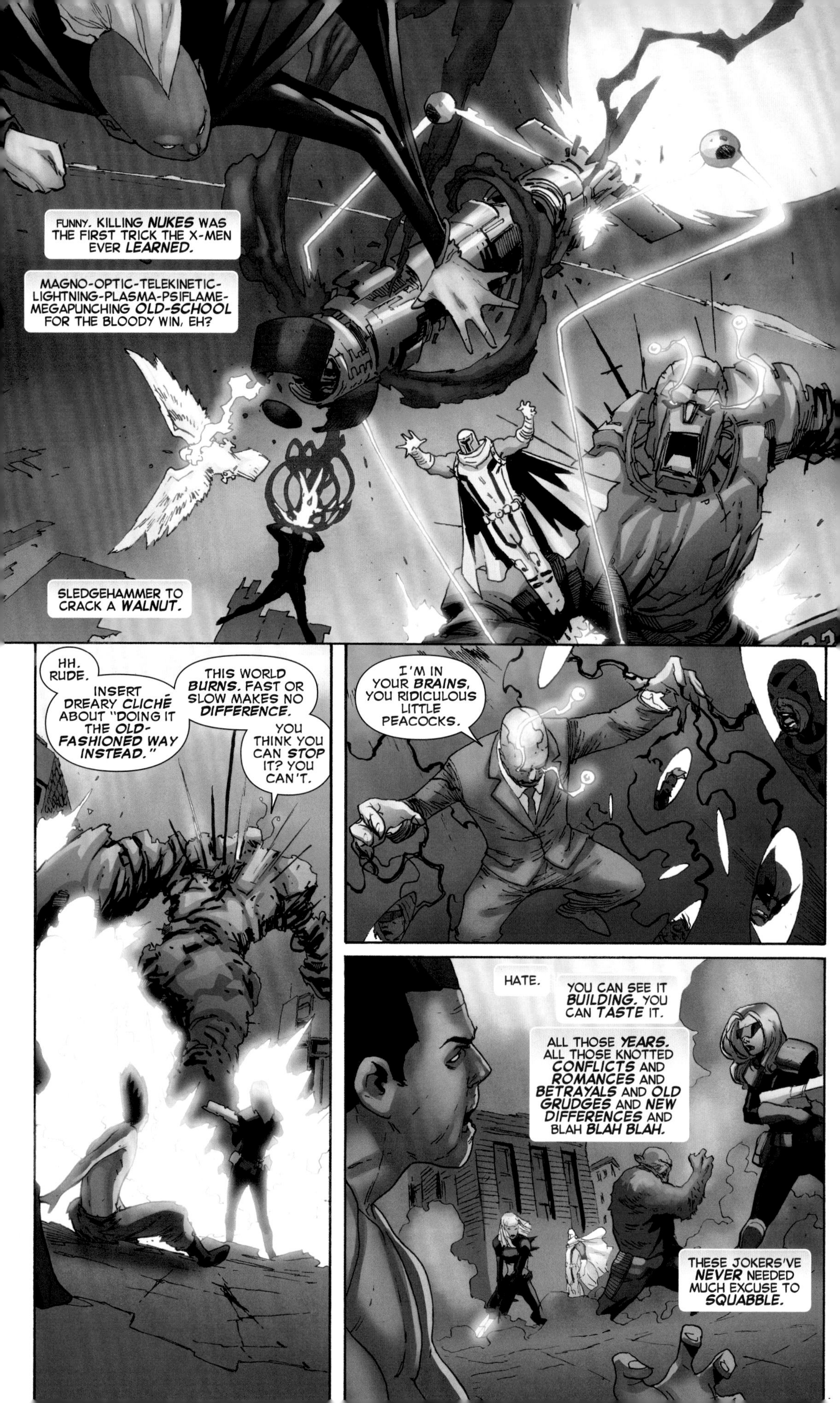
FUNNY. KILLING NUKES WAS THE FIRST TRICK THE X-MEN EVER LEARNED.
MAGNO-OPTIC-TELEKINETIC-LIGHTNING-PLASMA-PSIFLAME-MEGAPUNCHING OLD-SCHOOL FOR THE BLOODY WIN, EH?
SLEDGEHAMMER TO CRACK A WALNUT.
HH. RUDE.
INSERT DREARY CLICHÉ ABOUT "DOING IT THE OLD-FASHIONED WAY INSTEAD."
THIS WORLD BURNS. FAST OR SLOW MAKES NO DIFFERENCE.
YOU THINK YOU CAN STOP IT? YOU CAN'T.
I'M IN YOUR BRAINS, YOU RIDICULOUS LITTLE PEACOCKS.
HATE.
YOU CAN SEE IT BUILDING. YOU CAN TASTE IT.
ALL THOSE YEARS. ALL THOSE KNOTTED CONFLICTS AND ROMANCES AND BETRAYALS AND OLD GRUDGES AND NEW DIFFERENCES AND BLAH BLAH BLAH.
THESE JOKERS'VE NEVER NEEDED MUCH EXCUSE TO SQUABBLE.

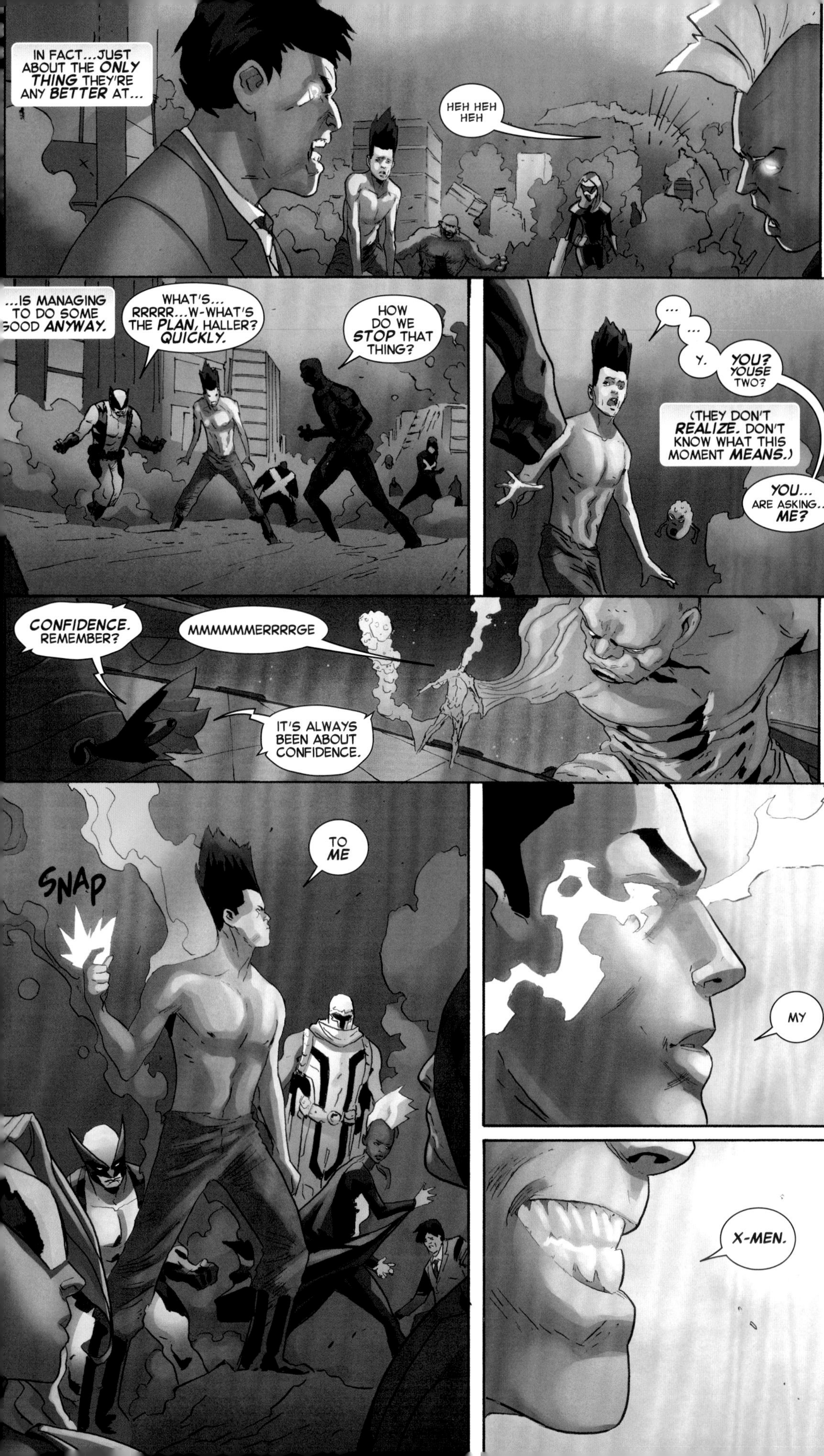
IN FACT...JUST ABOUT THE ONLY THING THEY'RE ANY BETTER AT...
HEH HEH HEH
...IS MANAGING TO DO SOME GOOD ANYWAY.
WHAT'S... RRRRR...W-WHAT'S THE PLAN, HALLER? QUICKLY.
HOW DO WE STOP THAT THING?
...
...
Y.
YOU? YOUSE TWO?
(THEY DON'T REALIZE. DON'T KNOW WHAT THIS MOMENT MEANS.)
YOU... ARE ASKING... ME?
CONFIDENCE. REMEMBER?
MMMMMMERRRRGE
IT'S ALWAYS BEEN ABOUT CONFIDENCE.
TO ME
SNAP
MY
X-MEN.

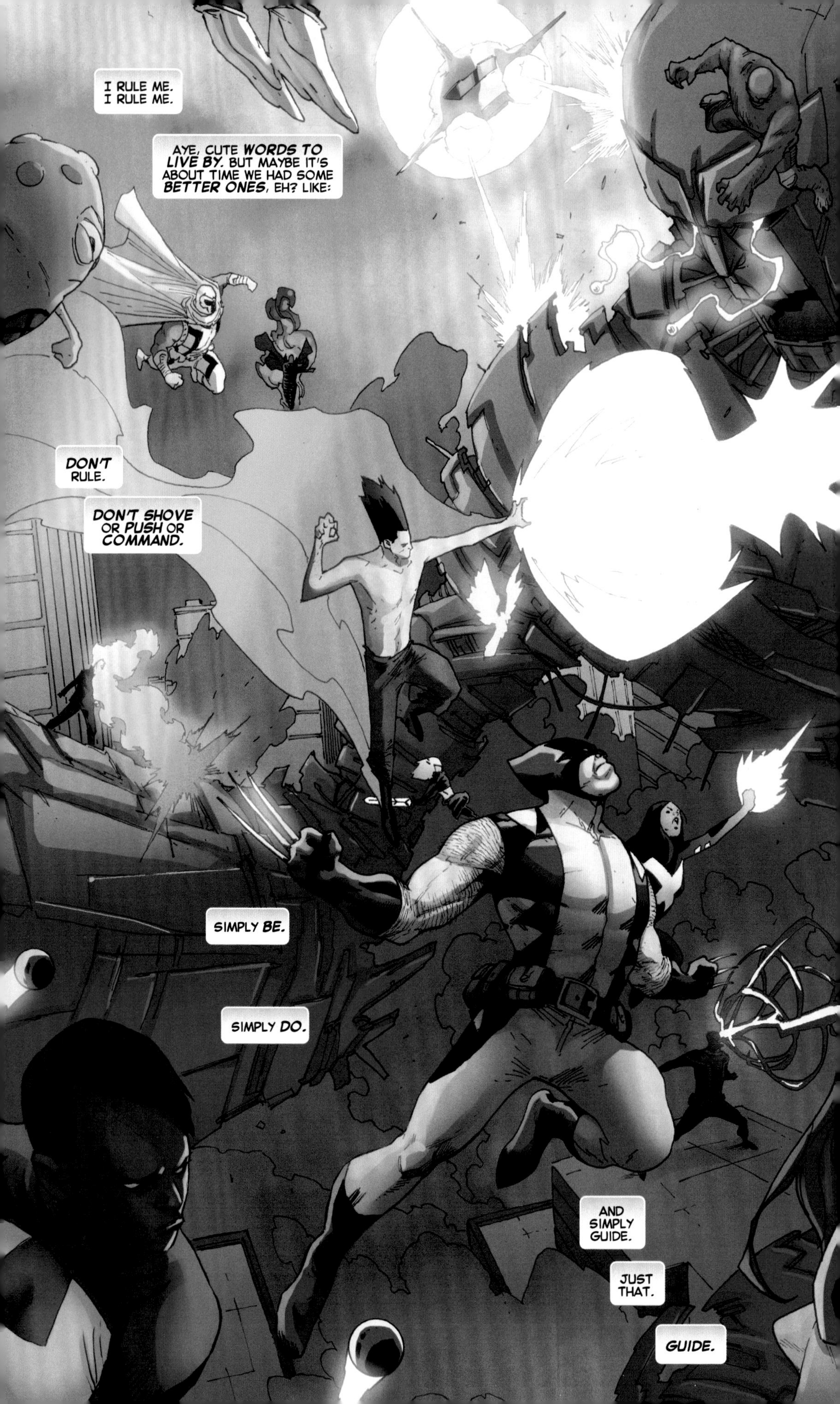
I RULE ME. I RULE ME.
AYE, CUTE WORDS TO LIVE BY. BUT MAYBE IT'S ABOUT TIME WE HAD SOME BETTER ONES, EH? LIKE:
DON'T RULE.
DON'T SHOVE OR PUSH OR COMMAND.
SIMPLY BE.
SIMPLY DO.
AND SIMPLY GUIDE.
JUST THAT.
GUIDE.

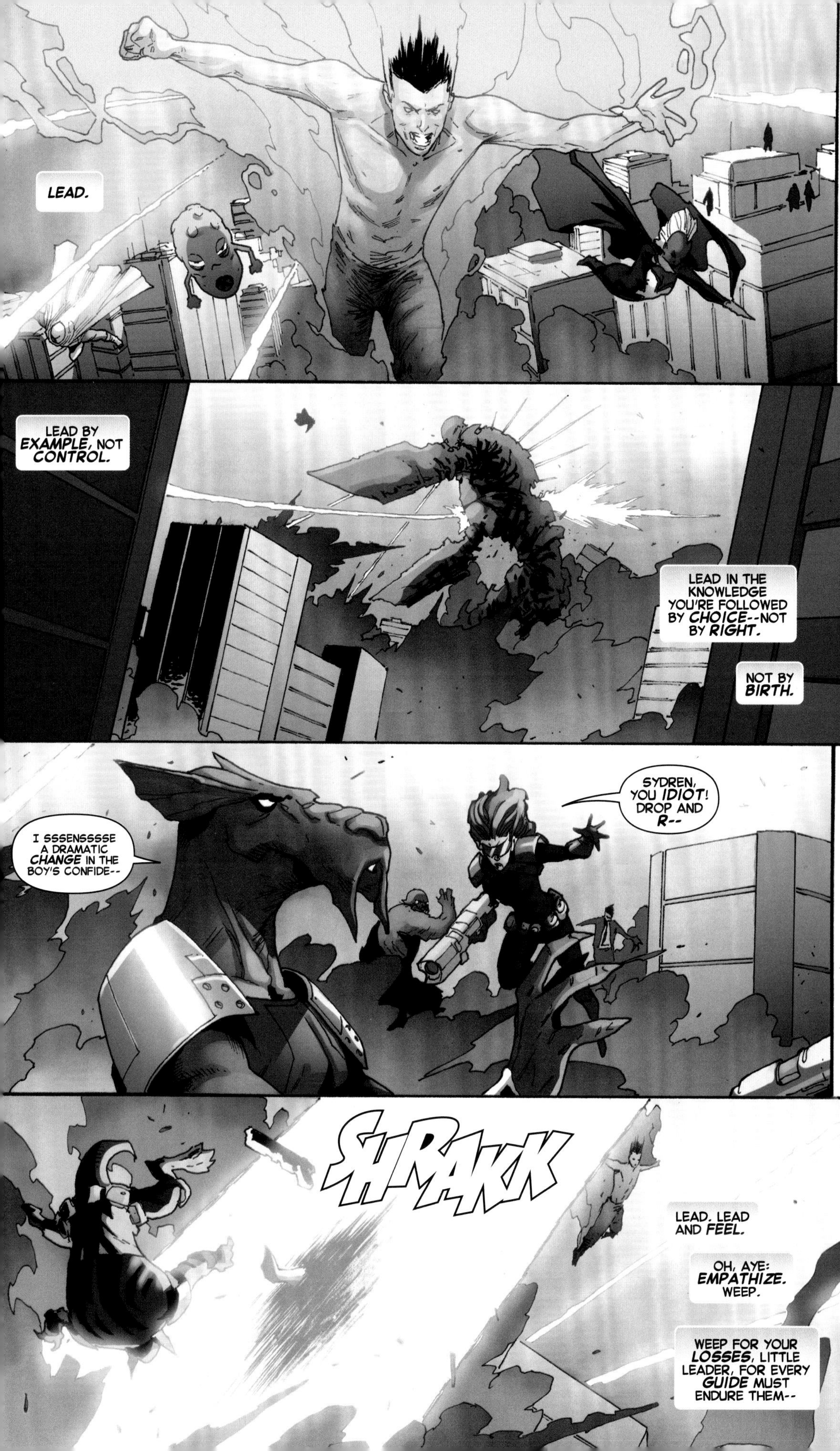
LEAD.
LEAD BY EXAMPLE, NOT CONTROL.
LEAD IN THE KNOWLEDGE YOU'RE FOLLOWED BY CHOICE--NOT BY RIGHT.
NOT BY BIRTH.
I SSSENSSSSE A DRAMATIC CHANGE IN THE BOY'S CONFIDE--
SYDREN, YOU IDIOT! DROP AND R--
SHRAKK
LEAD. LEAD AND FEEL.
OH, AYE: EMPATHIZE. WEEP.
WEEP FOR YOUR LOSSES, LITTLE LEADER, FOR EVERY GUIDE MUST ENDURE THEM--

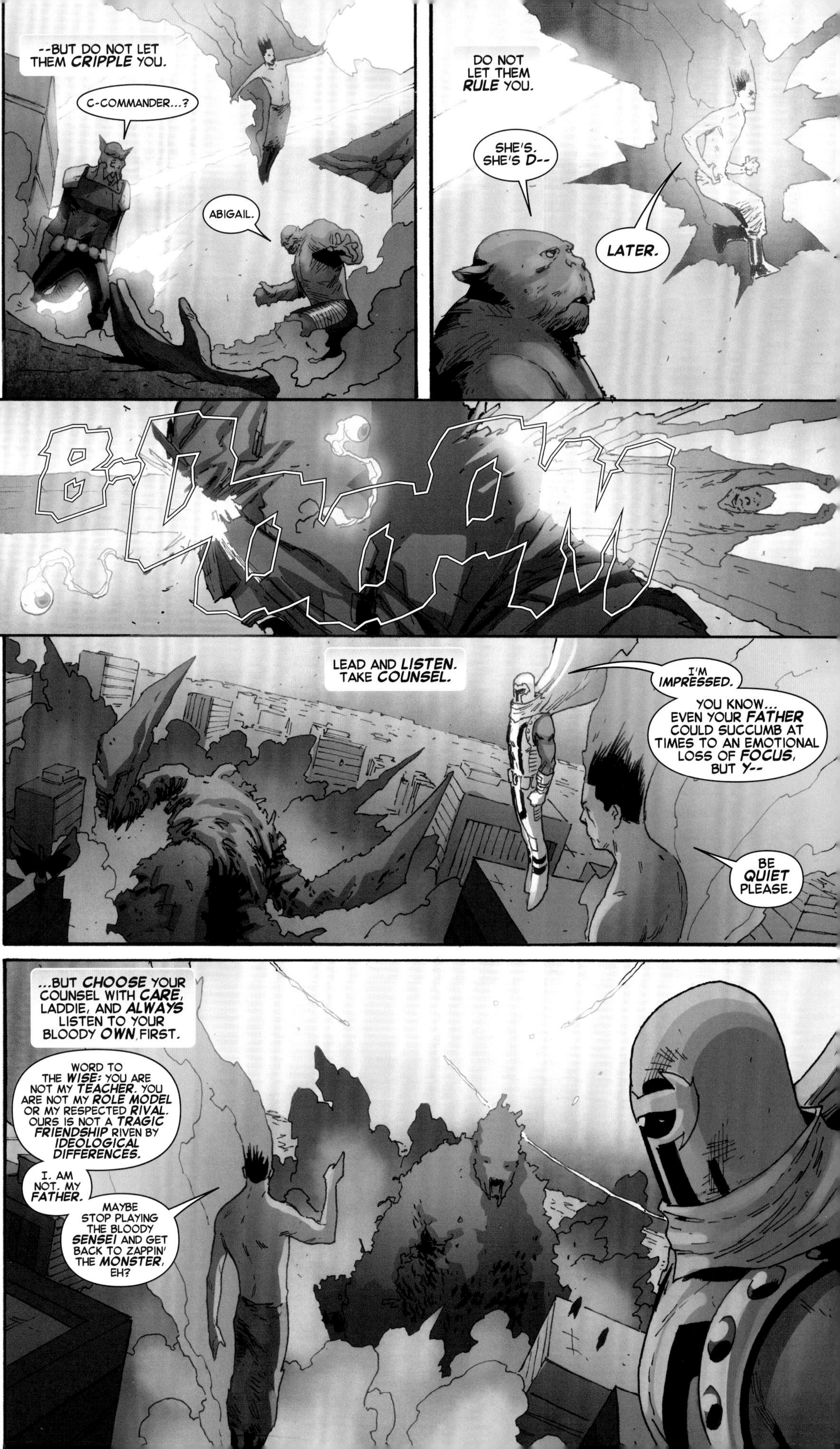
--BUT DO NOT LET THEM CRIPPLE YOU.
C-COMMANDER...?
ABIGAIL.
DO NOT LET THEM RULE YOU.
SHE'S. SHE'S D--
LATER.
BLOOOM
LEAD AND LISTEN. TAKE COUNSEL.
I'M IMPRESSED.
YOU KNOW... EVEN YOUR FATHER COULD SUCCUMB AT TIMES TO AN EMOTIONAL LOSS OF FOCUS, BUT Y--
BE QUIET PLEASE.
...BUT CHOOSE YOUR COUNSEL WITH CARE, LADDIE, AND ALWAYS LISTEN TO YOUR BLOODY OWN, FIRST.
WORD TO THE WISE: YOU ARE NOT MY TEACHER. YOU ARE NOT MY ROLE MODEL OR MY RESPECTED RIVAL. OURS IS NOT A TRAGIC FRIENDSHIP RIVEN BY IDEOLOGICAL DIFFERENCES.
I. AM NOT. MY FATHER.
MAYBE STOP PLAYING THE BLOODY SENSEI AND GET BACK TO ZAPPIN' THE MONSTER, EH?

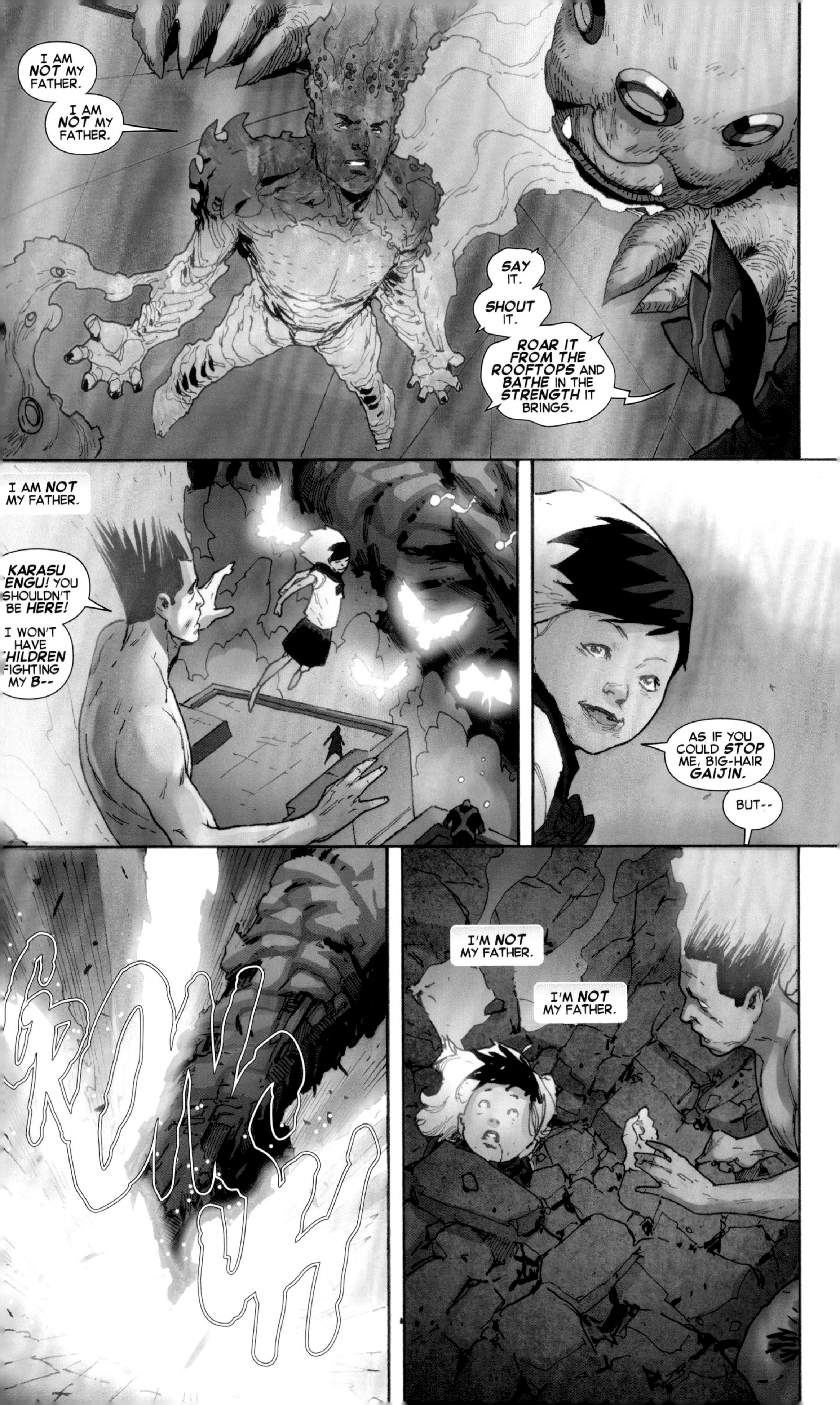
I AM NOT MY FATHER.
I AM NOT MY FATHER.
SAY IT.
SHOUT IT.
ROAR IT FROM THE ROOFTOPS AND BATHE IN THE STRENGTH IT BRINGS.
I AM NOT MY FATHER.
KARASU ENGU! YOU SHOULDN'T BE HERE!
I WON'T HAVE HILDREN FIGHTING MY B--
AS IF YOU COULD STOP ME, BIG-HAIR GAIJIN.
BUT--
I'M NOT MY FATHER.
I'M NOT MY FATHER.

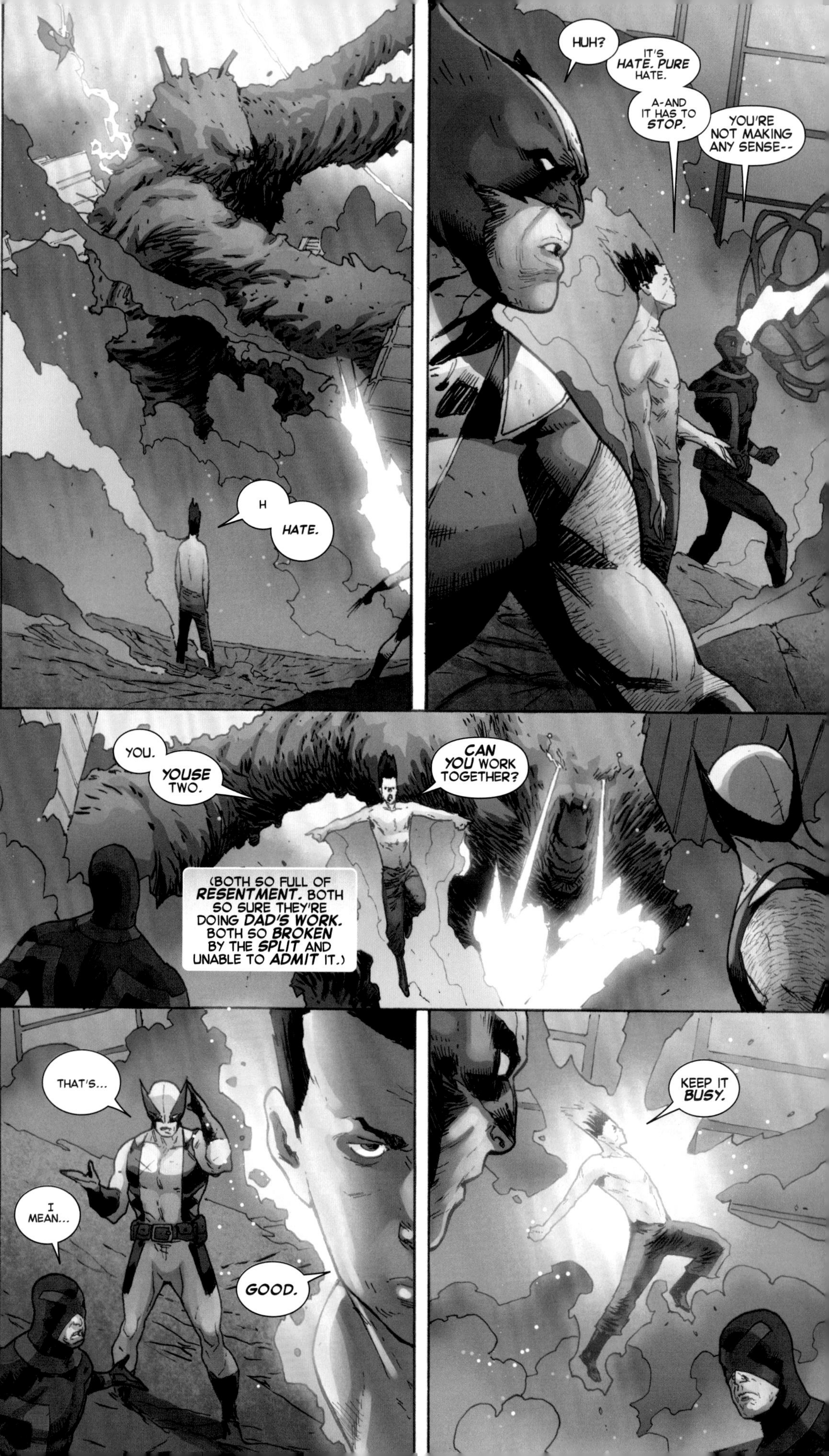
H
HATE.
HUH?
IT'S HATE. PURE HATE.
A-AND IT HAS TO STOP.
YOU'RE NOT MAKING ANY SENSE--
YOU. YOUSE TWO.
CAN YOU WORK TOGETHER?
(BOTH SO FULL OF RESENTMENT. BOTH SO SURE THEY'RE DOING DAD'S WORK. BOTH SO BROKEN BY THE SPLIT AND UNABLE TO ADMIT IT.)
THAT'S...
I MEAN...
GOOD.
KEEP IT BUSY.

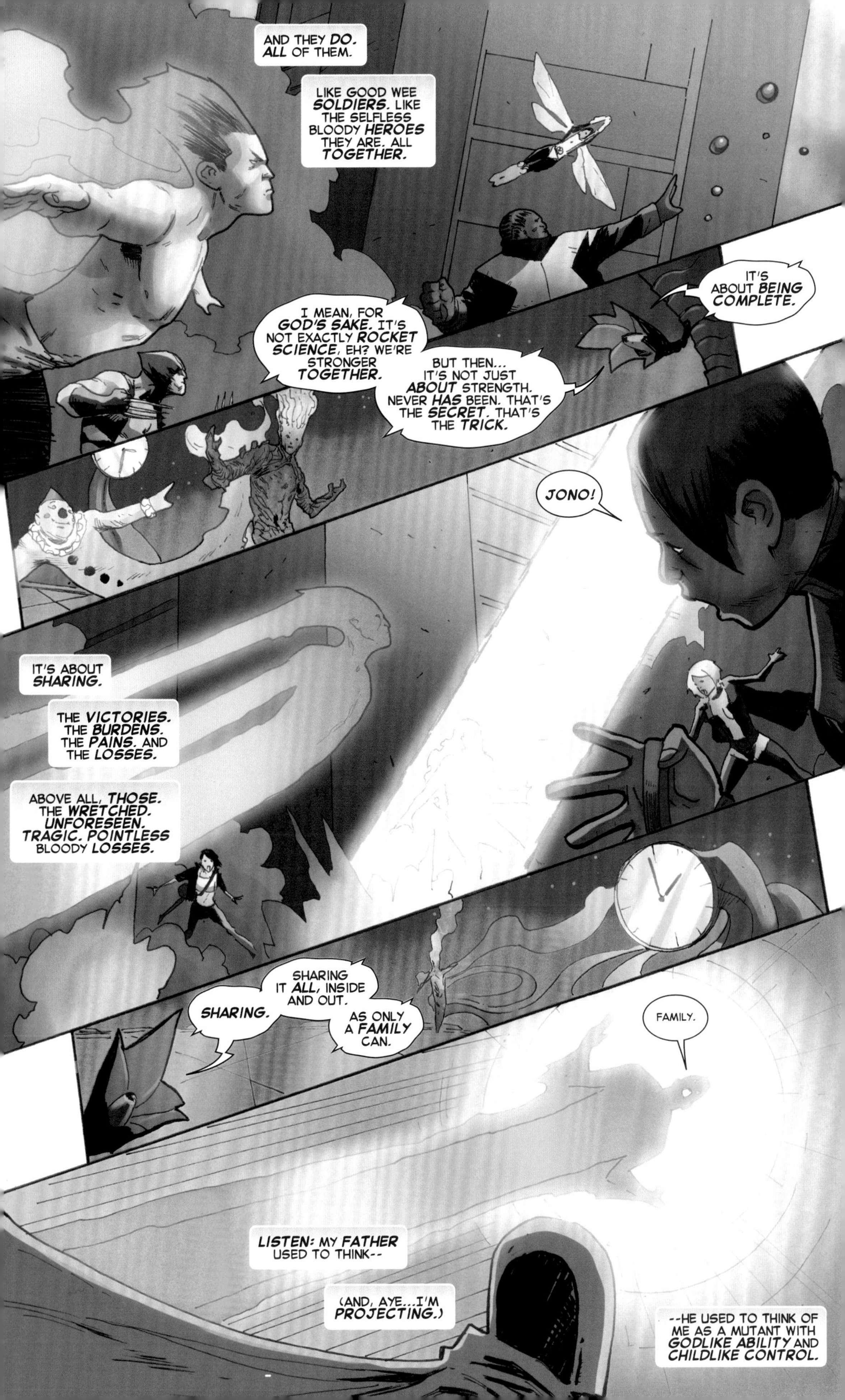
AND THEY DO. ALL OF THEM.
LIKE GOOD WEE SOLDIERS. LIKE THE SELFLESS BLOODY HEROES THEY ARE. ALL TOGETHER.
I MEAN, FOR GOD'S SAKE. IT'S NOT EXACTLY ROCKET SCIENCE, EH? WE'RE STRONGER TOGETHER.
BUT THEN... IT'S NOT JUST ABOUT STRENGTH. NEVER HAS BEEN. THAT'S THE SECRET. THAT'S THE TRICK.
IT'S ABOUT BEING COMPLETE.
JONO!
IT'S ABOUT SHARING.
THE VICTORIES. THE BURDENS. THE PAINS. AND THE LOSSES.
ABOVE ALL, THOSE. THE WRETCHED. UNFORESEEN. TRAGIC. POINTLESS BLOODY LOSSES.
SHARING.
SHARING IT ALL, INSIDE AND OUT.
AS ONLY A FAMILY CAN.
FAMILY.
LISTEN: MY FATHER USED TO THINK--
(AND, AYE...I'M PROJECTING.)
--HE USED TO THINK OF ME AS A MUTANT WITH GODLIKE ABILITY AND CHILDLIKE CONTROL.

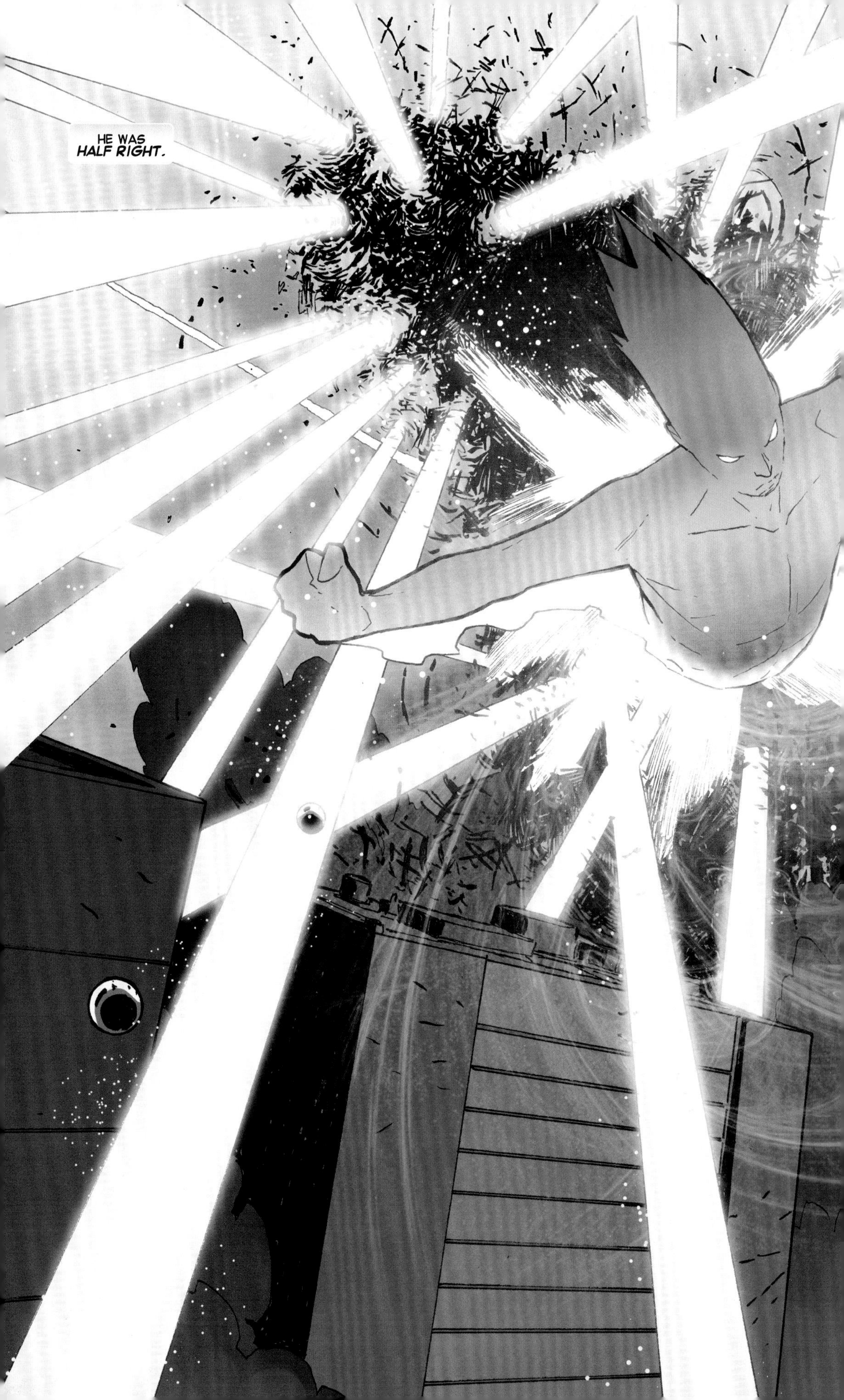
HE WAS
HALF RIGHT.

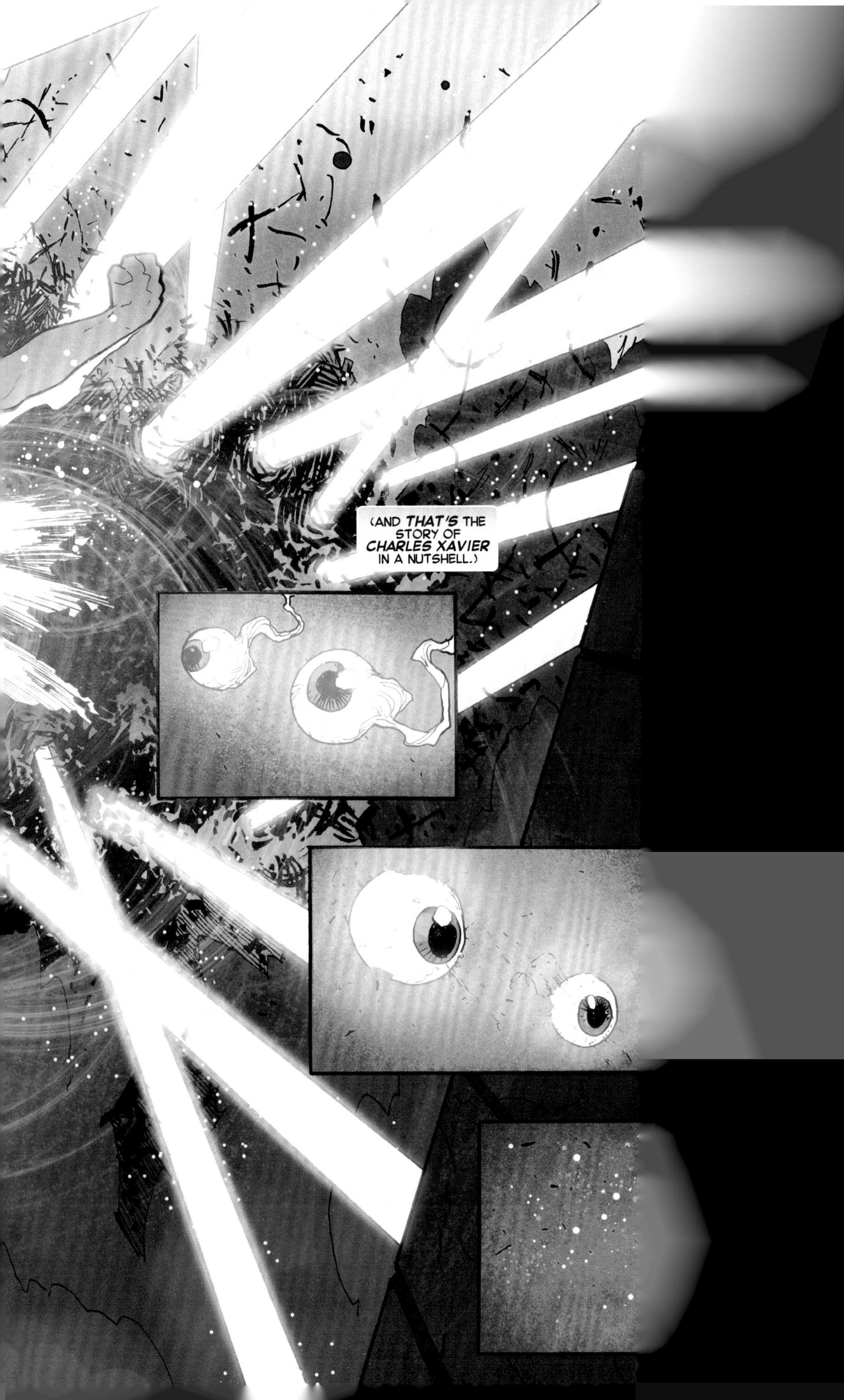
(AND THAT'S THE STORY OF CHARLES XAVIER IN A NUTSHELL.)

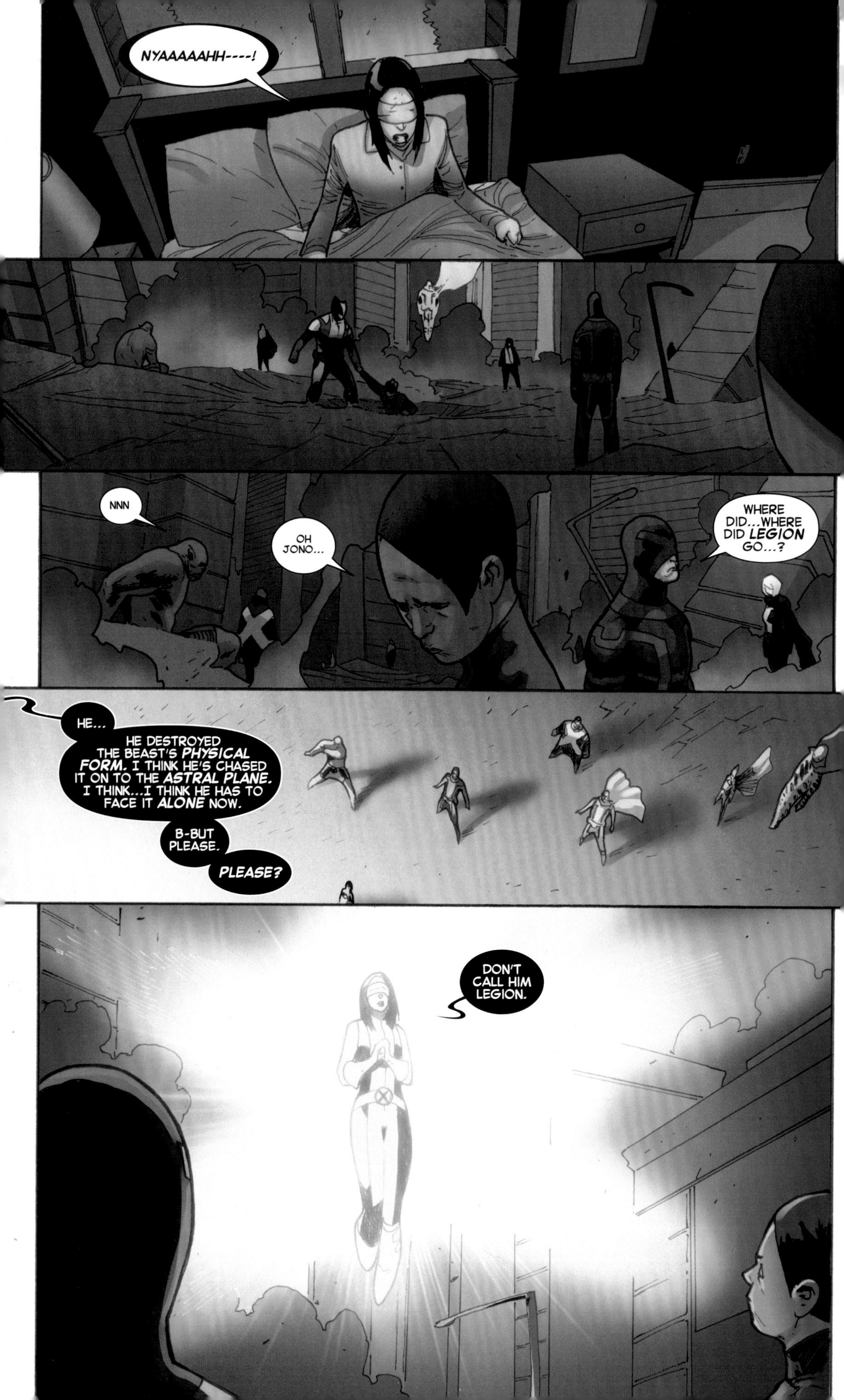
NYAAAAAHH----!
NNN
OH JONO...
WHERE DID...WHERE DID LEGION GO...?
HE...
HE DESTROYED THE BEAST'S PHYSICAL FORM. I THINK HE'S CHASED IT ON TO THE ASTRAL PLANE. I THINK...I THINK HE HAS TO FACE IT ALONE NOW.
B-BUT PLEASE.
PLEASE?
DON'T CALL HIM LEGION.

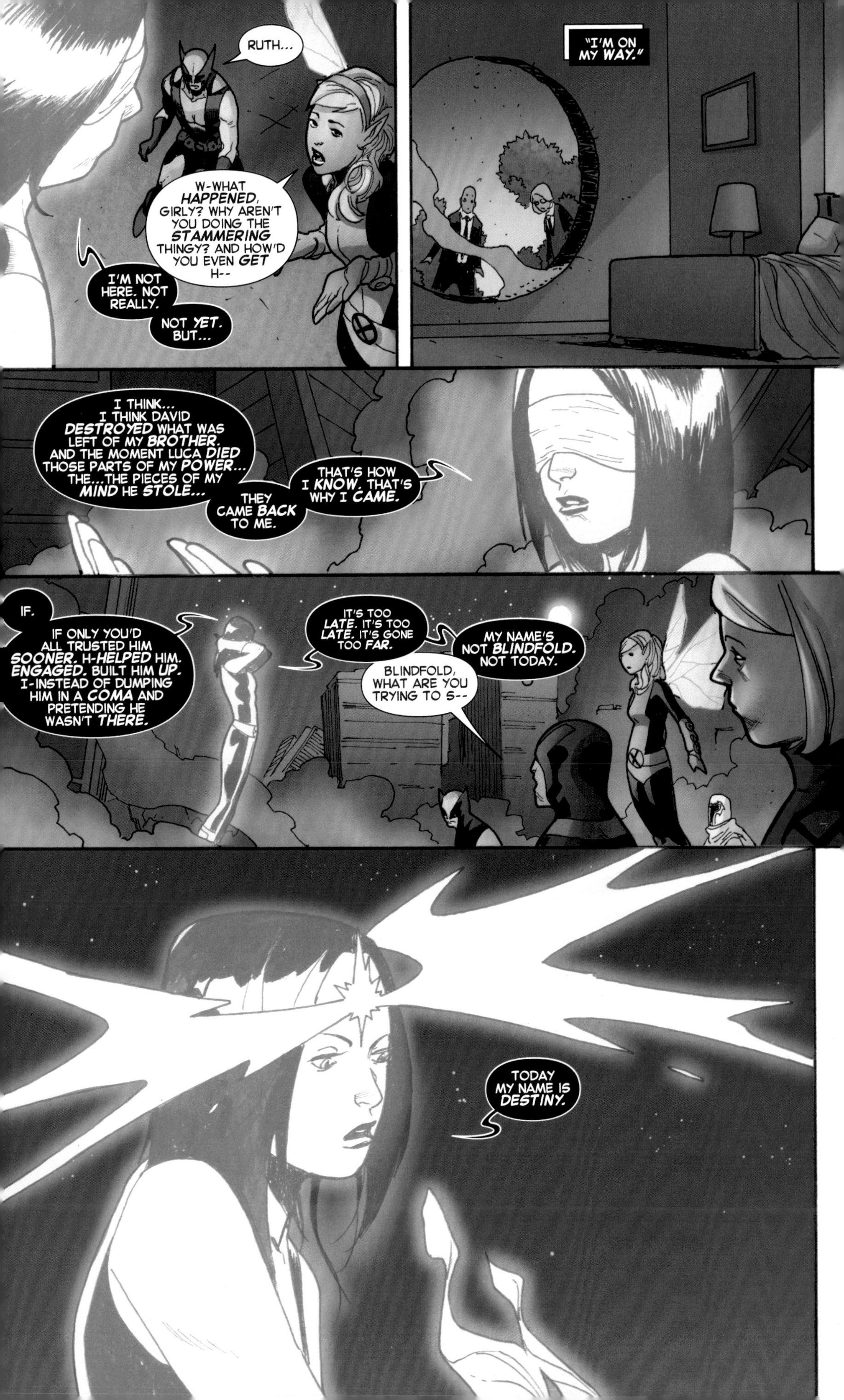
RUTH...
W-WHAT HAPPENED, GIRLY? WHY AREN'T YOU DOING THE STAMMERING THINGY? AND HOW'D YOU EVEN GET H--
I'M NOT HERE. NOT REALLY.
NOT YET. BUT...
"I'M ON MY WAY."
I THINK... I THINK DAVID DESTROYED WHAT WAS LEFT OF MY BROTHER. AND THE MOMENT LUCA DIED THOSE PARTS OF MY POWER... THE...THE PIECES OF MY MIND HE STOLE...
THEY CAME BACK TO ME.
THAT'S HOW I KNOW. THAT'S WHY I CAME.
IF.
IF ONLY YOU'D ALL TRUSTED HIM SOONER. H-HELPED HIM. ENGAGED. BUILT HIM UP. I-INSTEAD OF DUMPING HIM IN A COMA AND PRETENDING HE WASN'T THERE.
IT'S TOO LATE. IT'S TOO LATE. IT'S GONE TOO FAR.
MY NAME'S NOT BLINDFOLD. NOT TODAY.
BLINDFOLD, WHAT ARE YOU TRYING TO S--
TODAY MY NAME IS DESTINY.

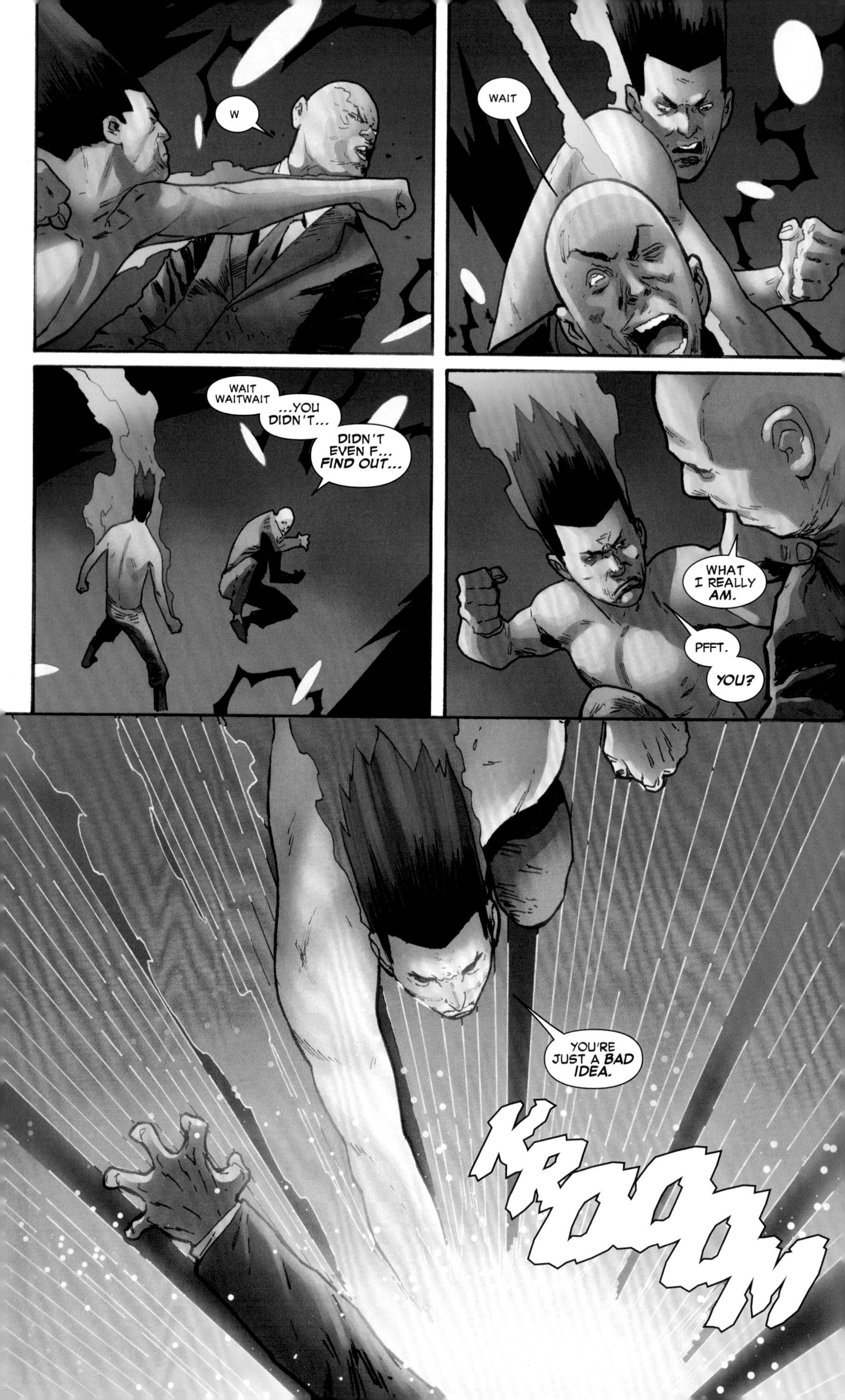
W
WAIT
WAIT WAITWAIT
...YOU DIDN'T...
DIDN'T EVEN F... FIND OUT...
WHAT I REALLY AM.
PFFT.
YOU?
YOU'RE JUST A BAD IDEA.
KROOOM

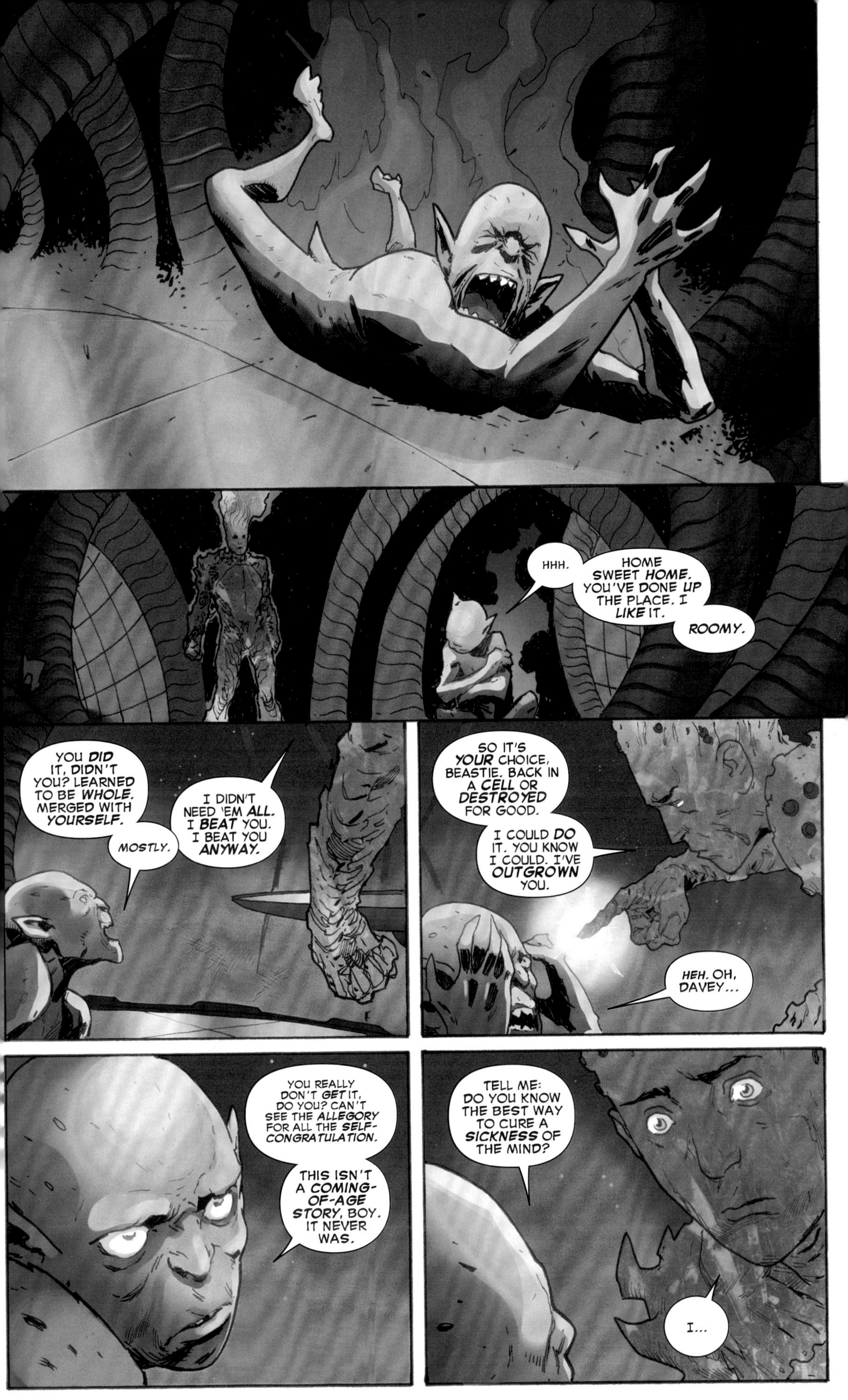
HHH.
HOME SWEET HOME. YOU'VE DONE UP THE PLACE. I LIKE IT.
ROOMY.
YOU DID IT, DIDN'T YOU? LEARNED TO BE WHOLE. MERGED WITH YOURSELF.
MOSTLY.
I DIDN'T NEED 'EM ALL. I BEAT YOU. I BEAT YOU ANYWAY.
SO IT'S YOUR CHOICE, BEASTIE. BACK IN A CELL OR DESTROYED FOR GOOD.
I COULD DO IT. YOU KNOW I COULD. I'VE OUTGROWN YOU.
HEH. OH, DAVEY...
YOU REALLY DON'T GET IT, DO YOU? CAN'T SEE THE ALLEGORY FOR ALL THE SELF-CONGRATULATION.
THIS ISN'T A COMING-OF-AGE STORY, BOY. IT NEVER WAS.
TELL ME: DO YOU KNOW THE BEST WAY TO CURE A SICKNESS OF THE MIND?
I...

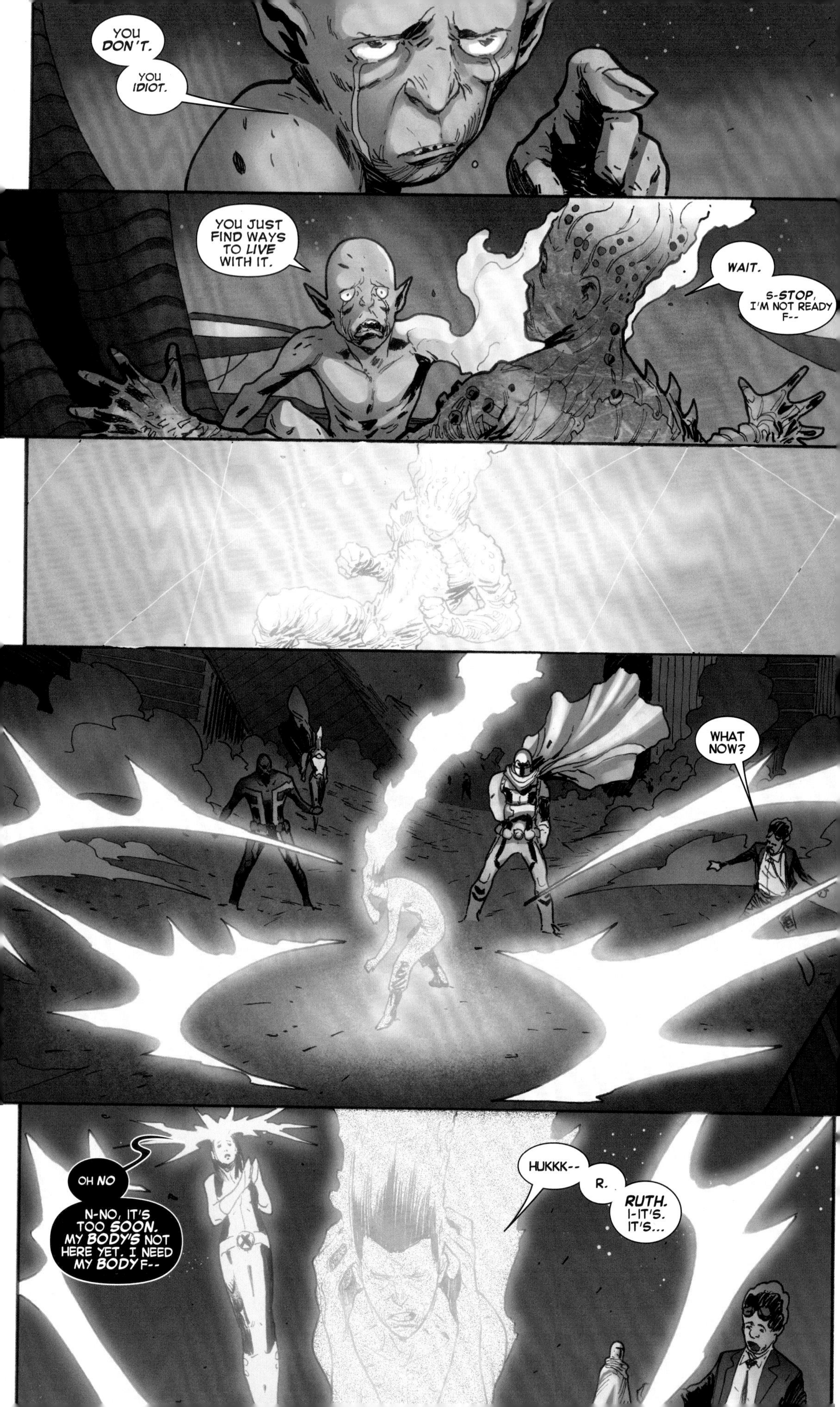
YOU DON'T.
YOU IDIOT.
YOU JUST FIND WAYS TO LIVE WITH IT.
WAIT.
S-STOP, I'M NOT READY F--
WHAT NOW?
OH NO
N-NO, IT'S TOO SOON. MY BODY'S NOT HERE YET. I NEED MY BODY F--
HUKKK--
R.
RUTH. I-IT'S. IT'S...

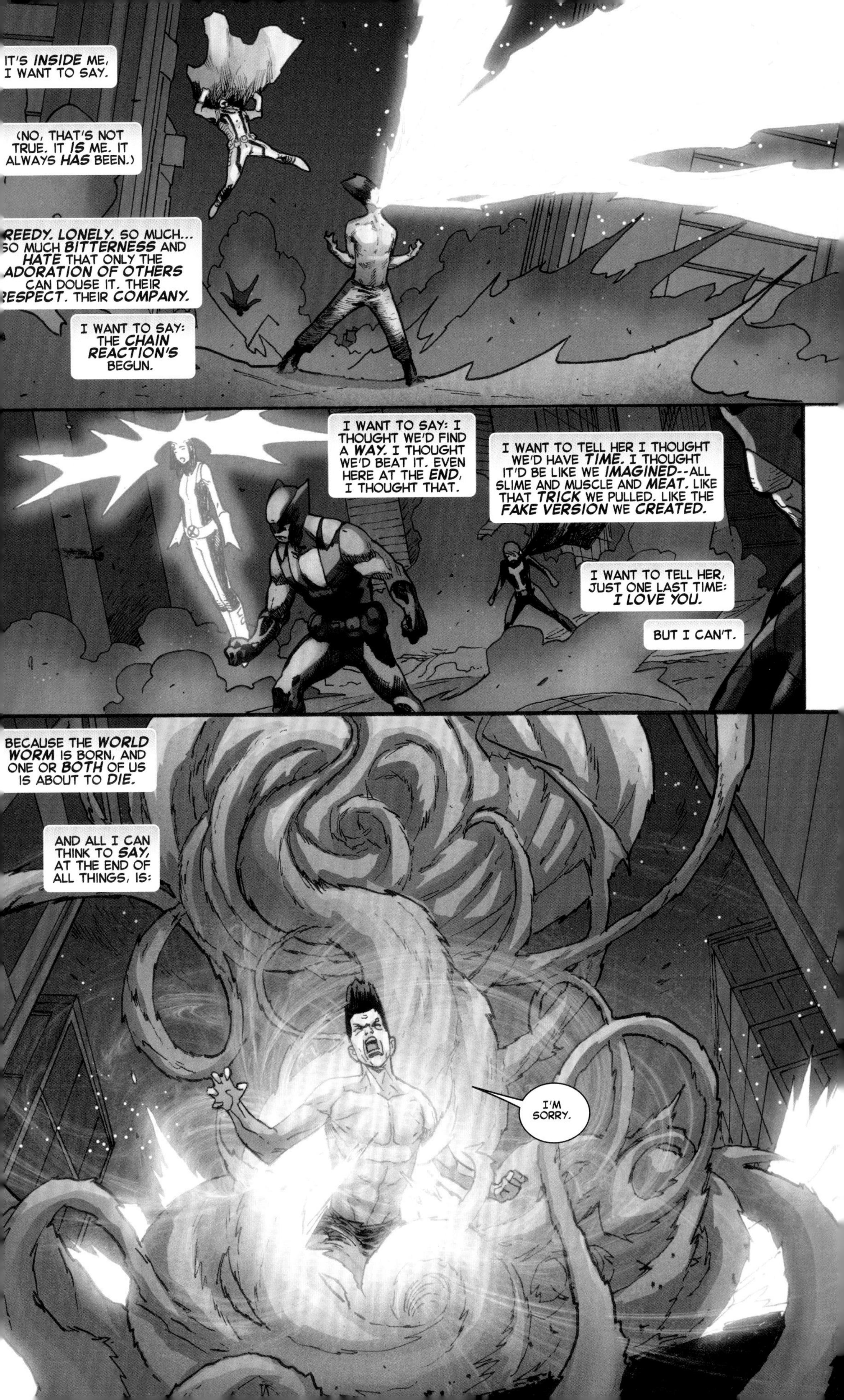

IT'S INSIDE ME, I WANT TO SAY.
(NO, THAT'S NOT TRUE. IT IS ME. IT ALWAYS HAS BEEN.)
REEDY. LONELY. SO MUCH... SO MUCH BITTERNESS AND HATE THAT ONLY THE ADORATION OF OTHERS CAN DOUSE IT. THEIR RESPECT. THEIR COMPANY.
I WANT TO SAY: THE CHAIN REACTION'S BEGUN.
I WANT TO SAY: I THOUGHT WE'D FIND A WAY. I THOUGHT WE'D BEAT IT. EVEN HERE AT THE END, I THOUGHT THAT.
I WANT TO TELL HER I THOUGHT WE'D HAVE TIME. I THOUGHT IT'D BE LIKE WE IMAGINED--ALL SLIME AND MUSCLE AND MEAT. LIKE THAT TRICK WE PULLED. LIKE THE FAKE VERSION WE CREATED.
I WANT TO TELL HER, JUST ONE LAST TIME: I LOVE YOU.
BUT I CAN'T.
BECAUSE THE WORLD WORM IS BORN, AND ONE OR BOTH OF US IS ABOUT TO DIE.
AND ALL I CAN THINK TO SAY, AT THE END OF ALL THINGS, IS:
I'M SORRY.

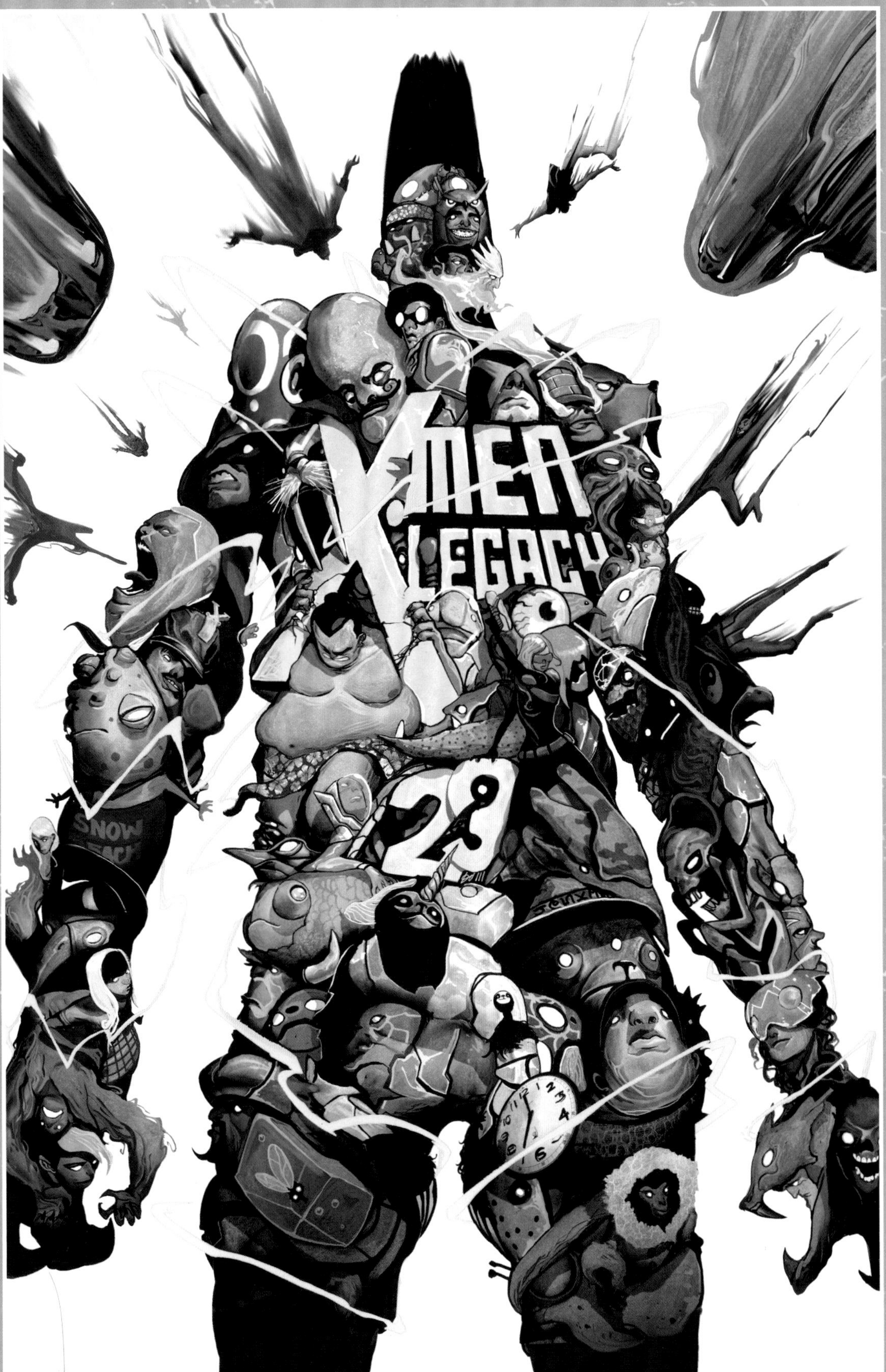
X-MEN
LEGACY
23

TWENTY-THREE

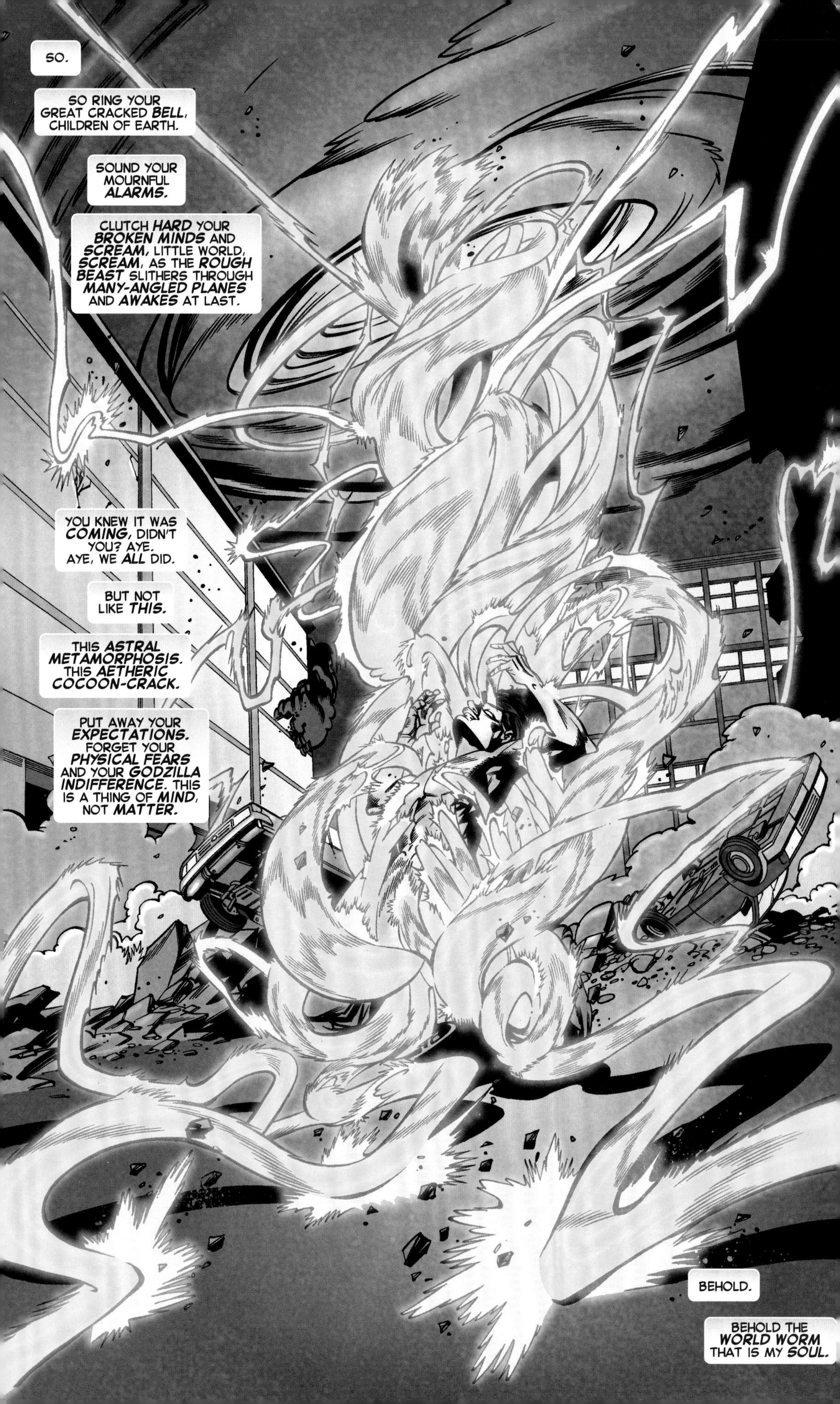
SO.
SO RING YOUR GREAT CRACKED BELL, CHILDREN OF EARTH.
SOUND YOUR MOURNFUL ALARMS.
CLUTCH HARD YOUR BROKEN MINDS AND SCREAM, LITTLE WORLD, SCREAM, AS THE ROUGH BEAST SLITHERS THROUGH MANY-ANGLED PLANES AND AWAKES AT LAST.
YOU KNEW IT WAS COMING, DIDN'T YOU? AYE. AYE, WE ALL DID.
BUT NOT LIKE THIS.
THIS ASTRAL METAMORPHOSIS. THIS AETHERIC COCOON-CRACK.
PUT AWAY YOUR EXPECTATIONS. FORGET YOUR PHYSICAL FEARS AND YOUR GODZILLA INDIFFERENCE. THIS IS A THING OF MIND, NOT MATTER.
BEHOLD.
BEHOLD THE WORLD WORM THAT IS MY SOUL.

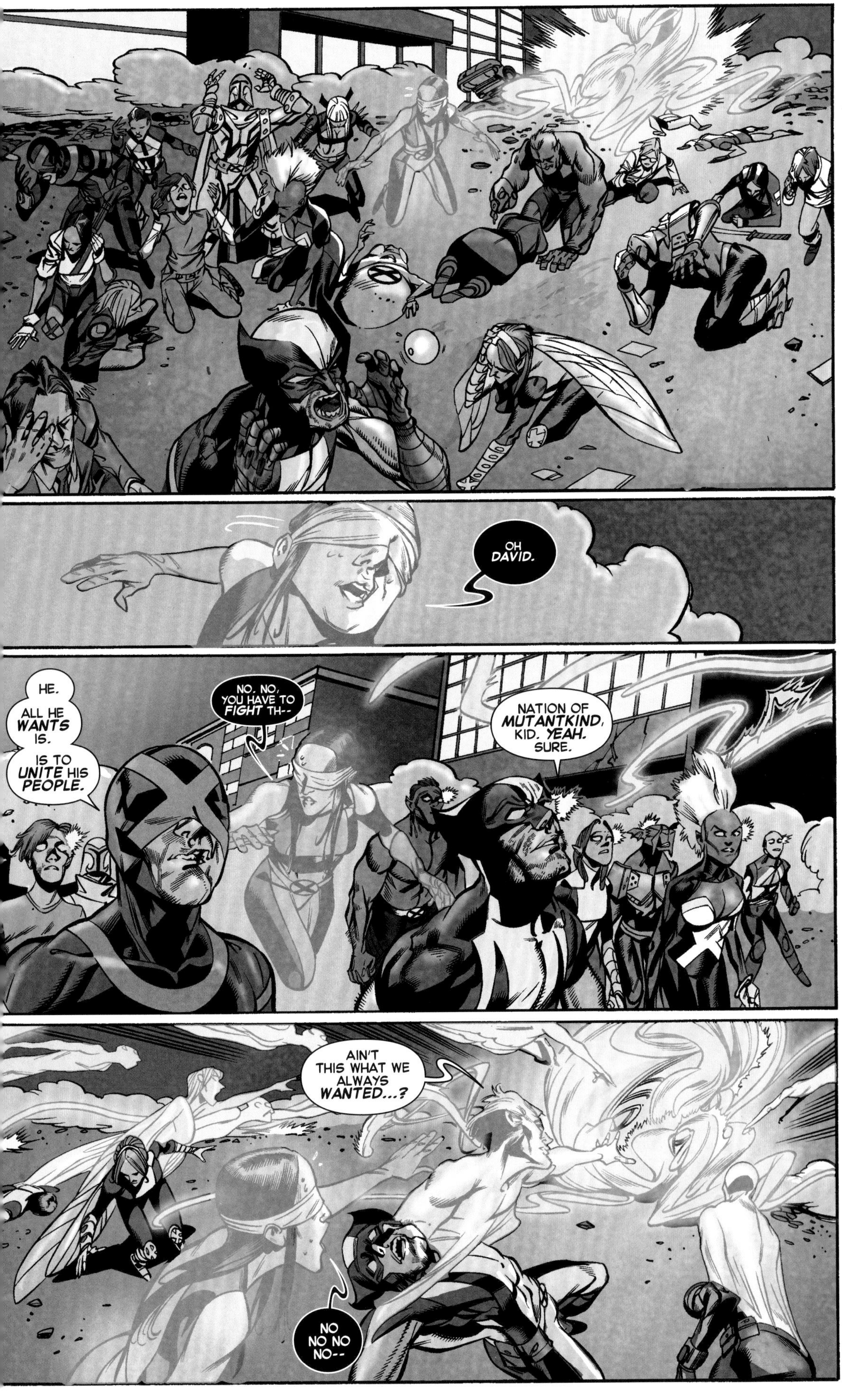

OH DAVID.
HE.
ALL HE WANTS IS.
IS TO UNITE HIS PEOPLE.
NO. NO, YOU HAVE TO FIGHT TH--
NATION OF MUTANTKIND, KID. YEAH. SURE.
AIN'T THIS WHAT WE ALWAYS WANTED...?
NO NO NO NO--

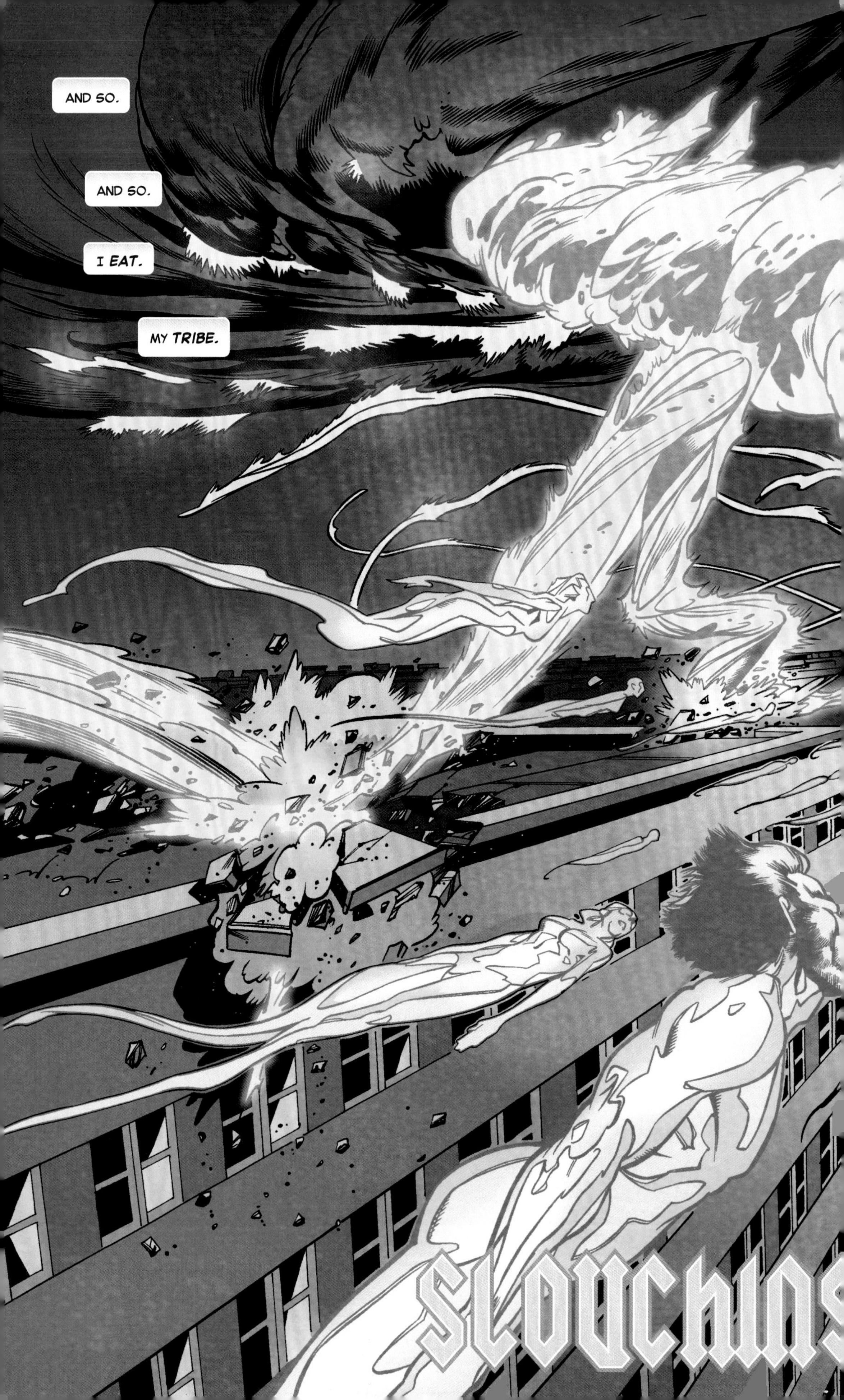
AND SO.
AND SO.
I EAT.
MY TRIBE.
SLOUCHIN

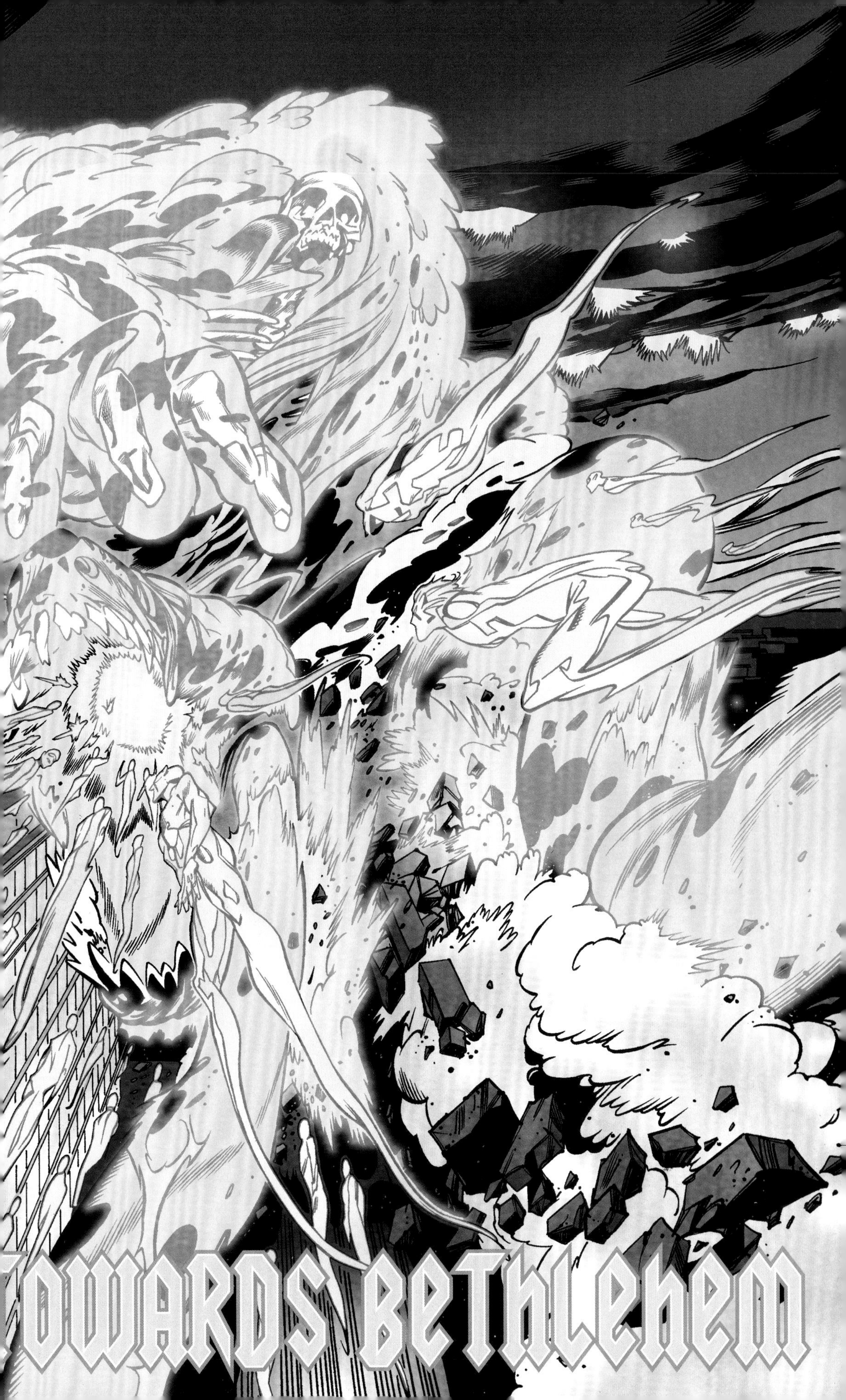
TOWARDS BETHLEHEM

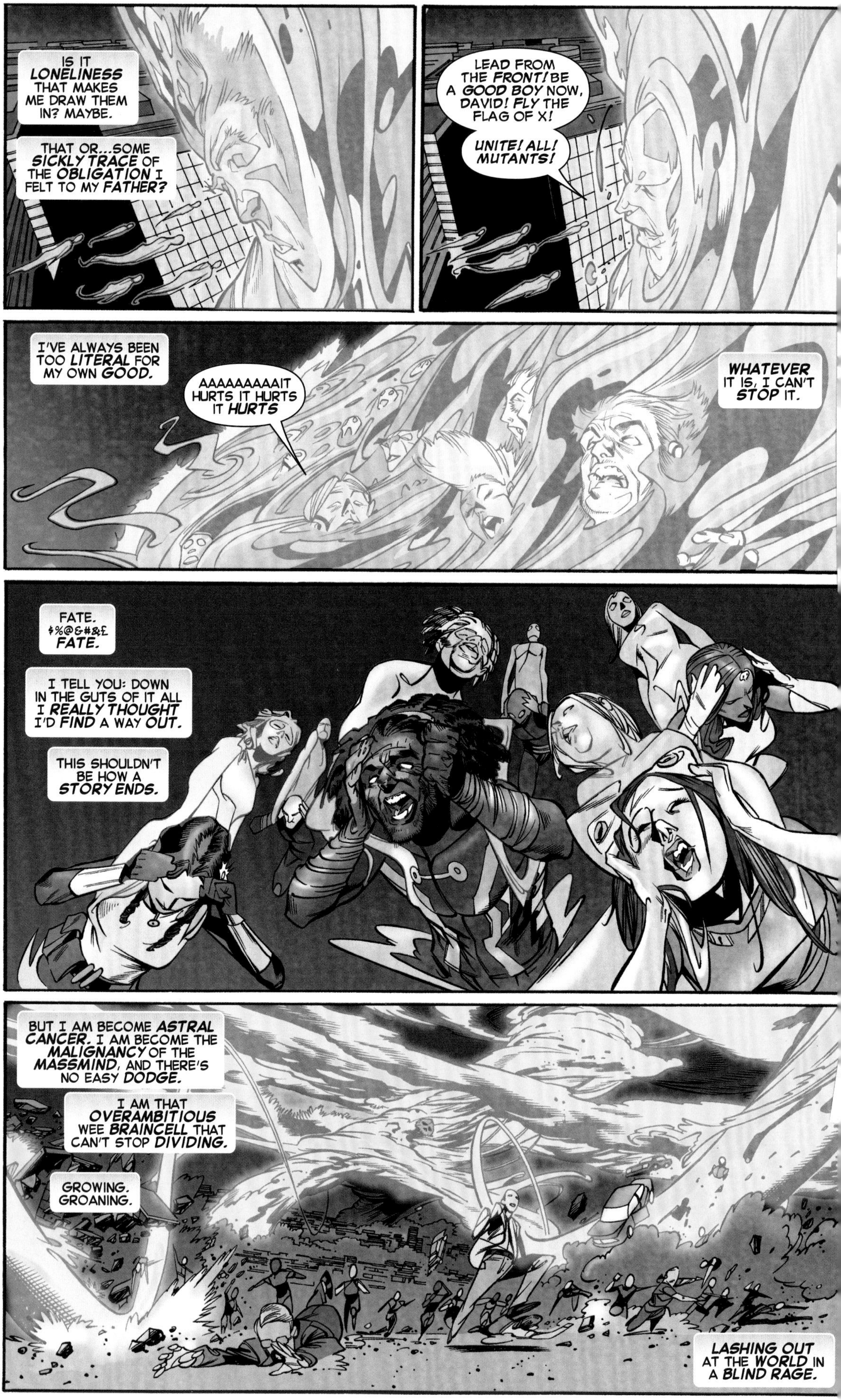

IS IT LONELINESS THAT MAKES ME DRAW THEM IN? MAYBE.
THAT OR...SOME SICKLY TRACE OF THE OBLIGATION I FELT TO MY FATHER?
LEAD FROM THE FRONT! BE A GOOD BOY NOW, DAVID! FLY THE FLAG OF X!
UNITE! ALL! MUTANTS!
I'VE ALWAYS BEEN TOO LITERAL FOR MY OWN GOOD.
AAAAAAAAAIT HURTS IT HURTS IT HURTS
WHATEVER IT IS, I CAN'T STOP IT.
FATE. $%@&#&£ FATE.
I TELL YOU: DOWN IN THE GUTS OF IT ALL I REALLY THOUGHT I'D FIND A WAY OUT.
THIS SHOULDN'T BE HOW A STORY ENDS.
BUT I AM BECOME ASTRAL CANCER. I AM BECOME THE MALIGNANCY OF THE MASSMIND, AND THERE'S NO EASY DODGE.
I AM THAT OVERAMBITIOUS WEE BRAINCELL THAT CAN'T STOP DIVIDING.
GROWING. GROANING.
LASHING OUT AT THE WORLD IN A BLIND RAGE.

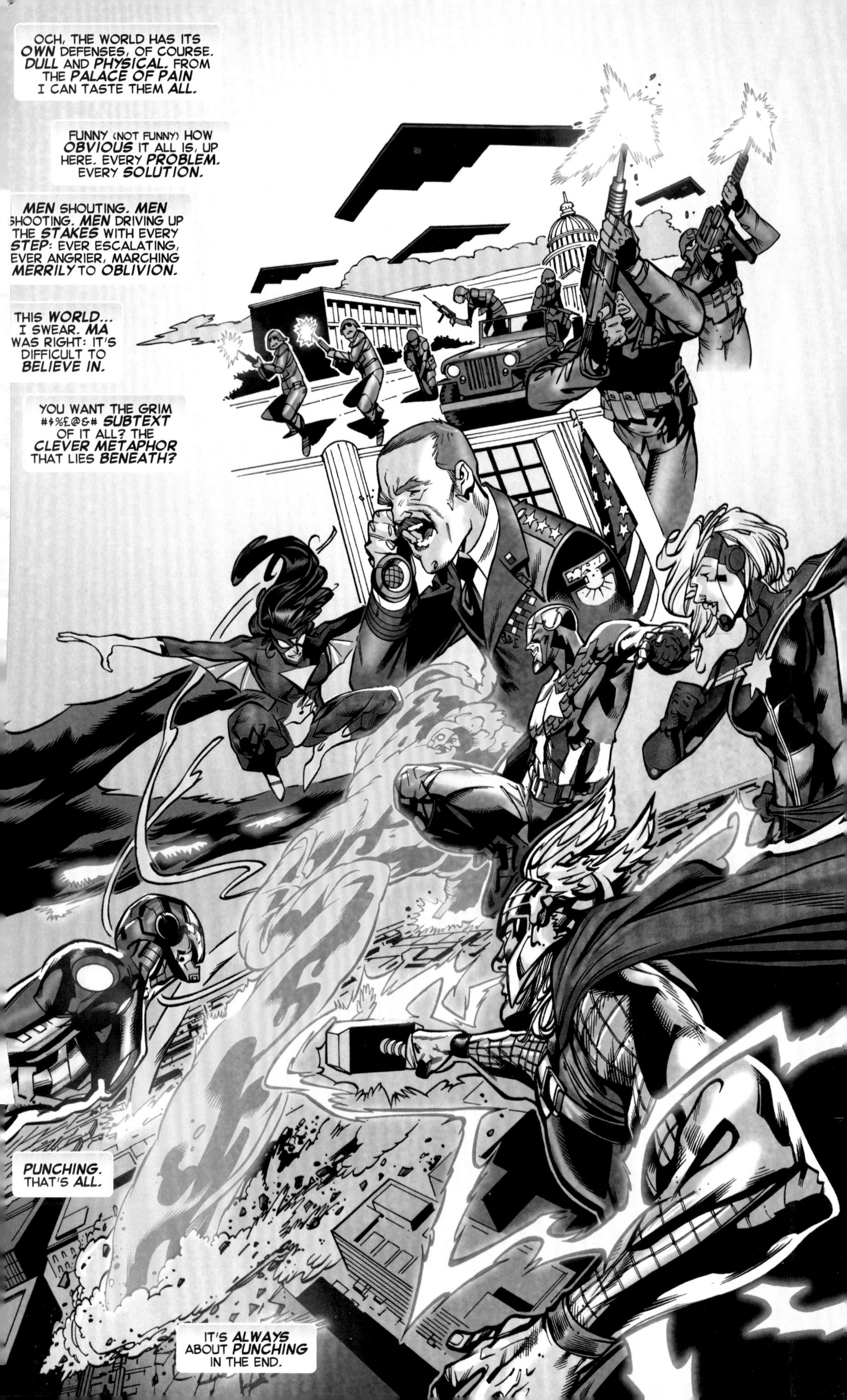

OCH, THE WORLD HAS ITS OWN DEFENSES, OF COURSE. DULL AND PHYSICAL. FROM THE PALACE OF PAIN I CAN TASTE THEM ALL.
FUNNY (NOT FUNNY) HOW OBVIOUS IT ALL IS, UP HERE. EVERY PROBLEM. EVERY SOLUTION.
MEN SHOUTING. MEN SHOOTING. MEN DRIVING UP THE STAKES WITH EVERY STEP: EVER ESCALATING, EVER ANGRIER, MARCHING MERRILY TO OBLIVION.
THIS WORLD... I SWEAR. MA WAS RIGHT: IT'S DIFFICULT TO BELIEVE IN.
YOU WANT THE GRIM #$%£@&# SUBTEXT OF IT ALL? THE CLEVER METAPHOR THAT LIES BENEATH?
PUNCHING. THAT'S ALL.
IT'S ALWAYS ABOUT PUNCHING IN THE END.

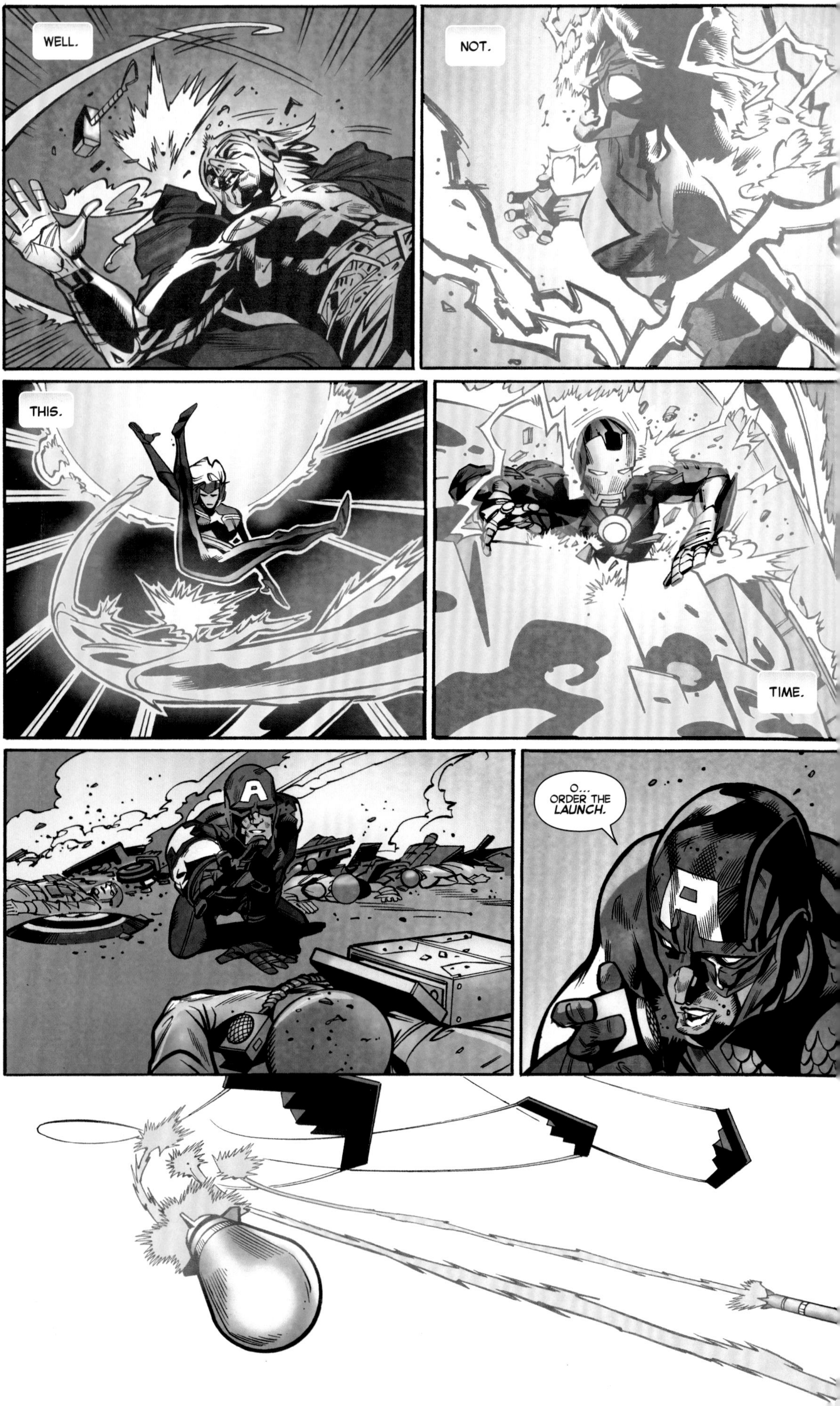
WELL.
NOT.
THIS.
TIME.
O... ORDER THE LAUNCH.

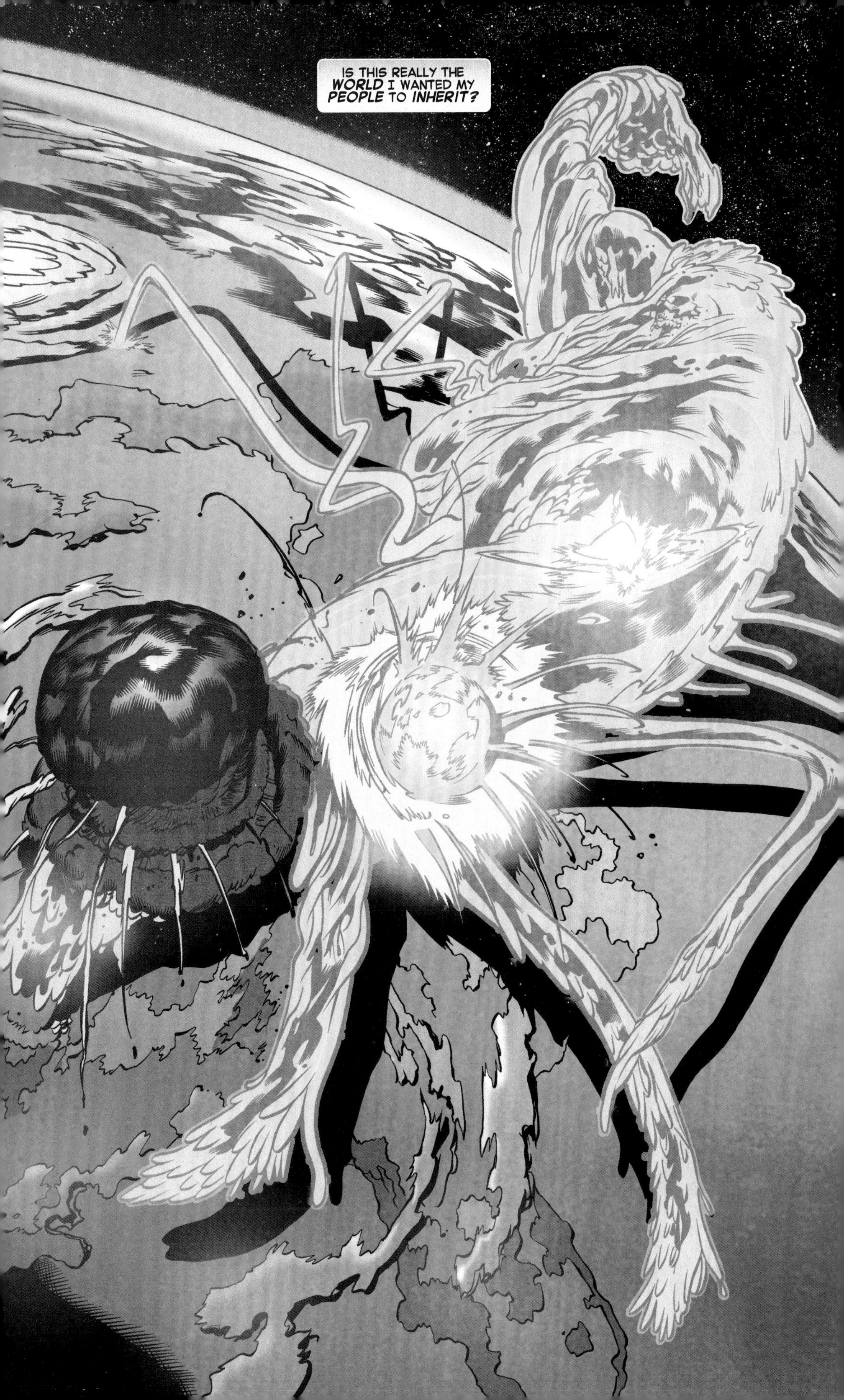
IS THIS REALLY THE *WORLD* I WANTED MY *PEOPLE* TO *INHERIT?*

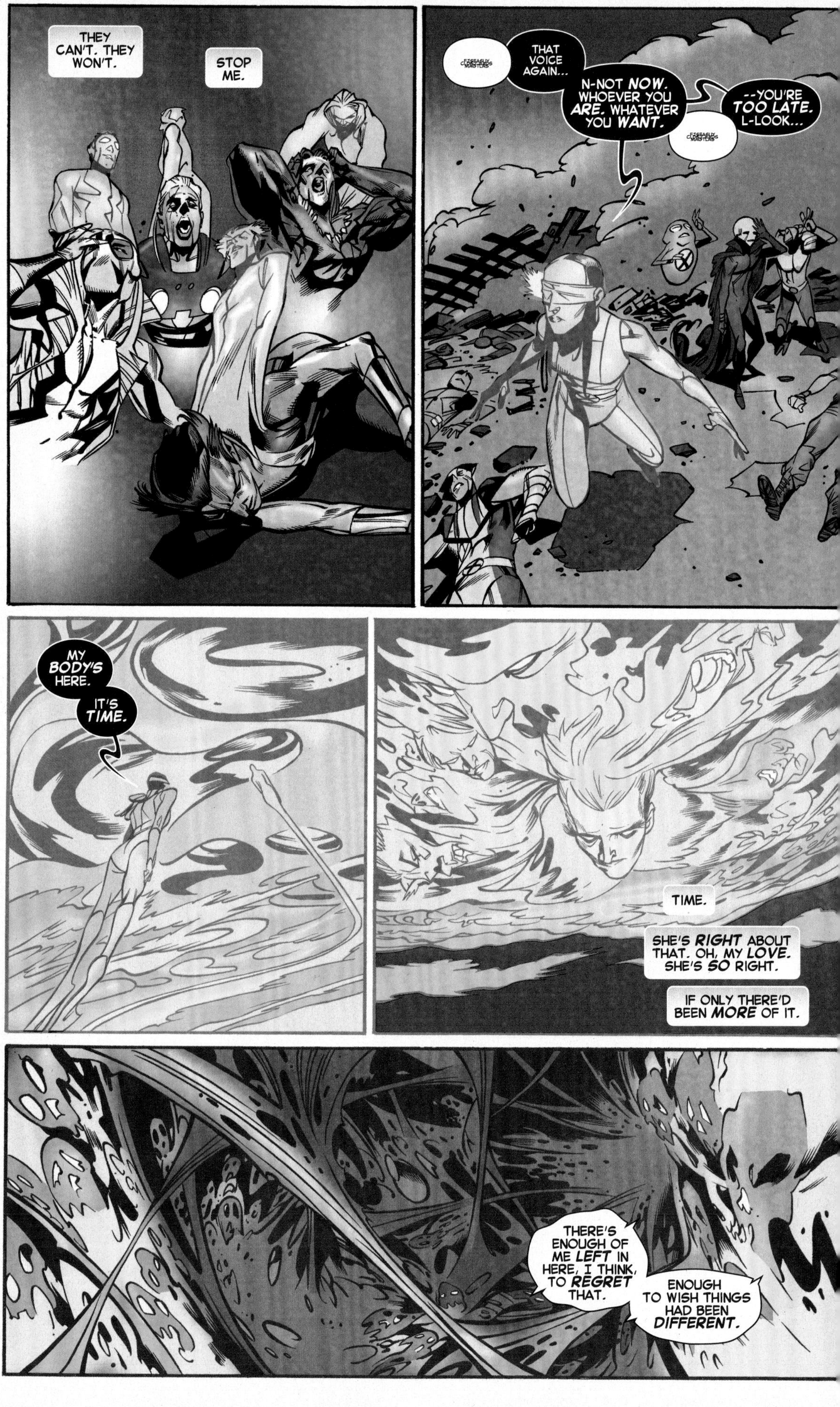

THEY CAN'T. THEY WON'T.
STOP ME.
THAT VOICE AGAIN...
N-NOT NOW. WHOEVER YOU ARE. WHATEVER YOU WANT.
--YOU'RE TOO LATE. L-LOOK...
MY BODY'S HERE.
IT'S TIME.
TIME.
SHE'S RIGHT ABOUT THAT. OH, MY LOVE. SHE'S SO RIGHT.
IF ONLY THERE'D BEEN MORE OF IT.
THERE'S ENOUGH OF ME LEFT IN HERE, I THINK, TO REGRET THAT.
ENOUGH TO WISH THINGS HAD BEEN DIFFERENT.

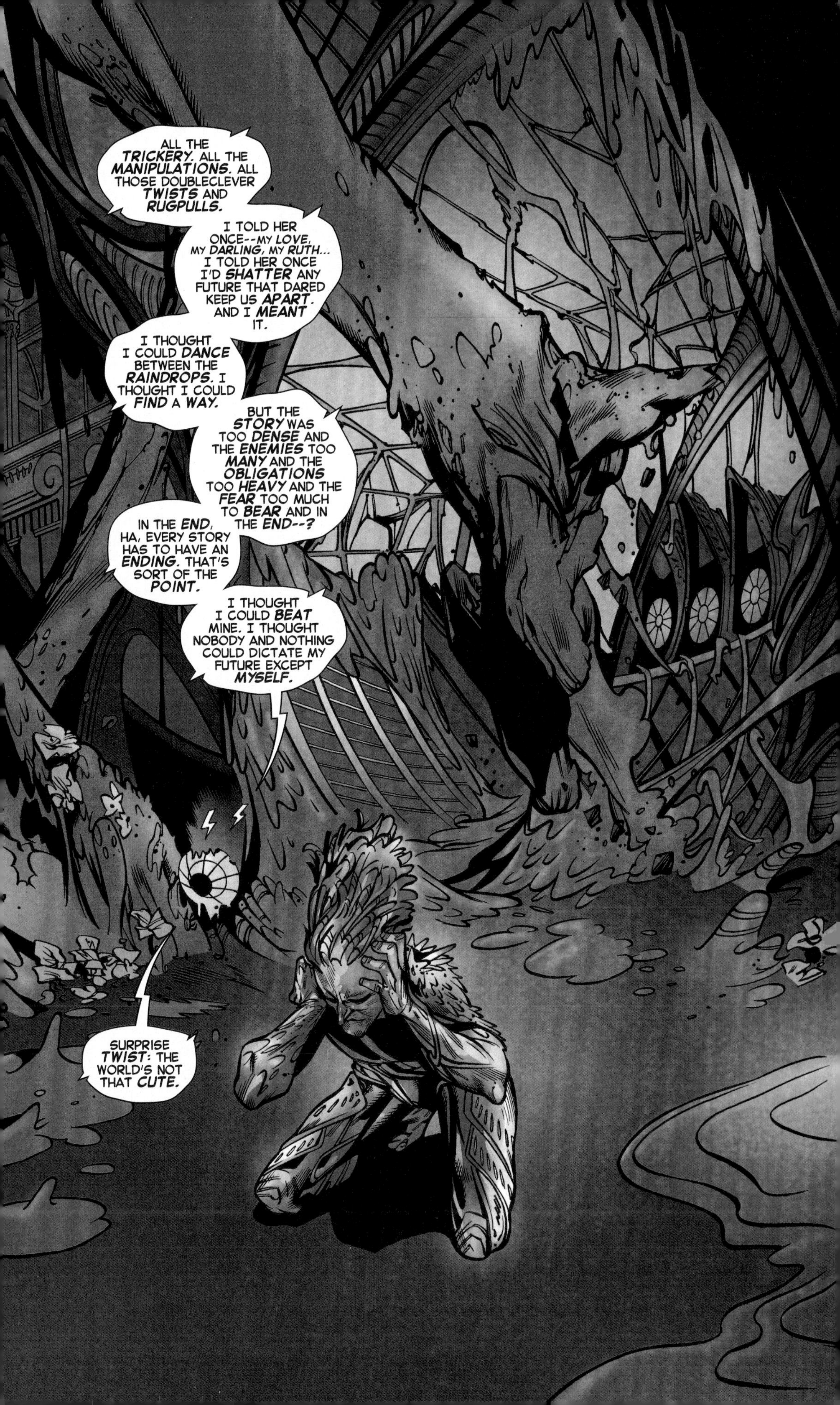
ALL THE TRICKERY. ALL THE MANIPULATIONS. ALL THOSE DOUBLECLEVER TWISTS AND RUGPULLS.
I TOLD HER ONCE--MY LOVE, MY DARLING, MY RUTH... I TOLD HER ONCE I'D SHATTER ANY FUTURE THAT DARED KEEP US APART. AND I MEANT IT.
I THOUGHT I COULD DANCE BETWEEN THE RAINDROPS. I THOUGHT I COULD FIND A WAY.
BUT THE STORY WAS TOO DENSE AND THE ENEMIES TOO MANY AND THE OBLIGATIONS TOO HEAVY AND THE FEAR TOO MUCH TO BEAR AND IN THE END--?
IN THE END, HA, EVERY STORY HAS TO HAVE AN ENDING. THAT'S SORT OF THE POINT.
I THOUGHT I COULD BEAT MINE. I THOUGHT NOBODY AND NOTHING COULD DICTATE MY FUTURE EXCEPT MYSELF.
SURPRISE TWIST: THE WORLD'S NOT THAT CUTE.

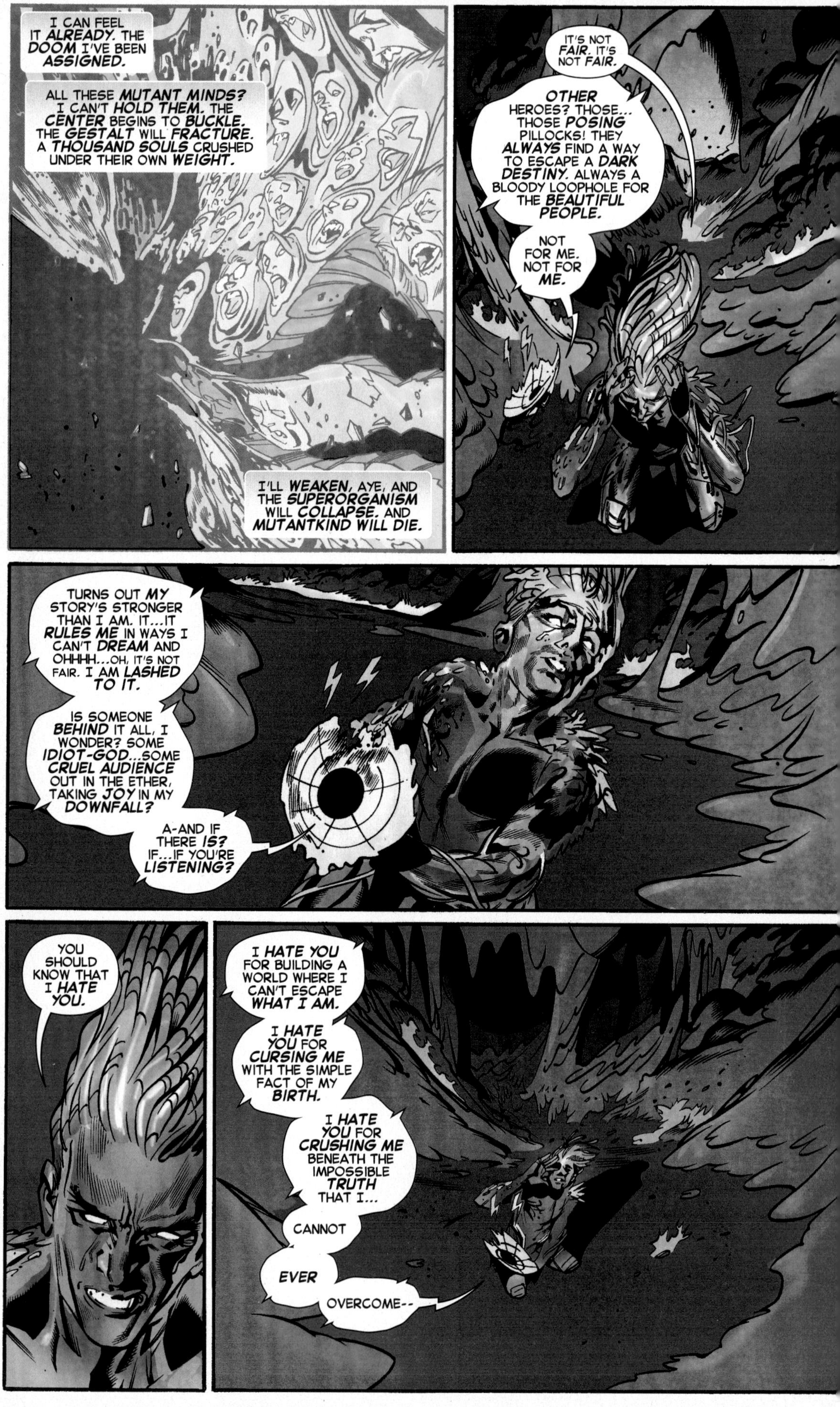

I CAN FEEL IT ALREADY. THE DOOM I'VE BEEN ASSIGNED.
ALL THESE MUTANT MINDS? I CAN'T HOLD THEM. THE CENTER BEGINS TO BUCKLE. THE GESTALT WILL FRACTURE. A THOUSAND SOULS CRUSHED UNDER THEIR OWN WEIGHT.
I'LL WEAKEN, AYE, AND THE SUPERORGANISM WILL COLLAPSE. AND MUTANTKIND WILL DIE.
IT'S NOT FAIR. IT'S NOT FAIR.
OTHER HEROES? THOSE... THOSE POSING PILLOCKS! THEY ALWAYS FIND A WAY TO ESCAPE A DARK DESTINY. ALWAYS A BLOODY LOOPHOLE FOR THE BEAUTIFUL PEOPLE.
NOT FOR ME. NOT FOR ME.
TURNS OUT MY STORY'S STRONGER THAN I AM. IT...IT RULES ME IN WAYS I CAN'T DREAM AND OHHHH...OH, IT'S NOT FAIR. I AM LASHED TO IT.
IS SOMEONE BEHIND IT ALL, I WONDER? SOME IDIOT-GOD...SOME CRUEL AUDIENCE OUT IN THE ETHER, TAKING JOY IN MY DOWNFALL?
A-AND IF THERE IS? IF...IF YOU'RE LISTENING?
YOU SHOULD KNOW THAT I HATE YOU.
I HATE YOU FOR BUILDING A WORLD WHERE I CAN'T ESCAPE WHAT I AM.
I HATE YOU FOR CURSING ME WITH THE SIMPLE FACT OF MY BIRTH.
I HATE YOU FOR CRUSHING ME BENEATH THE IMPOSSIBLE TRUTH THAT I...
CANNOT
EVER
OVERCOME--

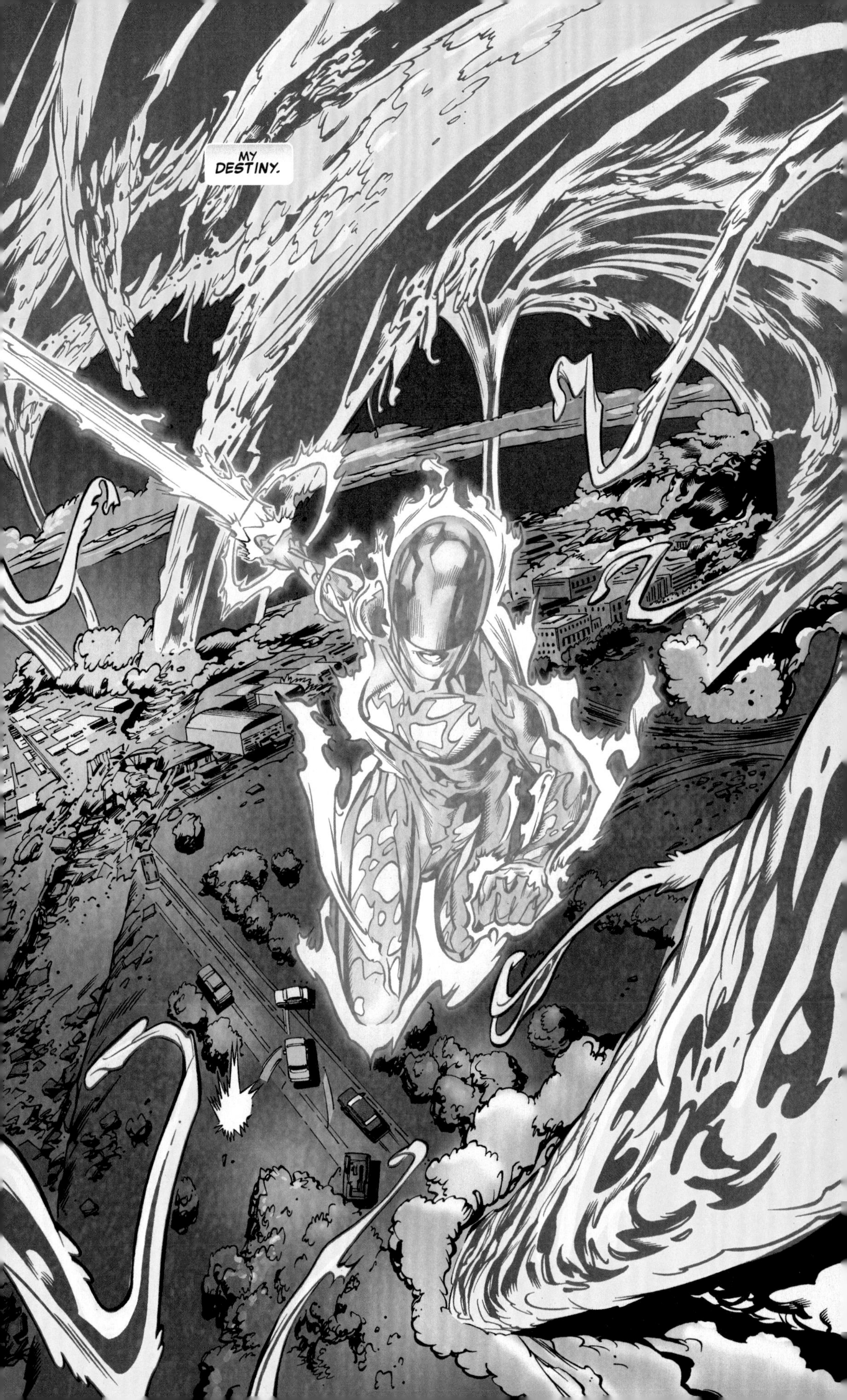
MY DESTINY.

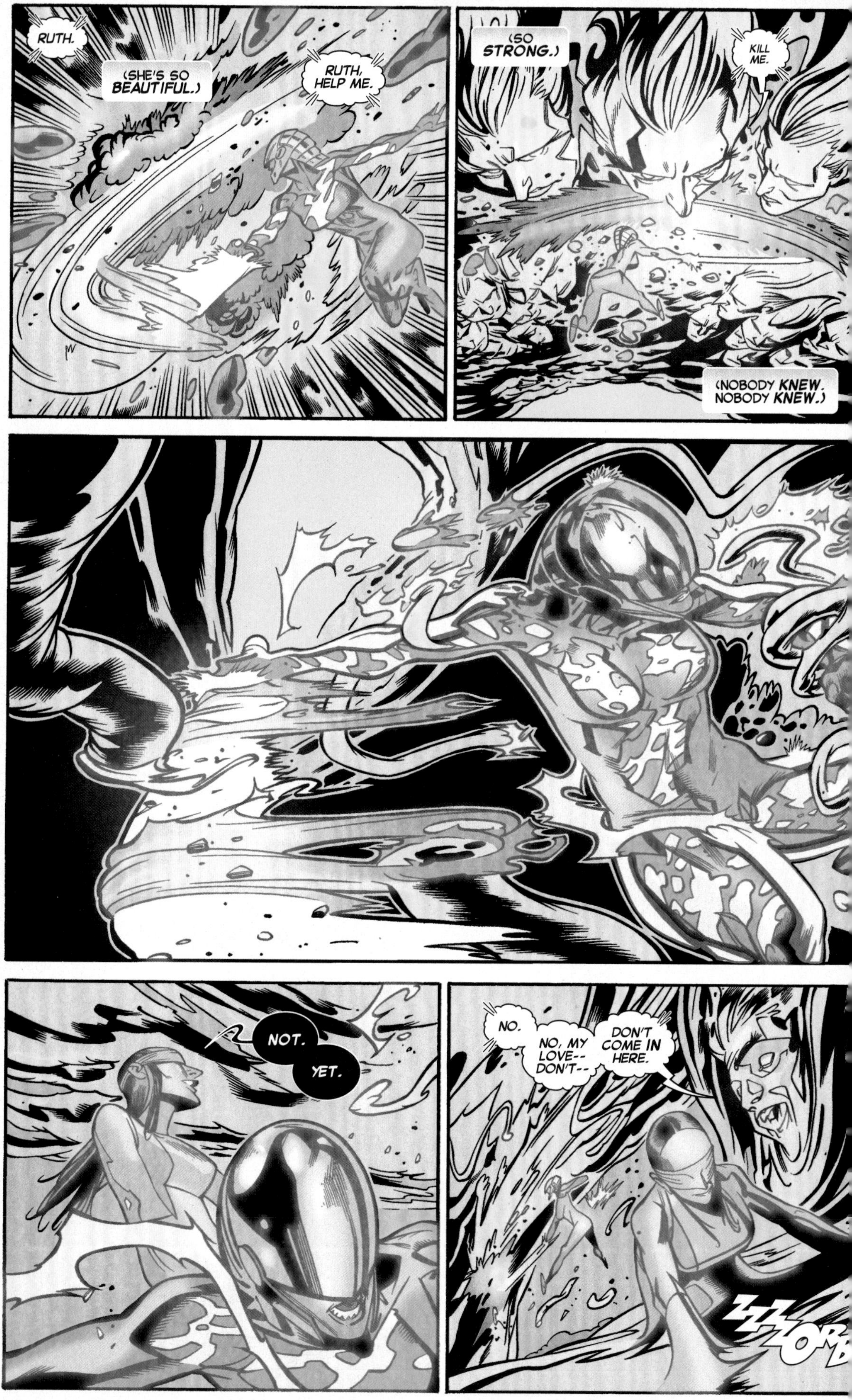
RUTH.
(SHE'S SO BEAUTIFUL.)
RUTH, HELP ME.
(SO STRONG.)
KILL ME.
(NOBODY KNEW. NOBODY KNEW.)
NOT.
YET.
NO.
NO, MY LOVE-- DON'T--
DON'T COME IN HERE.
ZZZORB

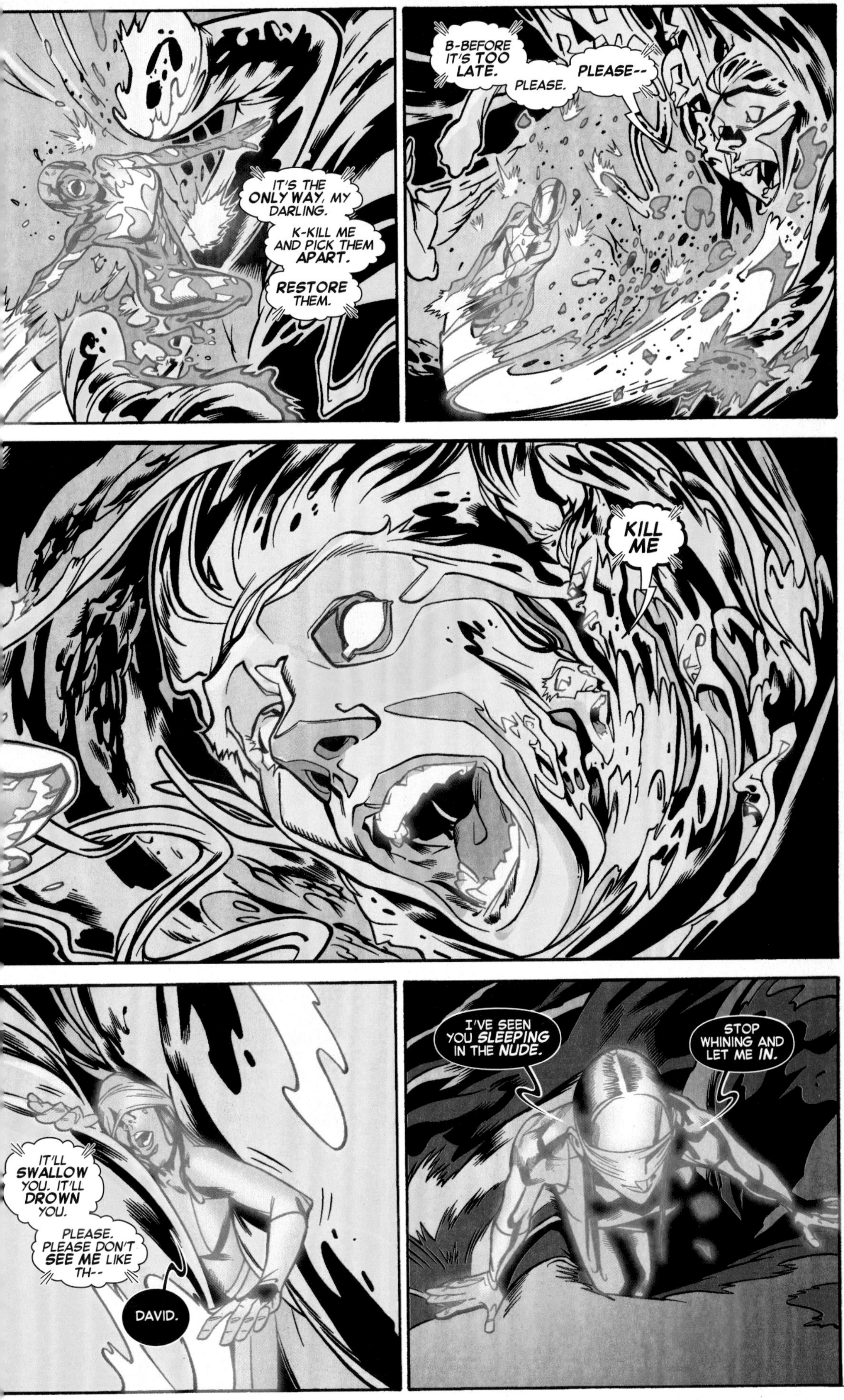
IT'S THE ONLY WAY, MY DARLING.
K-KILL ME AND PICK THEM APART.
RESTORE THEM.
B-BEFORE IT'S TOO LATE.
PLEASE.
PLEASE--
KILL ME
IT'LL SWALLOW YOU. IT'LL DROWN YOU.
PLEASE. PLEASE DON'T SEE ME LIKE TH--
DAVID.
I'VE SEEN YOU SLEEPING IN THE NUDE.
STOP WHINING AND LET ME IN.

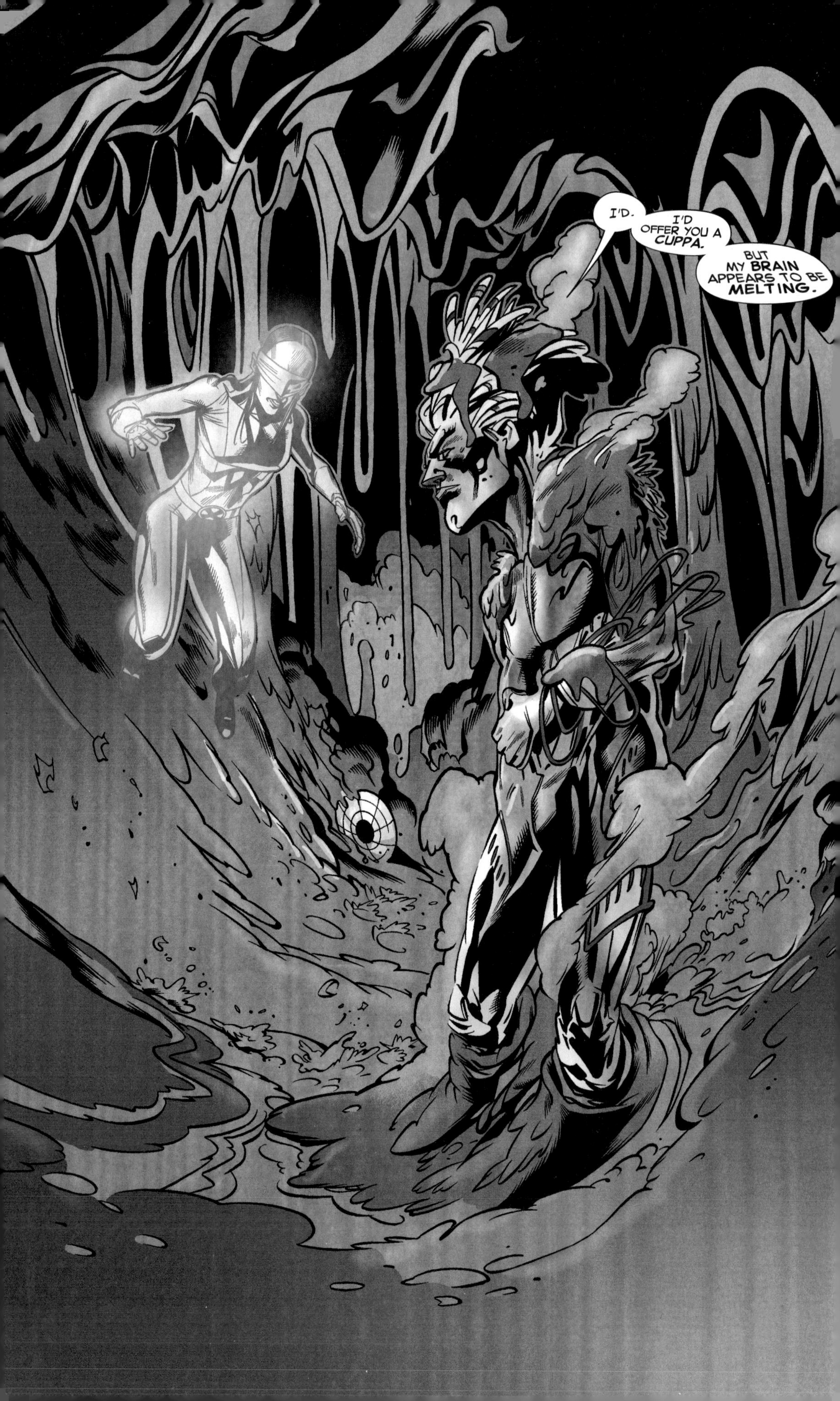

I'D.
I'D OFFER YOU A CUPPA.
BUT MY BRAIN APPEARS TO BE MELTING.

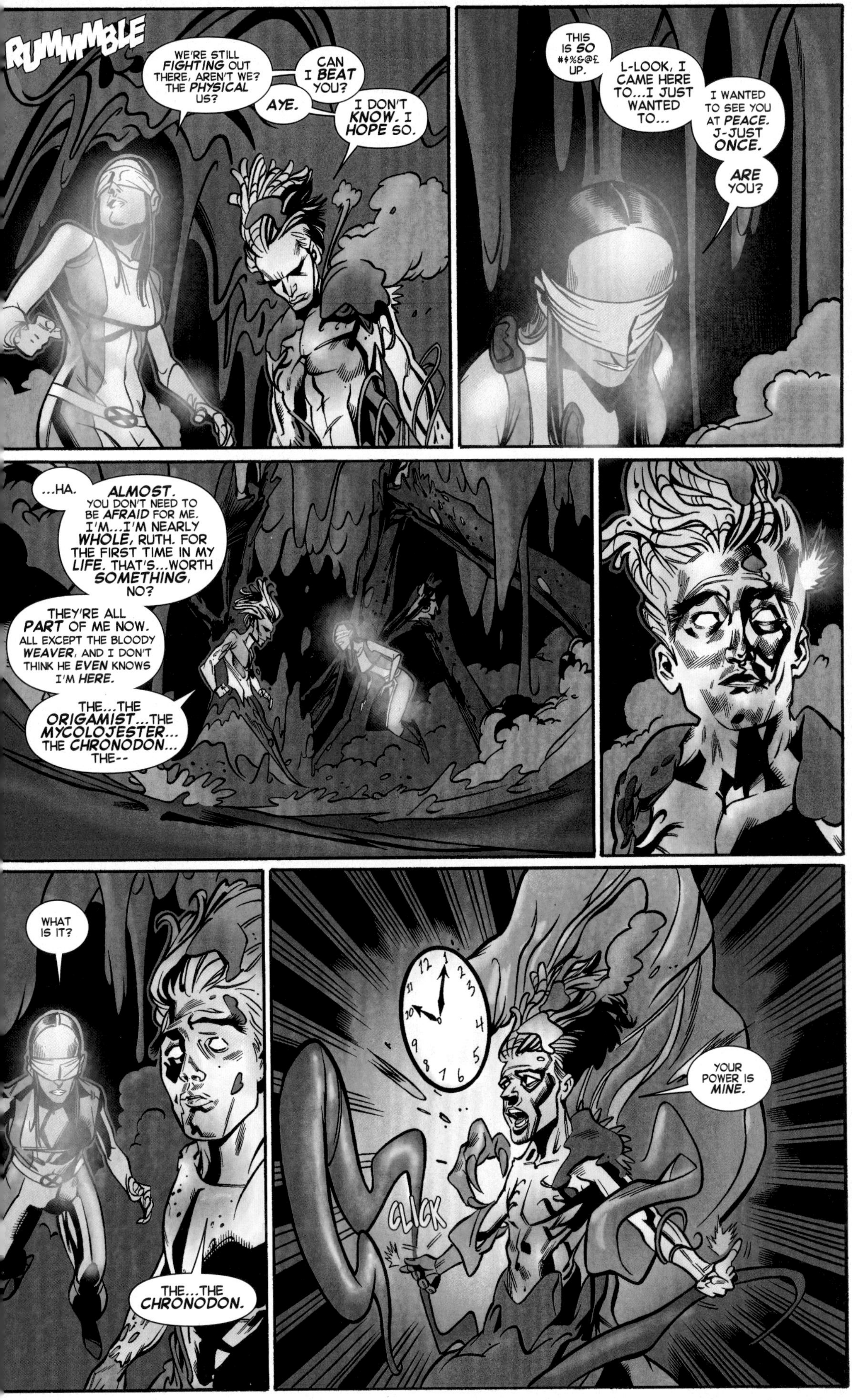
RUMMMBLE
WE'RE STILL FIGHTING OUT THERE, AREN'T WE? THE PHYSICAL US?
CAN I BEAT YOU?
AYE.
I DON'T KNOW. I HOPE SO.
THIS IS SO #$%&@£ UP.
L-LOOK, I CAME HERE TO...I JUST WANTED TO...
I WANTED TO SEE YOU AT PEACE. J-JUST ONCE.
ARE YOU?
...HA.
ALMOST. YOU DON'T NEED TO BE AFRAID FOR ME. I'M...I'M NEARLY WHOLE, RUTH. FOR THE FIRST TIME IN MY LIFE. THAT'S...WORTH SOMETHING, NO?
THEY'RE ALL PART OF ME NOW. ALL EXCEPT THE BLOODY WEAVER, AND I DON'T THINK HE EVEN KNOWS I'M HERE.
THE...THE ORIGAMIST...THE MYCOLOJESTER... THE CHRONODON... THE--
WHAT IS IT?
THE...THE CHRONODON.
CLICK
YOUR POWER IS MINE.

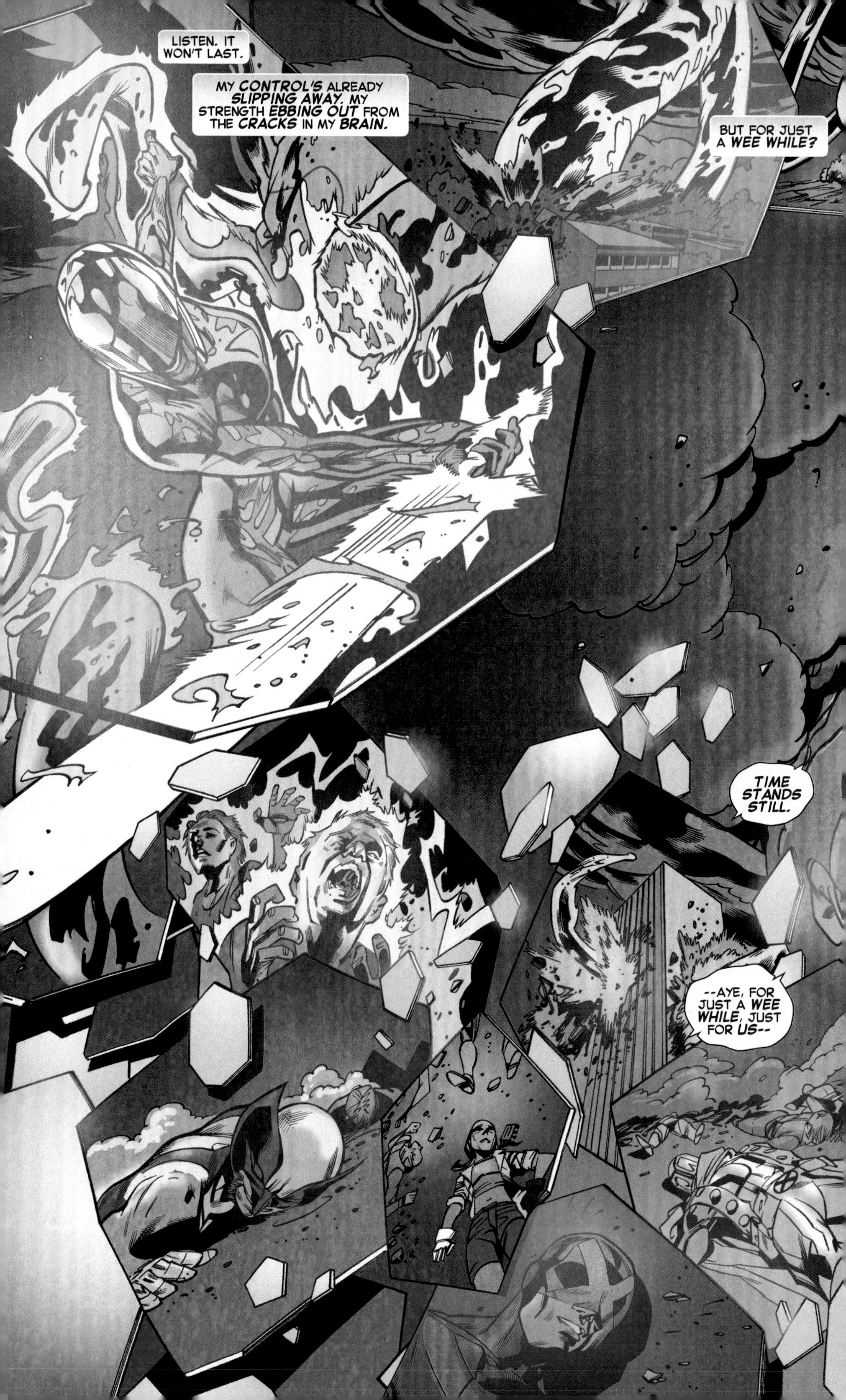
LISTEN. IT WON'T LAST.
MY CONTROL'S ALREADY SLIPPING AWAY. MY STRENGTH EBBING OUT FROM THE CRACKS IN MY BRAIN.
BUT FOR JUST A WEE WHILE?
TIME STANDS STILL.
--AYE, FOR JUST A WEE WHILE, JUST FOR US--

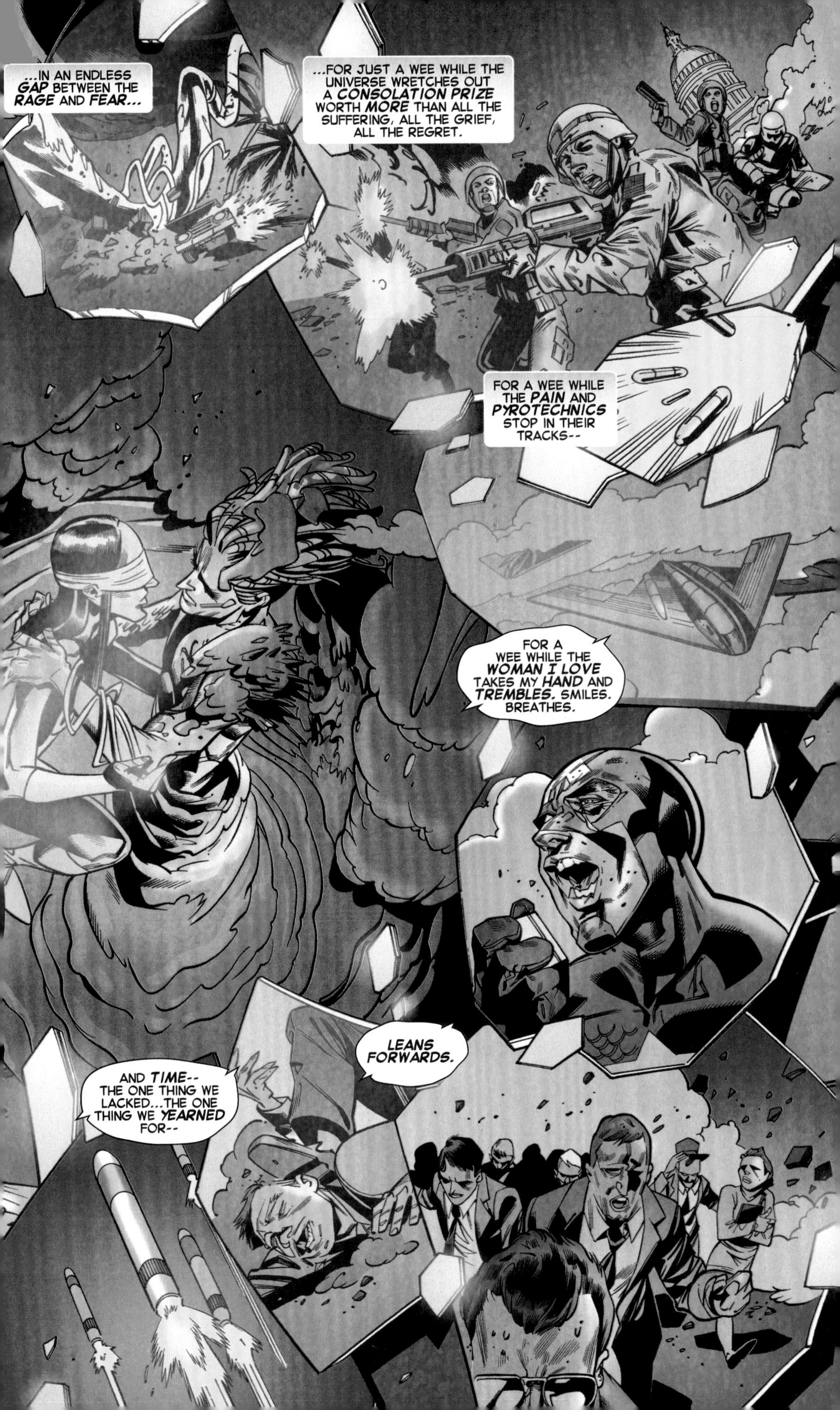
...IN AN ENDLESS GAP BETWEEN THE RAGE AND FEAR...
...FOR JUST A WEE WHILE THE UNIVERSE WRETCHES OUT A CONSOLATION PRIZE WORTH MORE THAN ALL THE SUFFERING, ALL THE GRIEF, ALL THE REGRET.
FOR A WEE WHILE THE PAIN AND PYROTECHNICS STOP IN THEIR TRACKS--
FOR A WEE WHILE THE WOMAN I LOVE TAKES MY HAND AND TREMBLES. SMILES. BREATHES.
LEANS FORWARDS.
AND TIME-- THE ONE THING WE LACKED...THE ONE THING WE YEARNED FOR--

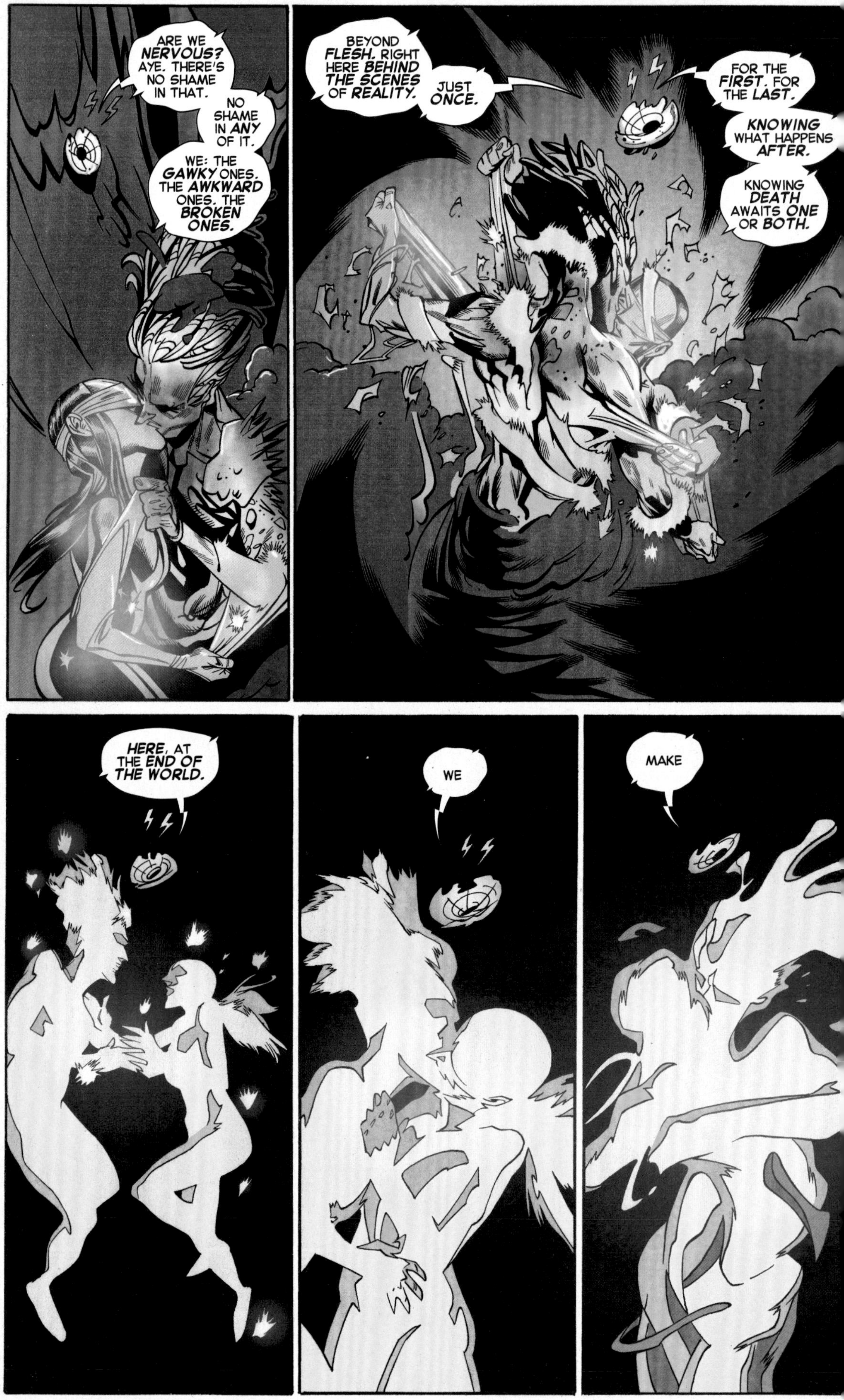
ARE WE NERVOUS? AYE. THERE'S NO SHAME IN THAT.
NO SHAME IN ANY OF IT.
WE: THE GAWKY ONES. THE AWKWARD ONES. THE BROKEN ONES.
BEYOND FLESH. RIGHT HERE BEHIND THE SCENES OF REALITY.
JUST ONCE.
FOR THE FIRST. FOR THE LAST.
KNOWING WHAT HAPPENS AFTER.
KNOWING DEATH AWAITS ONE OR BOTH.
HERE, AT THE END OF THE WORLD.
WE
MAKE

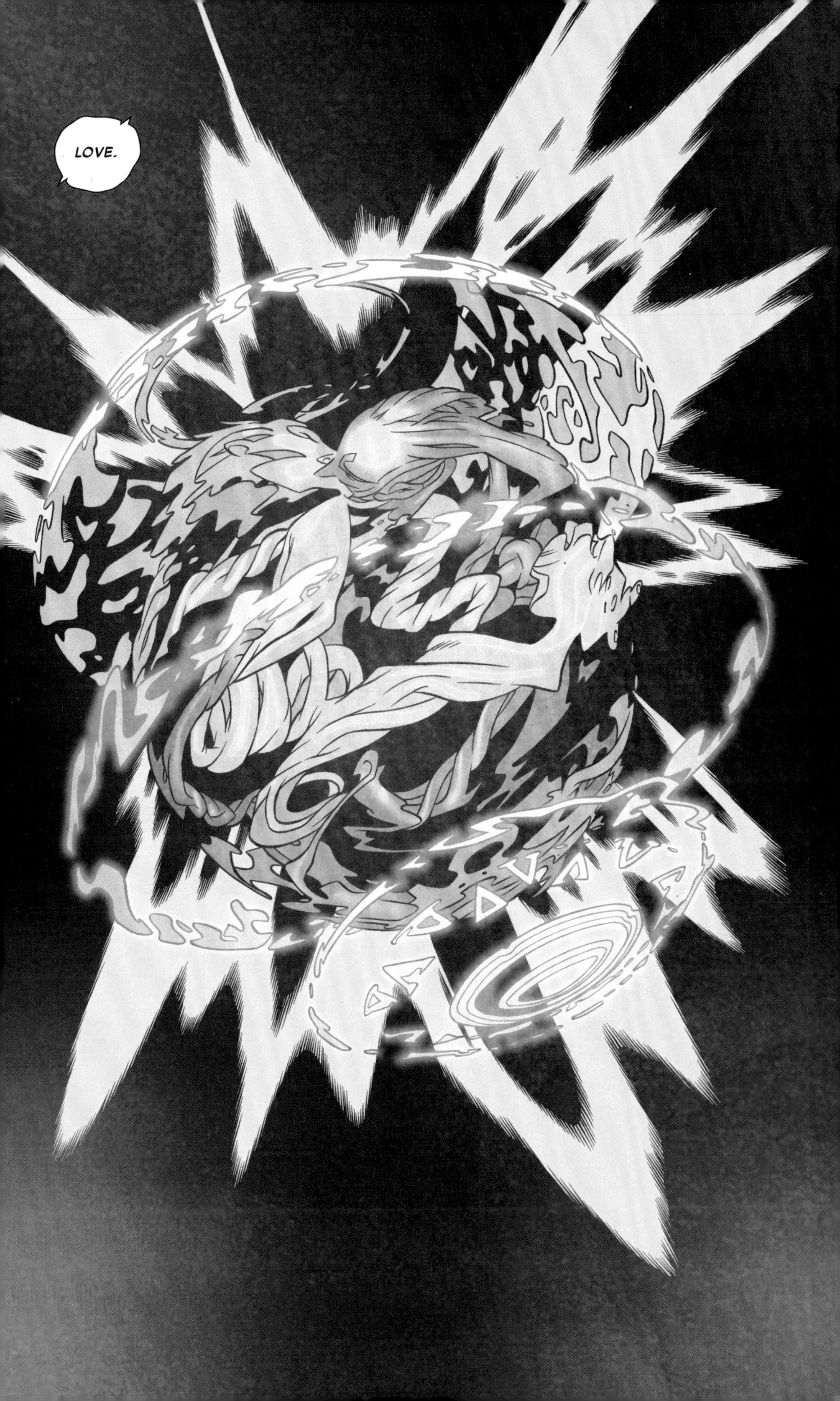
LOVE.

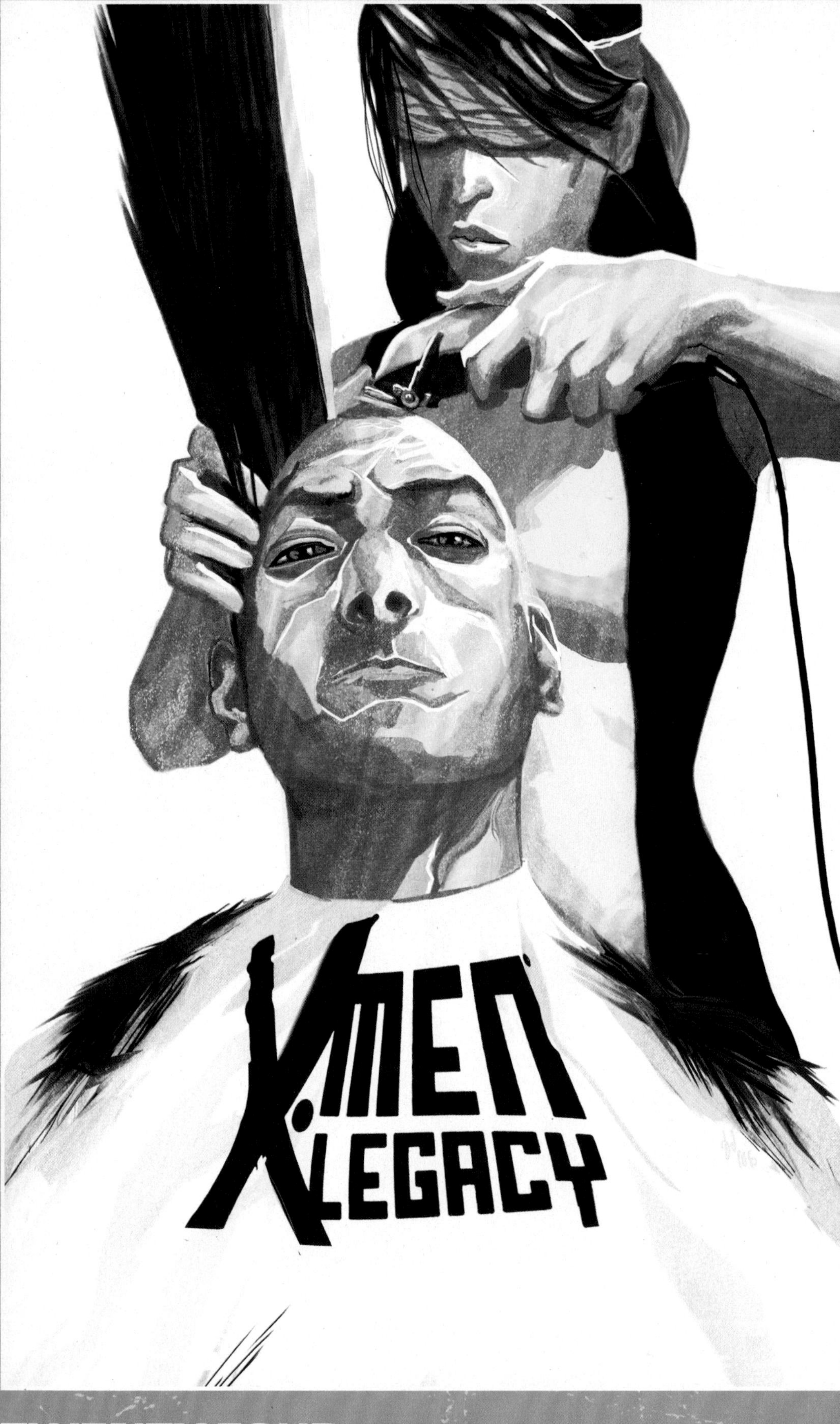
X-MEN
LEGACY

TWENTY-FOUR

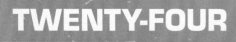

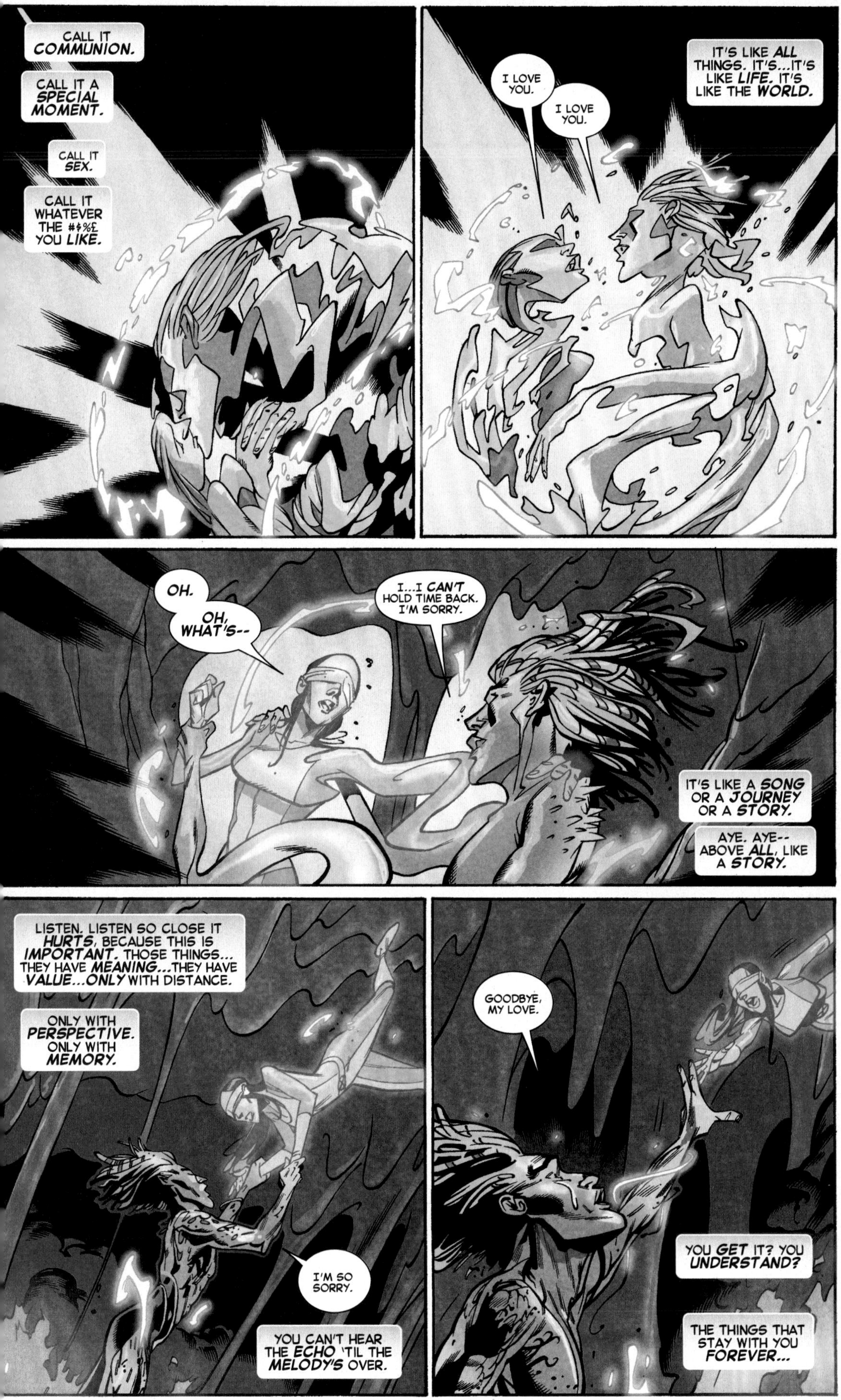
CALL IT COMMUNION.
CALL IT A SPECIAL MOMENT.
CALL IT SEX.
CALL IT WHATEVER THE #$%£ YOU LIKE.
I LOVE YOU.
I LOVE YOU.
IT'S LIKE ALL THINGS. IT'S...IT'S LIKE LIFE. IT'S LIKE THE WORLD.
OH.
OH, WHAT'S--
I...I CAN'T HOLD TIME BACK. I'M SORRY.
IT'S LIKE A SONG OR A JOURNEY OR A STORY.
AYE. AYE-- ABOVE ALL, LIKE A STORY.
LISTEN. LISTEN SO CLOSE IT HURTS, BECAUSE THIS IS IMPORTANT. THOSE THINGS... THEY HAVE MEANING...THEY HAVE VALUE...ONLY WITH DISTANCE.
ONLY WITH PERSPECTIVE. ONLY WITH MEMORY.
I'M SO SORRY.
YOU CAN'T HEAR THE ECHO 'TIL THE MELODY'S OVER.
GOODBYE, MY LOVE.
YOU GET IT? YOU UNDERSTAND?
THE THINGS THAT STAY WITH YOU FOREVER...

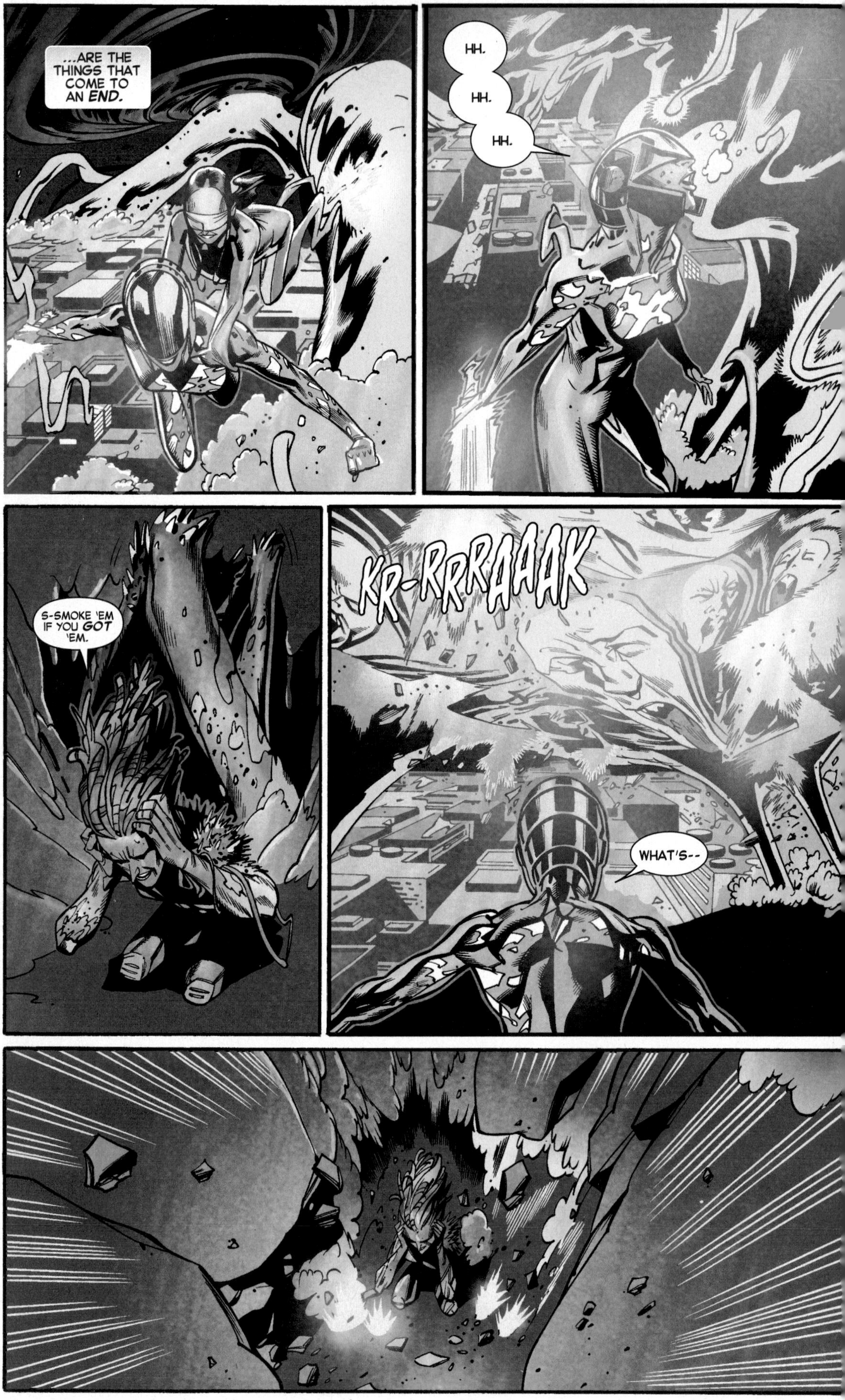

...ARE THE THINGS THAT COME TO AN *END.*
HH.
HH.
HH.
S-SMOKE 'EM IF YOU **GOT** 'EM.
KR-RRRAAAK
WHAT'S--

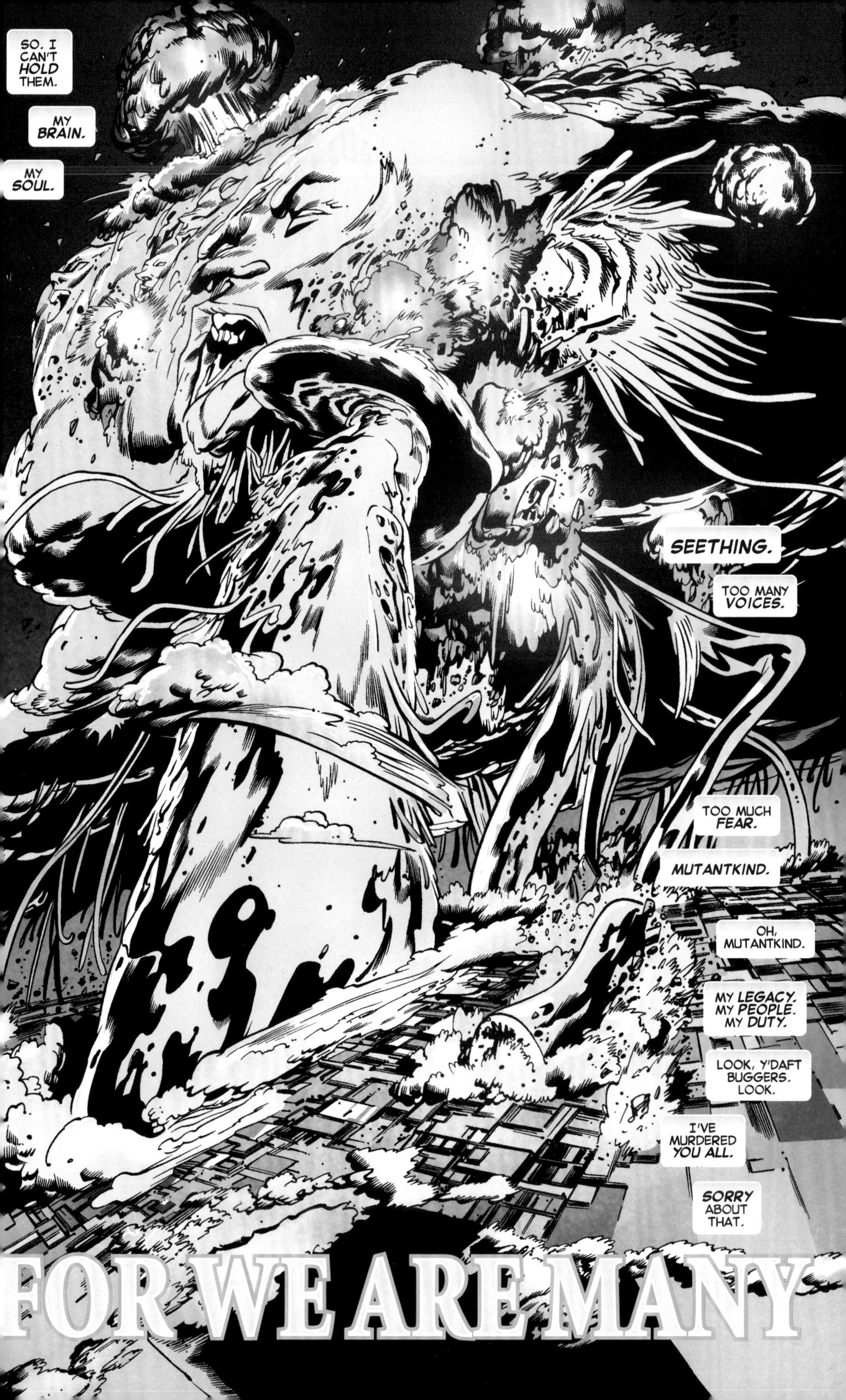

SO. I CAN'T HOLD THEM.
MY BRAIN.
MY SOUL.
SEETHING.
TOO MANY VOICES.
TOO MUCH FEAR.
MUTANTKIND.
OH, MUTANTKIND.
MY LEGACY. MY PEOPLE. MY DUTY.
LOOK, Y'DAFT BUGGERS. LOOK.
I'VE MURDERED YOU ALL.
SORRY ABOUT THAT.
FOR WE ARE MANY

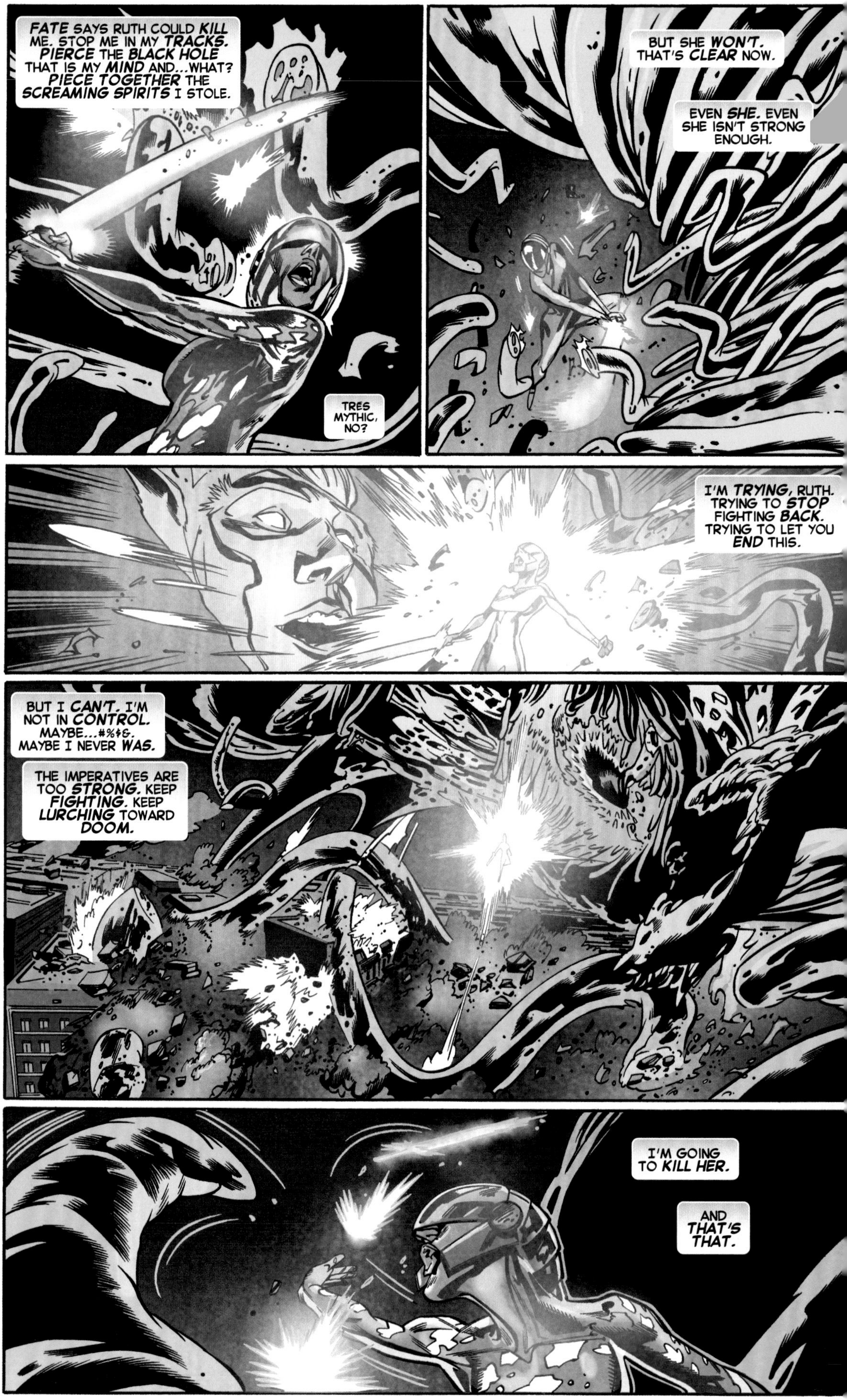
FATE SAYS RUTH COULD KILL ME. STOP ME IN MY TRACKS. PIERCE THE BLACK HOLE THAT IS MY MIND AND...WHAT? PIECE TOGETHER THE SCREAMING SPIRITS I STOLE.
TRES MYTHIC, NO?
BUT SHE WON'T. THAT'S CLEAR NOW.
EVEN SHE. EVEN SHE ISN'T STRONG ENOUGH.
I'M TRYING, RUTH. TRYING TO STOP FIGHTING BACK. TRYING TO LET YOU END THIS.
BUT I CAN'T. I'M NOT IN CONTROL. MAYBE...#%$&. MAYBE I NEVER WAS.
THE IMPERATIVES ARE TOO STRONG. KEEP FIGHTING. KEEP LURCHING TOWARD DOOM.
I'M GOING TO KILL HER.
AND THAT'S THAT.

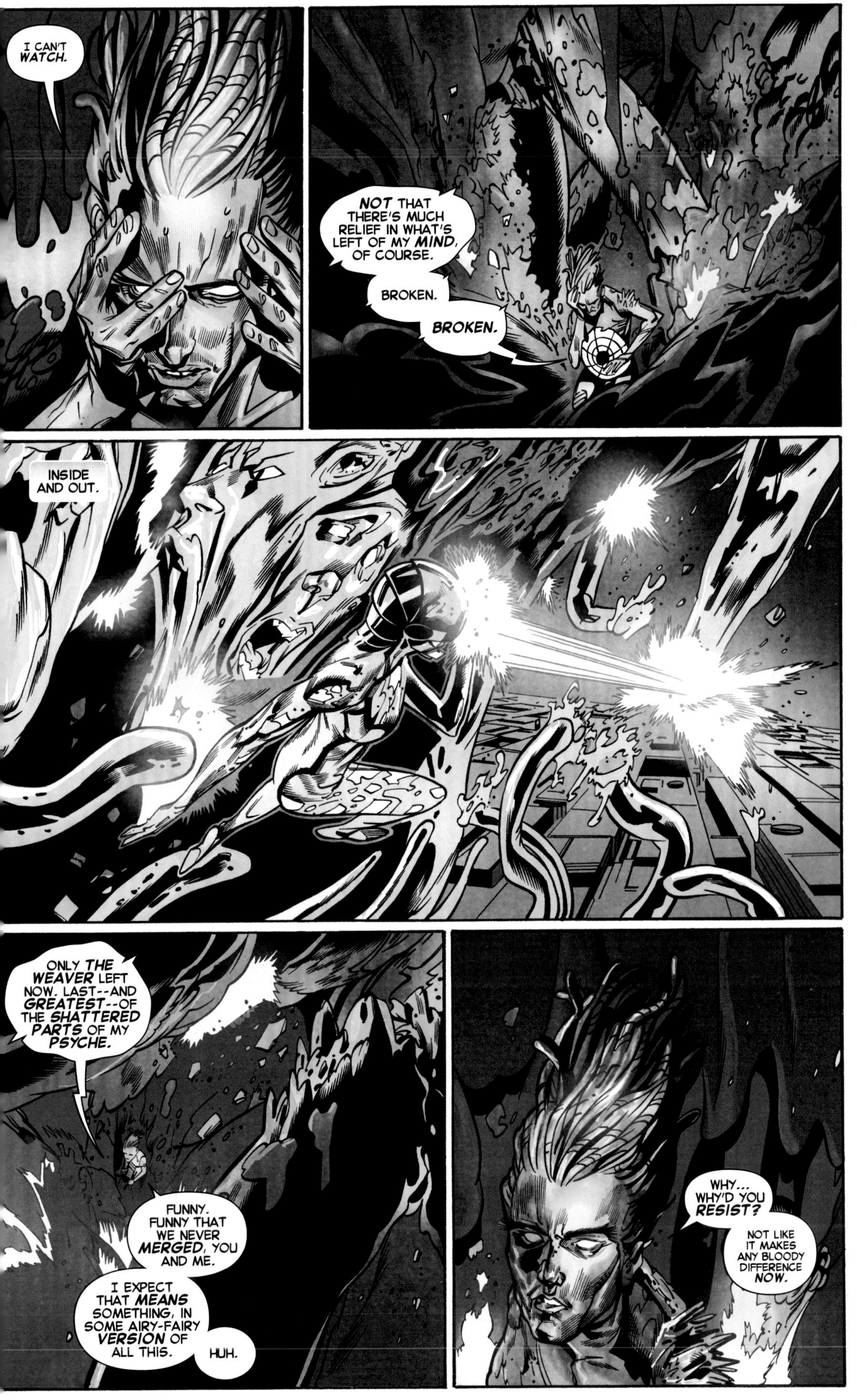
I CAN'T WATCH.
NOT THAT THERE'S MUCH RELIEF IN WHAT'S LEFT OF MY MIND, OF COURSE.
BROKEN.
BROKEN.
INSIDE AND OUT.
ONLY THE WEAVER LEFT NOW. LAST--AND GREATEST--OF THE SHATTERED PARTS OF MY PSYCHE.
FUNNY. FUNNY THAT WE NEVER MERGED, YOU AND ME.
I EXPECT THAT MEANS SOMETHING, IN SOME AIRY-FAIRY VERSION OF ALL THIS.
HUH.
WHY... WHY'D YOU RESIST?
NOT LIKE IT MAKES ANY BLOODY DIFFERENCE NOW.

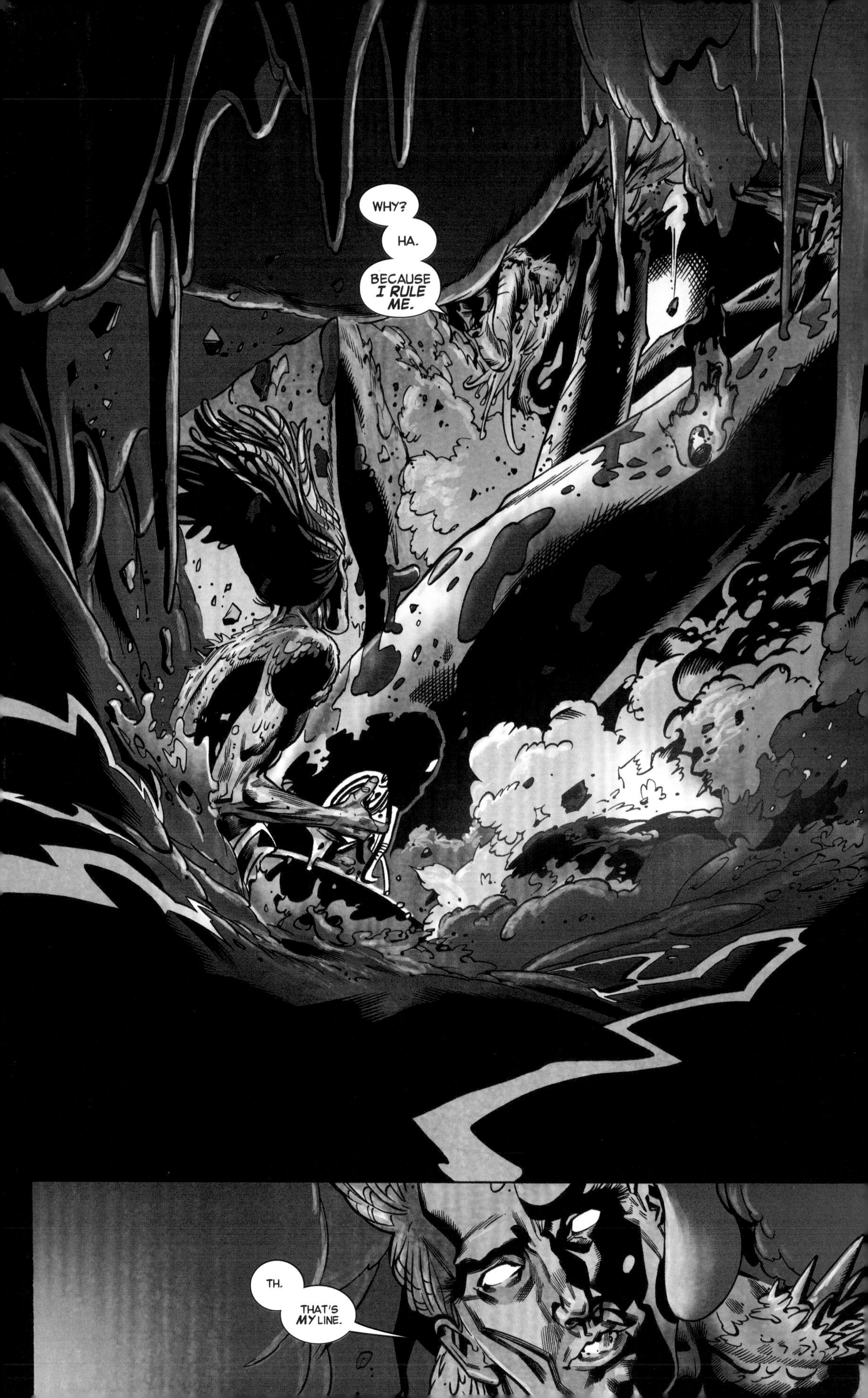
WHY?
HA.
BECAUSE *I RULE ME.*
TH.
THAT'S *MY* LINE.

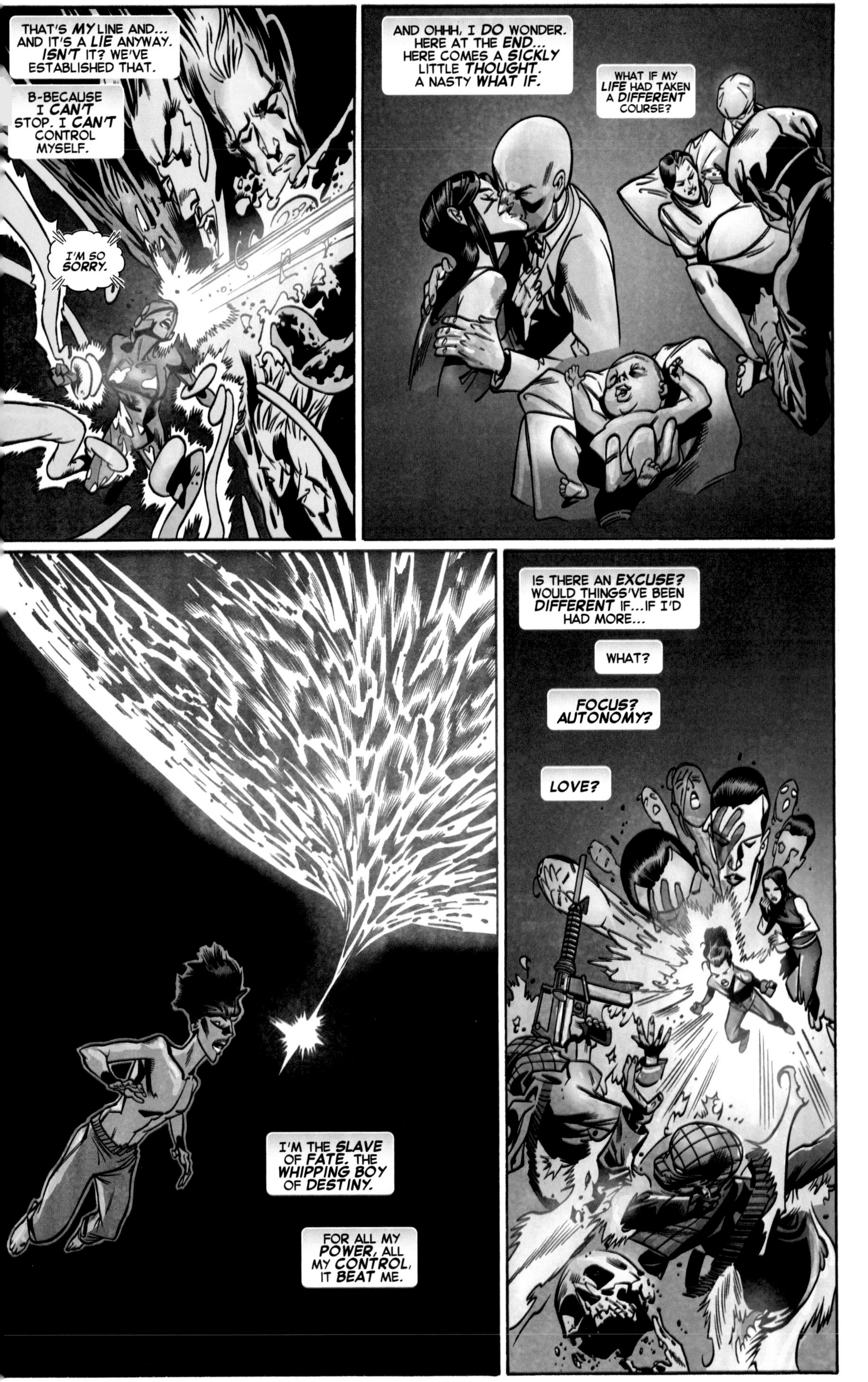

THAT'S MY LINE AND... AND IT'S A LIE ANYWAY. ISN'T IT? WE'VE ESTABLISHED THAT.
B-BECAUSE I CAN'T STOP. I CAN'T CONTROL MYSELF.
I'M SO SORRY.
AND OHHH, I DO WONDER. HERE AT THE END... HERE COMES A SICKLY LITTLE THOUGHT. A NASTY WHAT IF.
WHAT IF MY LIFE HAD TAKEN A DIFFERENT COURSE?
IS THERE AN EXCUSE? WOULD THINGS'VE BEEN DIFFERENT IF...IF I'D HAD MORE...
WHAT?
FOCUS? AUTONOMY?
LOVE?
I'M THE SLAVE OF FATE. THE WHIPPING BOY OF DESTINY.
FOR ALL MY POWER, ALL MY CONTROL, IT BEAT ME.

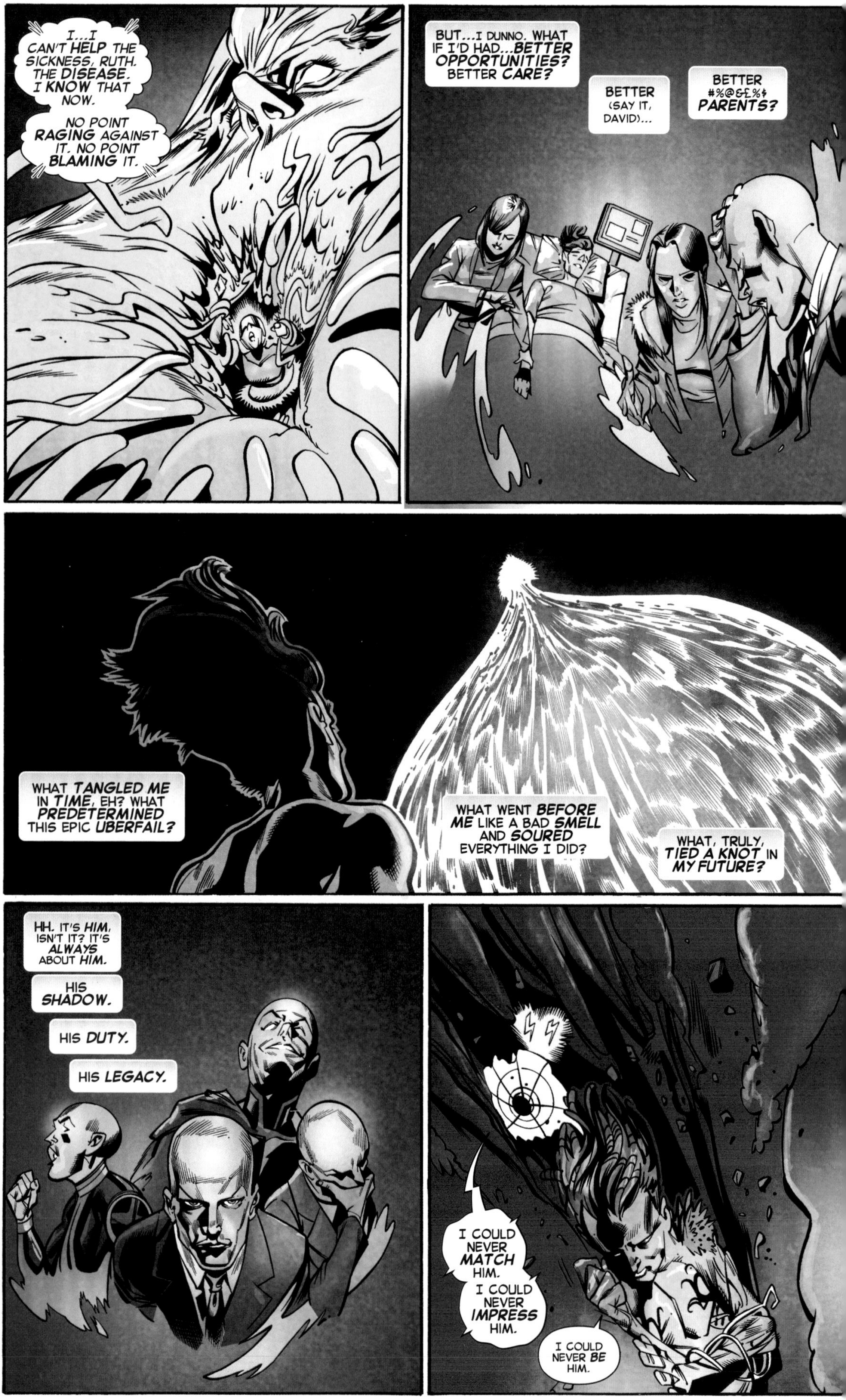
I...I CAN'T HELP THE SICKNESS, RUTH. THE DISEASE. I KNOW THAT NOW.
NO POINT RAGING AGAINST IT. NO POINT BLAMING IT.
BUT...I DUNNO. WHAT IF I'D HAD...BETTER OPPORTUNITIES? BETTER CARE?
BETTER (SAY IT, DAVID)...
BETTER #%@&£%$ PARENTS?
WHAT TANGLED ME IN TIME, EH? WHAT PREDETERMINED THIS EPIC UBERFAIL?
WHAT WENT BEFORE ME LIKE A BAD SMELL AND SOURED EVERYTHING I DID?
WHAT, TRULY, TIED A KNOT IN MY FUTURE?
HH. IT'S HIM, ISN'T IT? IT'S ALWAYS ABOUT HIM.
HIS SHADOW.
HIS DUTY.
HIS LEGACY.
I COULD NEVER MATCH HIM.
I COULD NEVER IMPRESS HIM.
I COULD NEVER BE HIM.

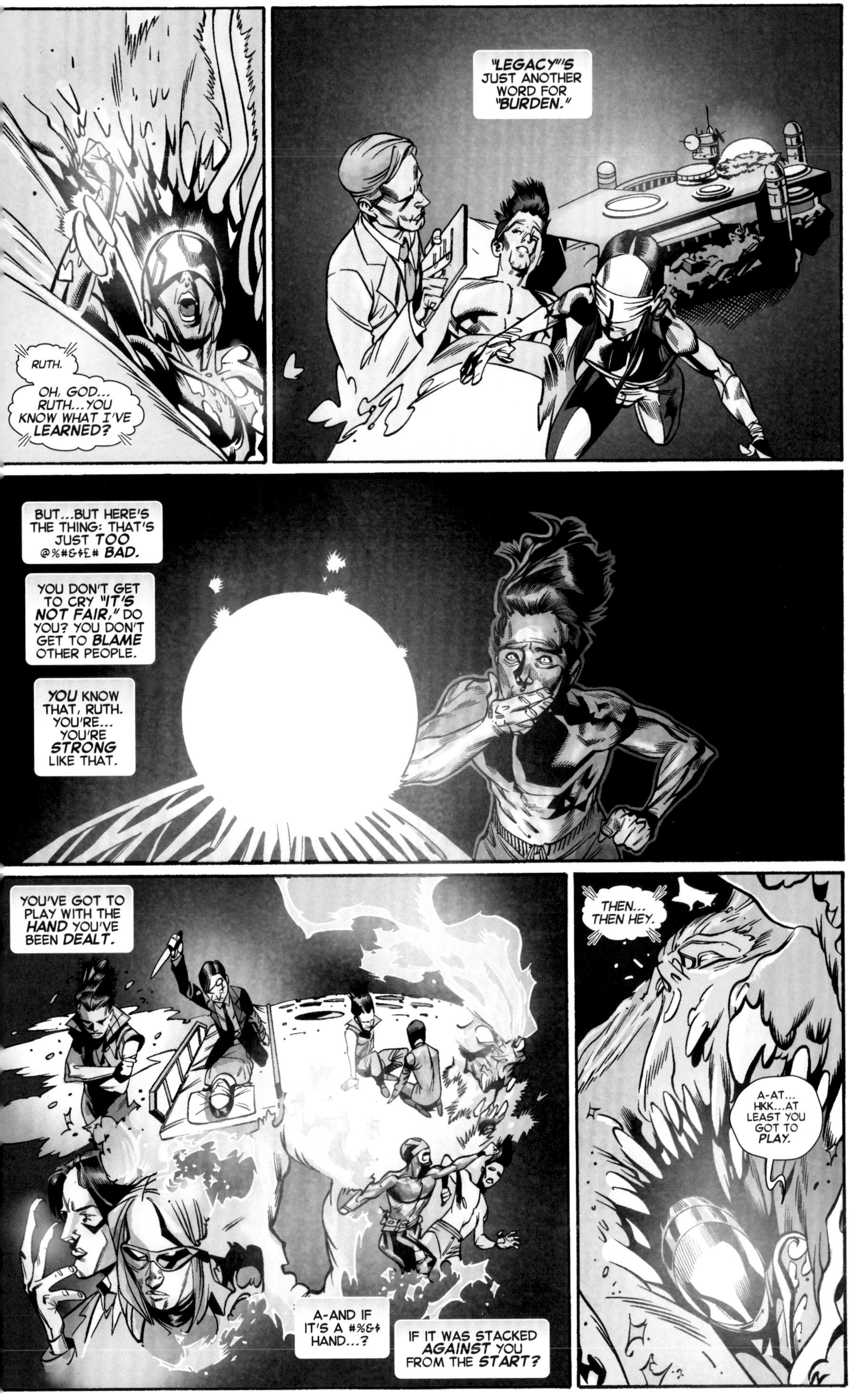
RUTH.
OH, GOD... RUTH...YOU KNOW WHAT I'VE LEARNED?
"LEGACY"'S JUST ANOTHER WORD FOR "BURDEN."
BUT...BUT HERE'S THE THING: THAT'S JUST TOO @%#&$£# BAD.
YOU DON'T GET TO CRY "IT'S NOT FAIR," DO YOU? YOU DON'T GET TO BLAME OTHER PEOPLE.
YOU KNOW THAT, RUTH. YOU'RE... YOU'RE STRONG LIKE THAT.
YOU'VE GOT TO PLAY WITH THE HAND YOU'VE BEEN DEALT.
A-AND IF IT'S A #%&$ HAND...?
IF IT WAS STACKED AGAINST YOU FROM THE START?
THEN... THEN HEY.
A-AT... HKK...AT LEAST YOU GOT TO PLAY.

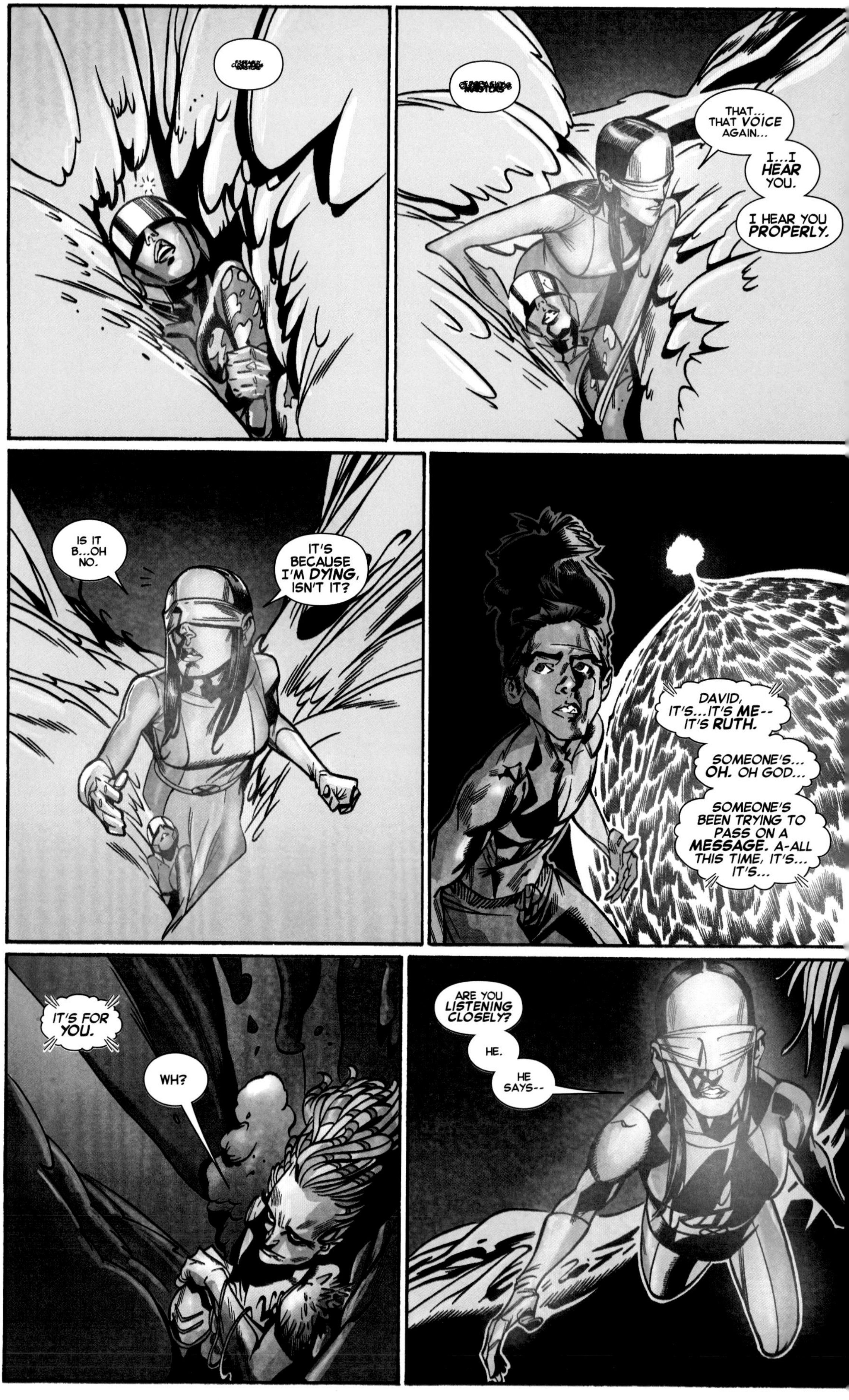
THAT... THAT VOICE AGAIN...
I...I HEAR YOU.
I HEAR YOU PROPERLY.
IS IT B...OH NO.
IT'S BECAUSE I'M DYING, ISN'T IT?
DAVID, IT'S...IT'S ME-- IT'S RUTH.
SOMEONE'S... OH. OH GOD...
SOMEONE'S BEEN TRYING TO PASS ON A MESSAGE. A-ALL THIS TIME, IT'S... IT'S...
IT'S FOR YOU.
WH?
ARE YOU LISTENING CLOSELY?
HE.
HE SAYS--

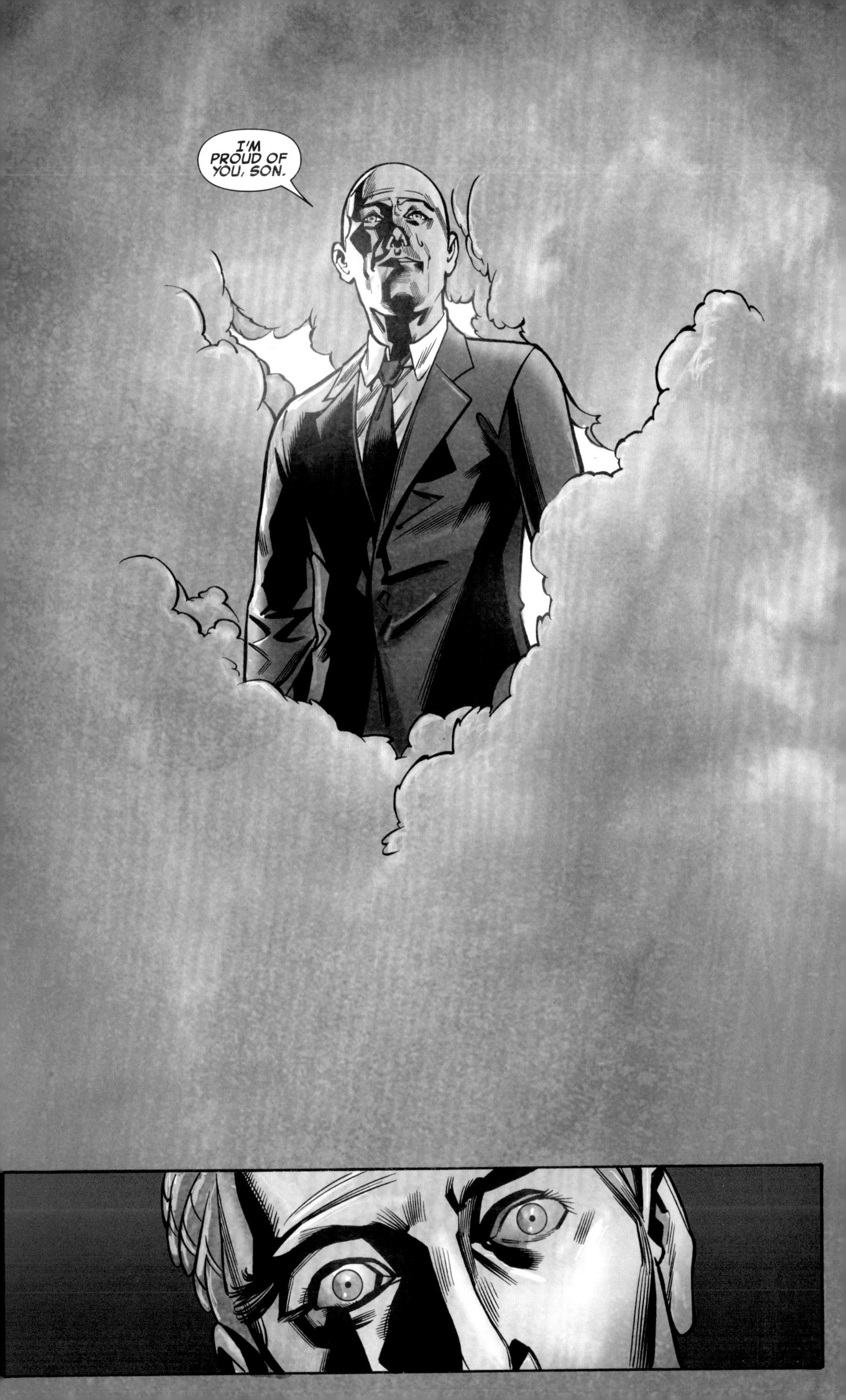
I'M PROUD OF YOU, SON.

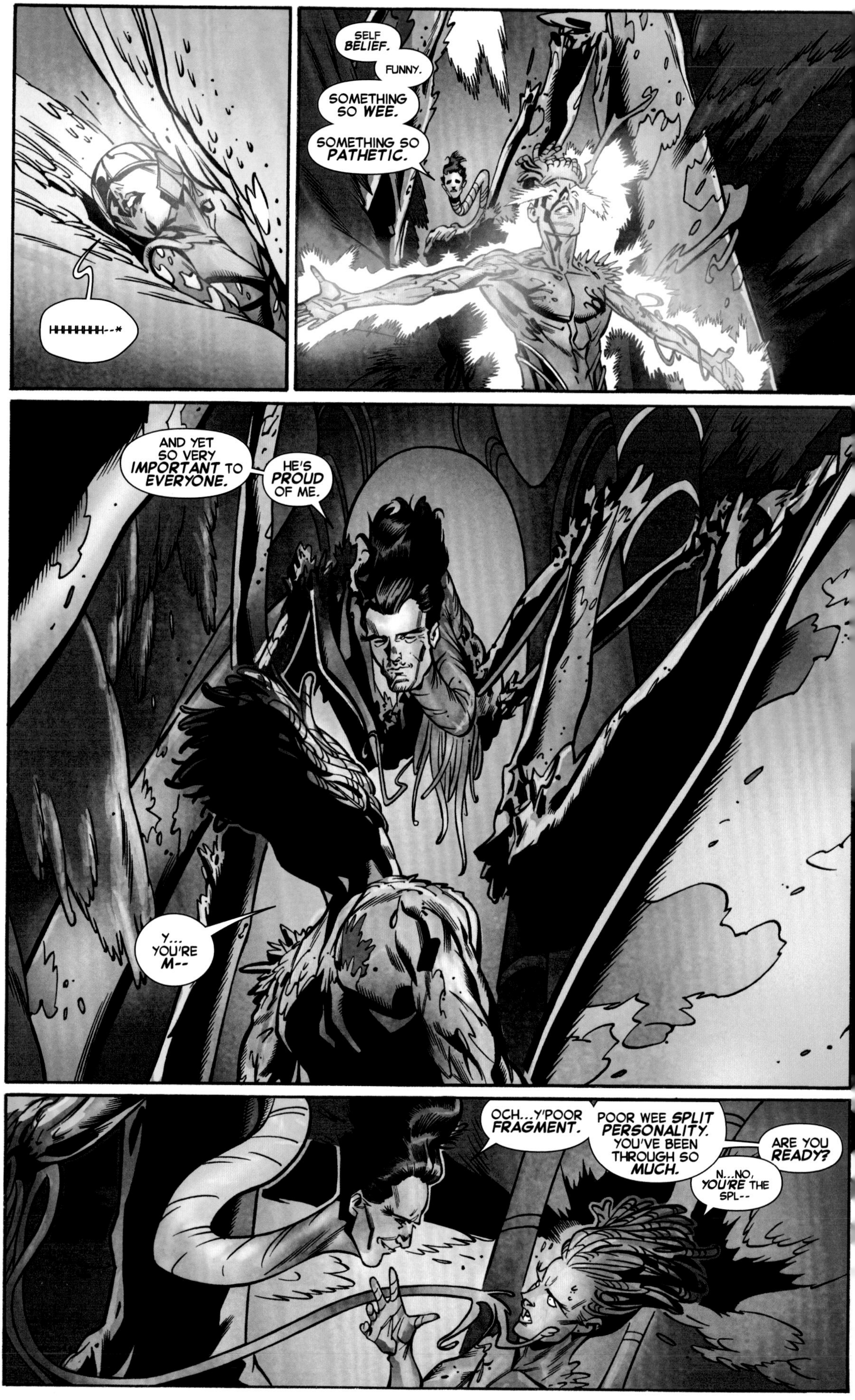
HHHHHHHH--*
SELF BELIEF.
FUNNY.
SOMETHING SO WEE.
SOMETHING SO PATHETIC.
AND YET SO VERY IMPORTANT TO EVERYONE.
HE'S PROUD OF ME.
Y... YOU'RE M--
OCH...Y'POOR FRAGMENT.
POOR WEE SPLIT PERSONALITY. YOU'VE BEEN THROUGH SO MUCH.
ARE YOU READY?
N...NO, YOU'RE THE SPL--

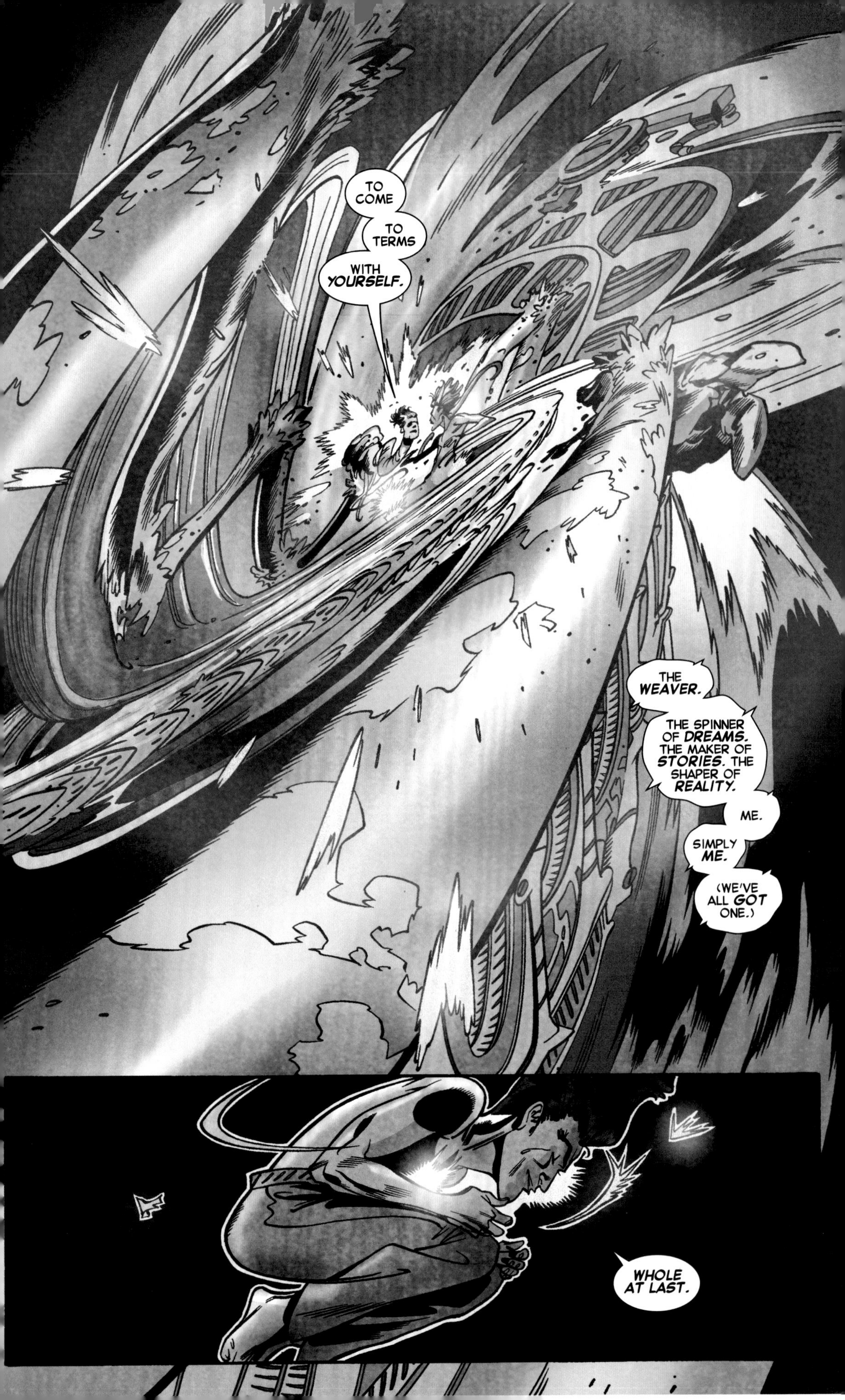
TO COME
TO TERMS
WITH YOURSELF.
THE WEAVER.
THE SPINNER OF DREAMS. THE MAKER OF STORIES. THE SHAPER OF REALITY.
ME.
SIMPLY ME.
(WE'VE ALL GOT ONE.)
WHOLE AT LAST.

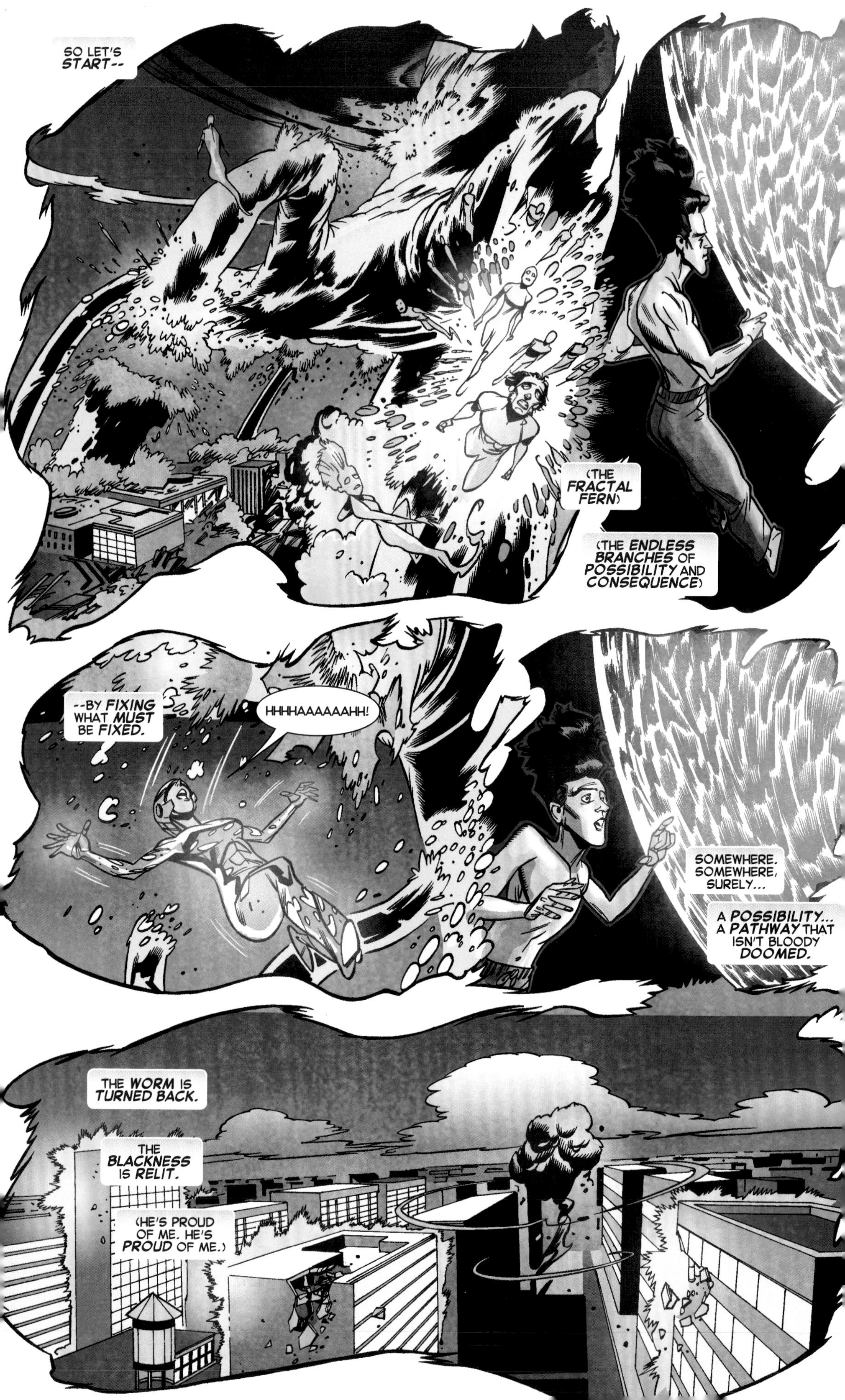
SO LET'S START--
(THE FRACTAL FERN)
(THE ENDLESS BRANCHES OF POSSIBILITY AND CONSEQUENCE)
--BY FIXING WHAT MUST BE FIXED.
HHHHAAAAAAAHH!
SOMEWHERE. SOMEWHERE, SURELY...
A POSSIBILITY... A PATHWAY THAT ISN'T BLOODY DOOMED.
THE WORM IS TURNED BACK.
THE BLACKNESS IS RELIT.
(HE'S PROUD OF ME. HE'S PROUD OF ME.)

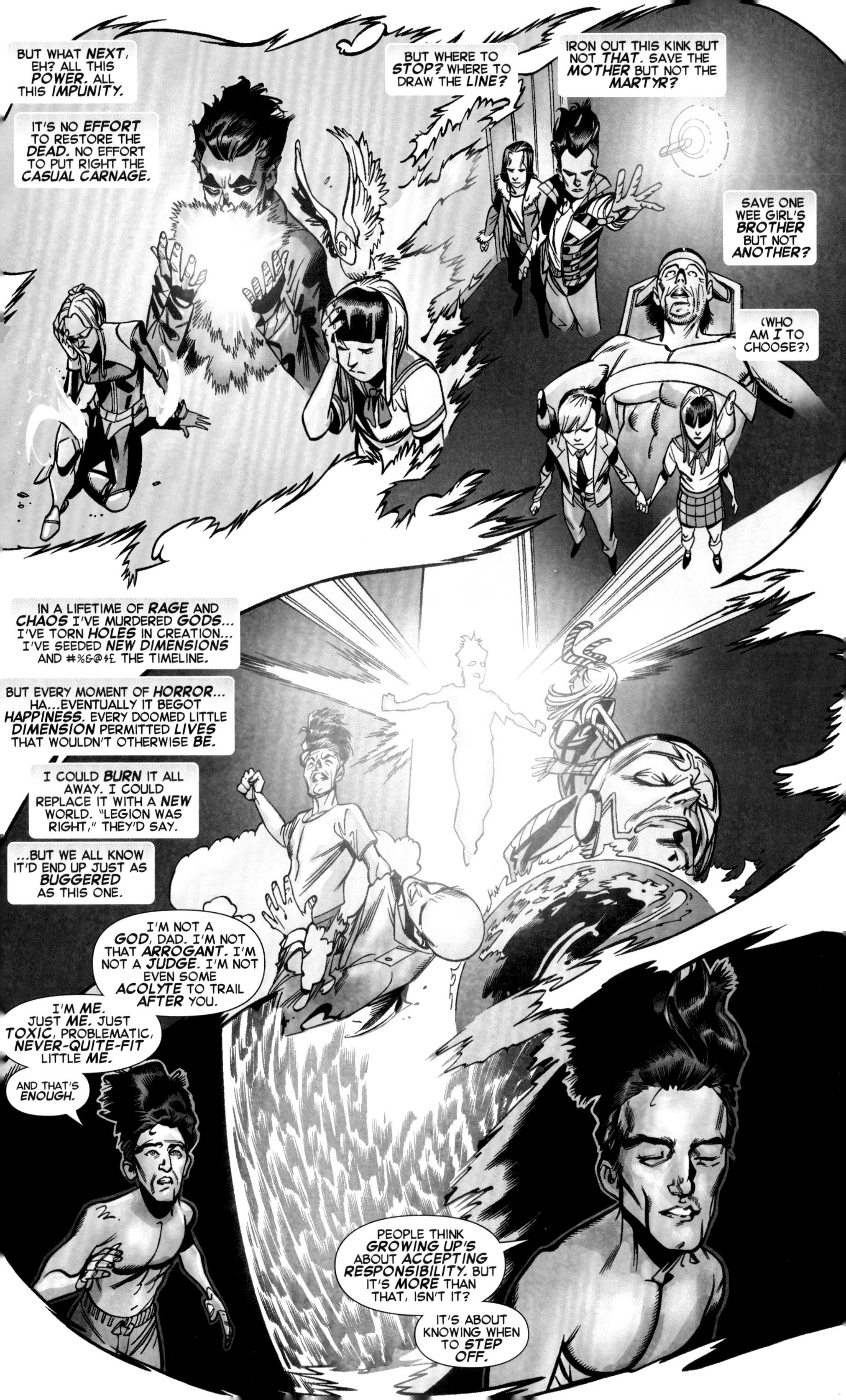

BUT WHAT NEXT, EH? ALL THIS POWER. ALL THIS IMPUNITY.
IT'S NO EFFORT TO RESTORE THE DEAD. NO EFFORT TO PUT RIGHT THE CASUAL CARNAGE.
BUT WHERE TO STOP? WHERE TO DRAW THE LINE?
IRON OUT THIS KINK BUT NOT THAT. SAVE THE MOTHER BUT NOT THE MARTYR?
SAVE ONE WEE GIRL'S BROTHER BUT NOT ANOTHER?
(WHO AM I TO CHOOSE?)
IN A LIFETIME OF RAGE AND CHAOS I'VE MURDERED GODS... I'VE TORN HOLES IN CREATION... I'VE SEEDED NEW DIMENSIONS AND #%&@$£ THE TIMELINE.
BUT EVERY MOMENT OF HORROR... HA...EVENTUALLY IT BEGOT HAPPINESS. EVERY DOOMED LITTLE DIMENSION PERMITTED LIVES THAT WOULDN'T OTHERWISE BE.
I COULD BURN IT ALL AWAY. I COULD REPLACE IT WITH A NEW WORLD. "LEGION WAS RIGHT," THEY'D SAY.
...BUT WE ALL KNOW IT'D END UP JUST AS BUGGERED AS THIS ONE.
I'M NOT A GOD, DAD. I'M NOT THAT ARROGANT. I'M NOT A JUDGE. I'M NOT EVEN SOME ACOLYTE TO TRAIL AFTER YOU.
I'M ME. JUST ME. JUST TOXIC, PROBLEMATIC, NEVER-QUITE-FIT LITTLE ME.
AND THAT'S ENOUGH.
PEOPLE THINK GROWING UP'S ABOUT ACCEPTING RESPONSIBILITY. BUT IT'S MORE THAN THAT, ISN'T IT?
IT'S ABOUT KNOWING WHEN TO STEP OFF.

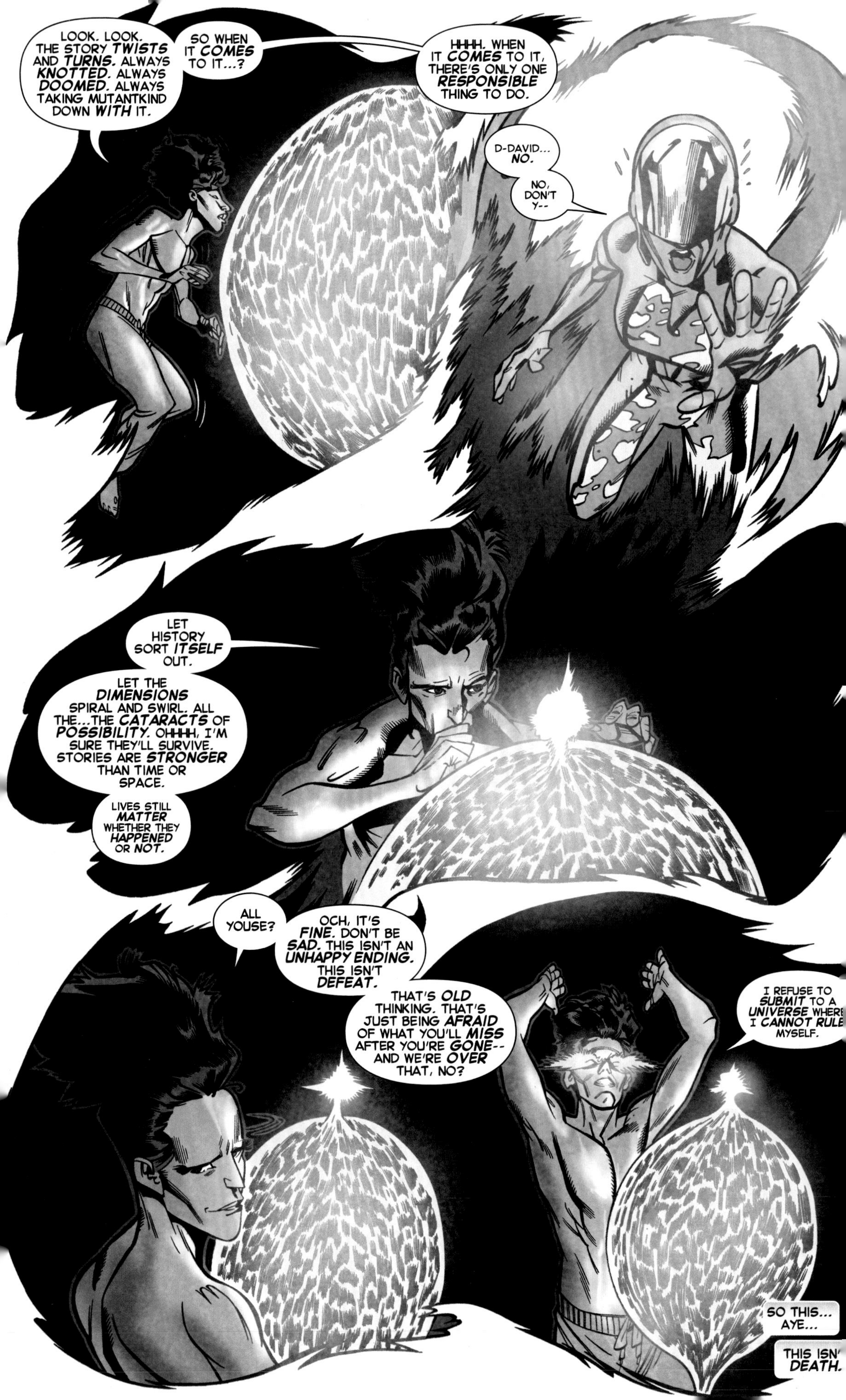
LOOK. LOOK. THE STORY TWISTS AND TURNS. ALWAYS KNOTTED. ALWAYS DOOMED. ALWAYS TAKING MUTANTKIND DOWN WITH IT.
SO WHEN IT COMES TO IT...?
HHHH. WHEN IT COMES TO IT, THERE'S ONLY ONE RESPONSIBLE THING TO DO.
D-DAVID... NO.
NO, DON'T Y--
LET HISTORY SORT ITSELF OUT.
LET THE DIMENSIONS SPIRAL AND SWIRL. ALL THE...THE CATARACTS OF POSSIBILITY. OHHHH, I'M SURE THEY'LL SURVIVE. STORIES ARE STRONGER THAN TIME OR SPACE.
LIVES STILL MATTER WHETHER THEY HAPPENED OR NOT.
ALL YOUSE?
OCH, IT'S FINE. DON'T BE SAD. THIS ISN'T AN UNHAPPY ENDING. THIS ISN'T DEFEAT.
THAT'S OLD THINKING. THAT'S JUST BEING AFRAID OF WHAT YOU'LL MISS AFTER YOU'RE GONE-- AND WE'RE OVER THAT, NO?
I REFUSE TO SUBMIT TO A UNIVERSE WHERE I CANNOT RULE MYSELF.
SO THIS... AYE...
THIS ISN' DEATH.

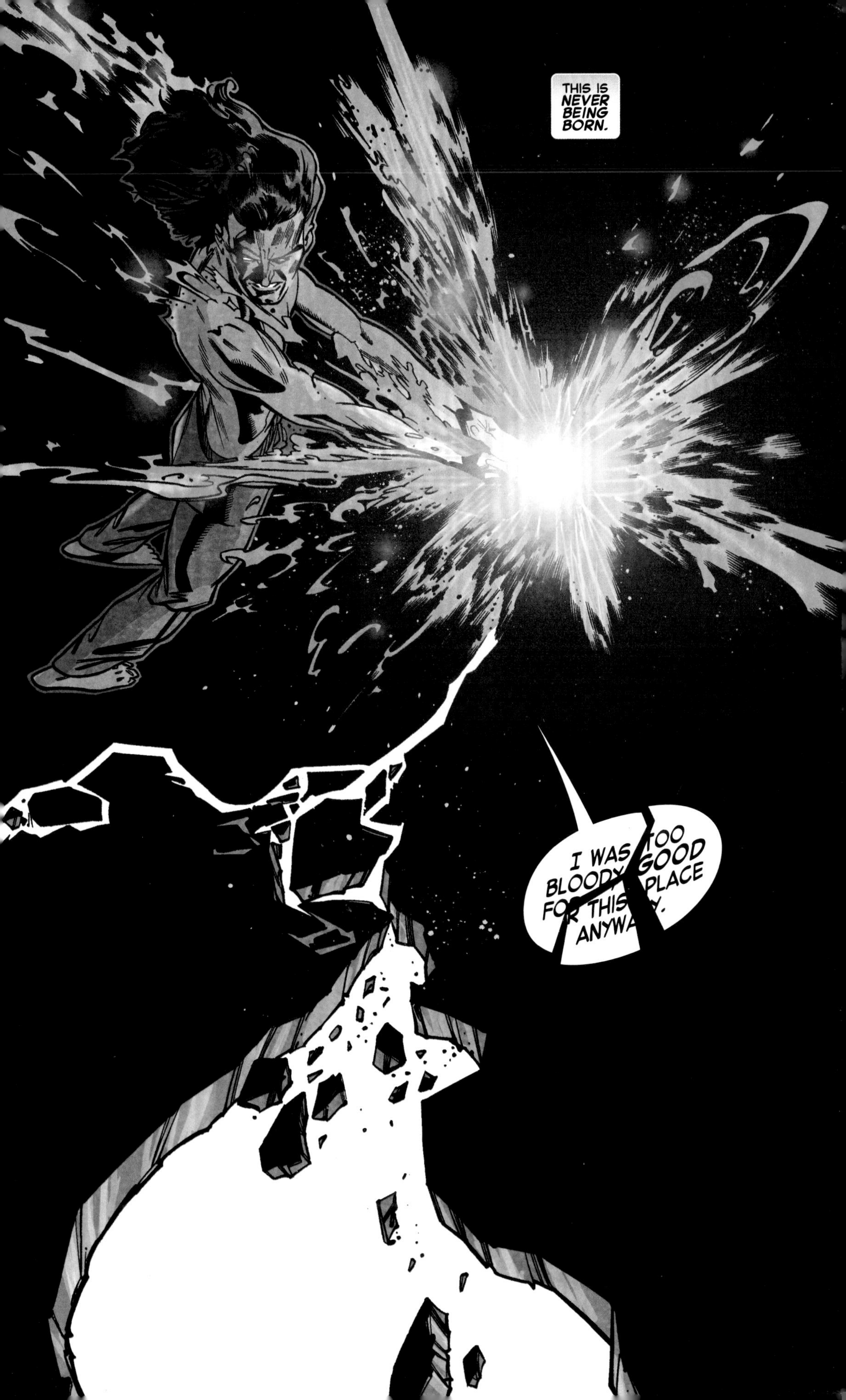
THIS IS NEVER BEING BORN.
I WAS TOO BLOODY GOOD FOR THIS PLACE ANYWA

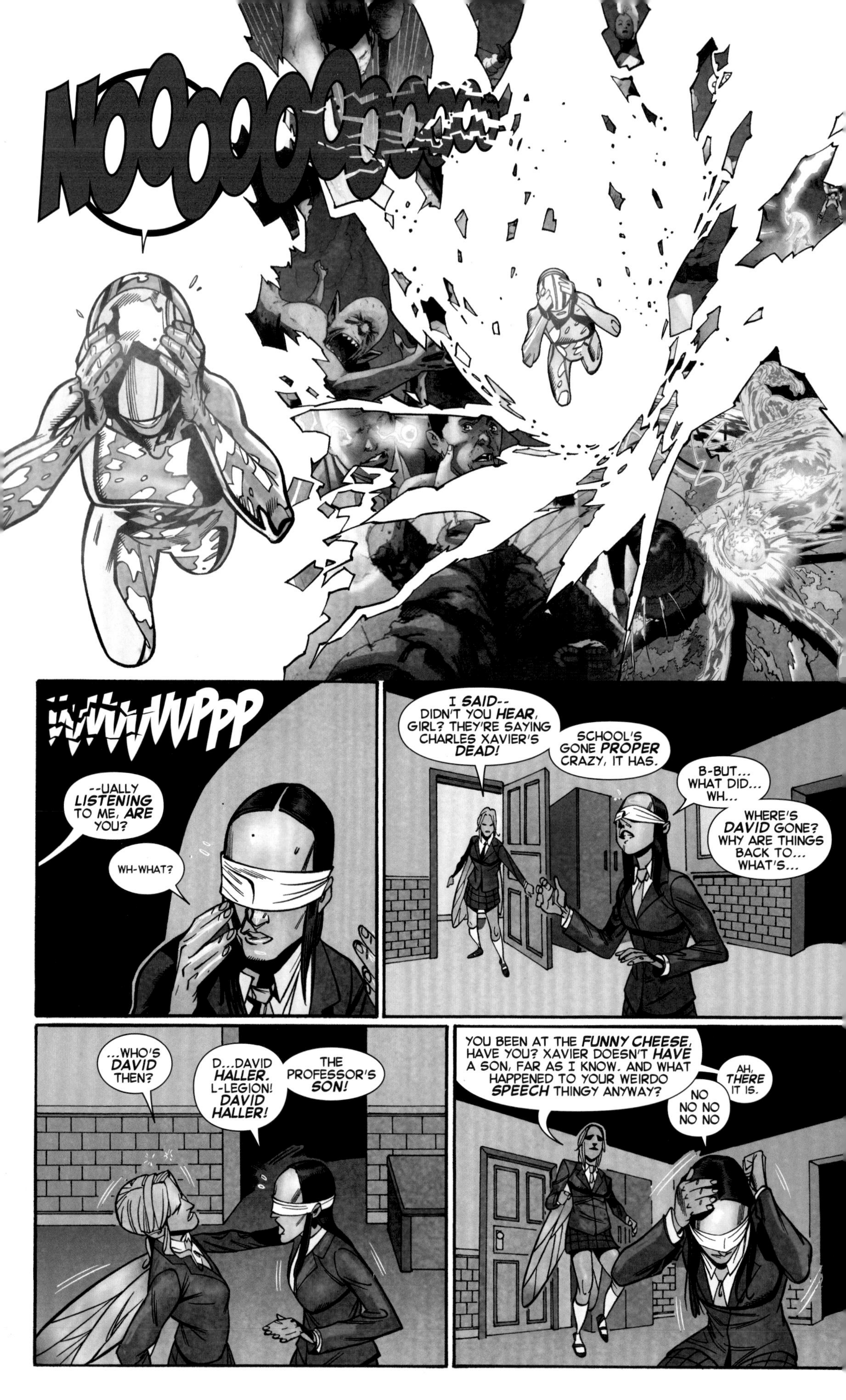
NOOOOOOOOOOOO
WWWWUPPP
--UALLY LISTENING TO ME, ARE YOU?
WH-WHAT?
I SAID-- DIDN'T YOU HEAR, GIRL? THEY'RE SAYING CHARLES XAVIER'S DEAD!
SCHOOL'S GONE PROPER CRAZY, IT HAS.
B-BUT... WHAT DID... WH...
WHERE'S DAVID GONE? WHY ARE THINGS BACK TO... WHAT'S...
...WHO'S DAVID THEN?
D...DAVID HALLER. L-LEGION! DAVID HALLER!
THE PROFESSOR'S SON!
YOU BEEN AT THE FUNNY CHEESE, HAVE YOU? XAVIER DOESN'T HAVE A SON, FAR AS I KNOW. AND WHAT HAPPENED TO YOUR WEIRDO SPEECH THINGY ANYWAY?
AH, THERE IT IS.
NO NO NO NO NO

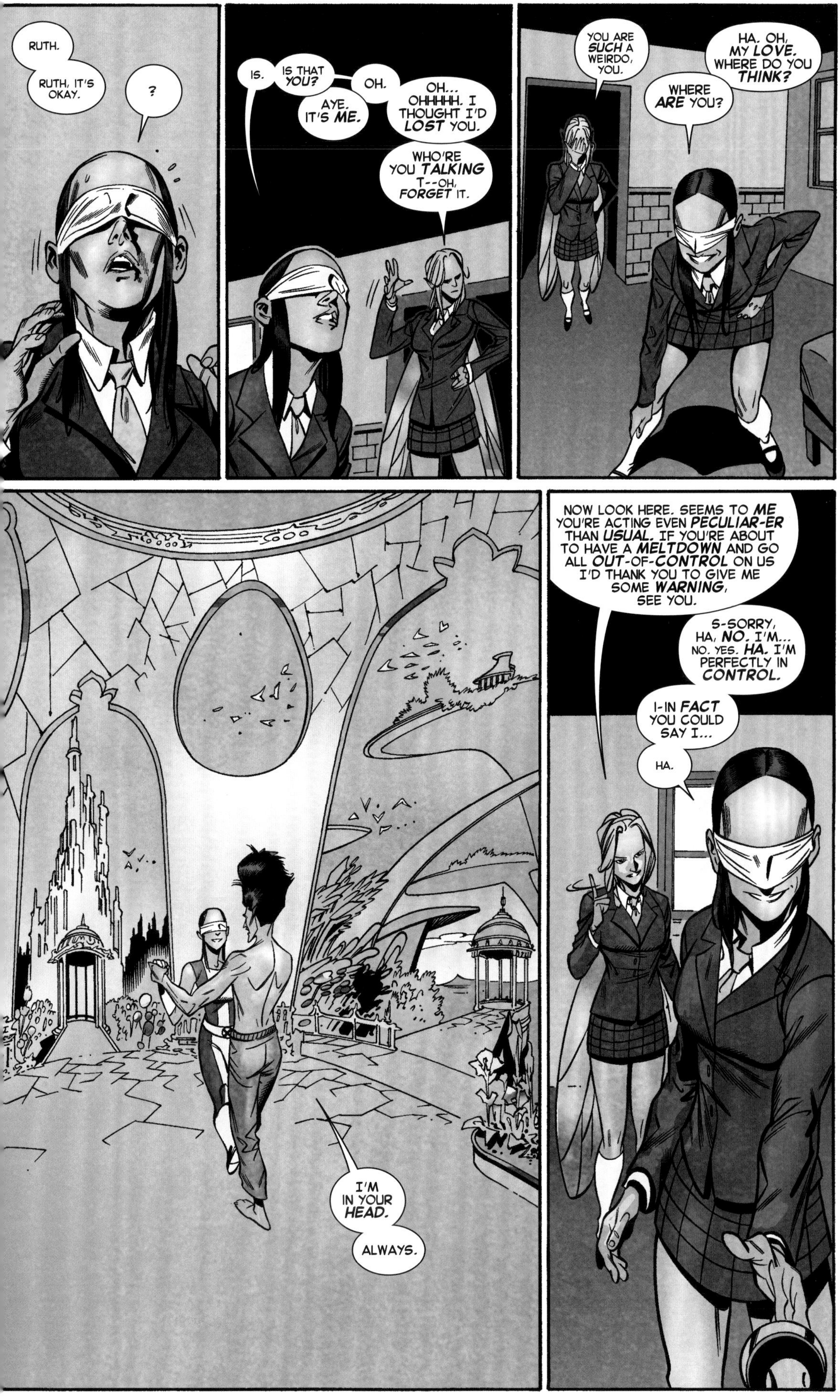

RUTH.
RUTH, IT'S OKAY.
?
IS.
IS THAT YOU?
AYE. IT'S ME.
OH.
OH... OHHHHH. I THOUGHT I'D LOST YOU.
WHO'RE YOU TALKING T--OH, FORGET IT.
YOU ARE SUCH A WEIRDO, YOU.
WHERE ARE YOU?
HA. OH, MY LOVE. WHERE DO YOU THINK?
I'M IN YOUR HEAD.
ALWAYS.
NOW LOOK HERE. SEEMS TO ME YOU'RE ACTING EVEN PECULIAR-ER THAN USUAL. IF YOU'RE ABOUT TO HAVE A MELTDOWN AND GO ALL OUT-OF-CONTROL ON US I'D THANK YOU TO GIVE ME SOME WARNING, SEE YOU.
S-SORRY, HA, NO. I'M... NO. YES. HA. I'M PERFECTLY IN CONTROL.
I-IN FACT YOU COULD SAY I...
HA.

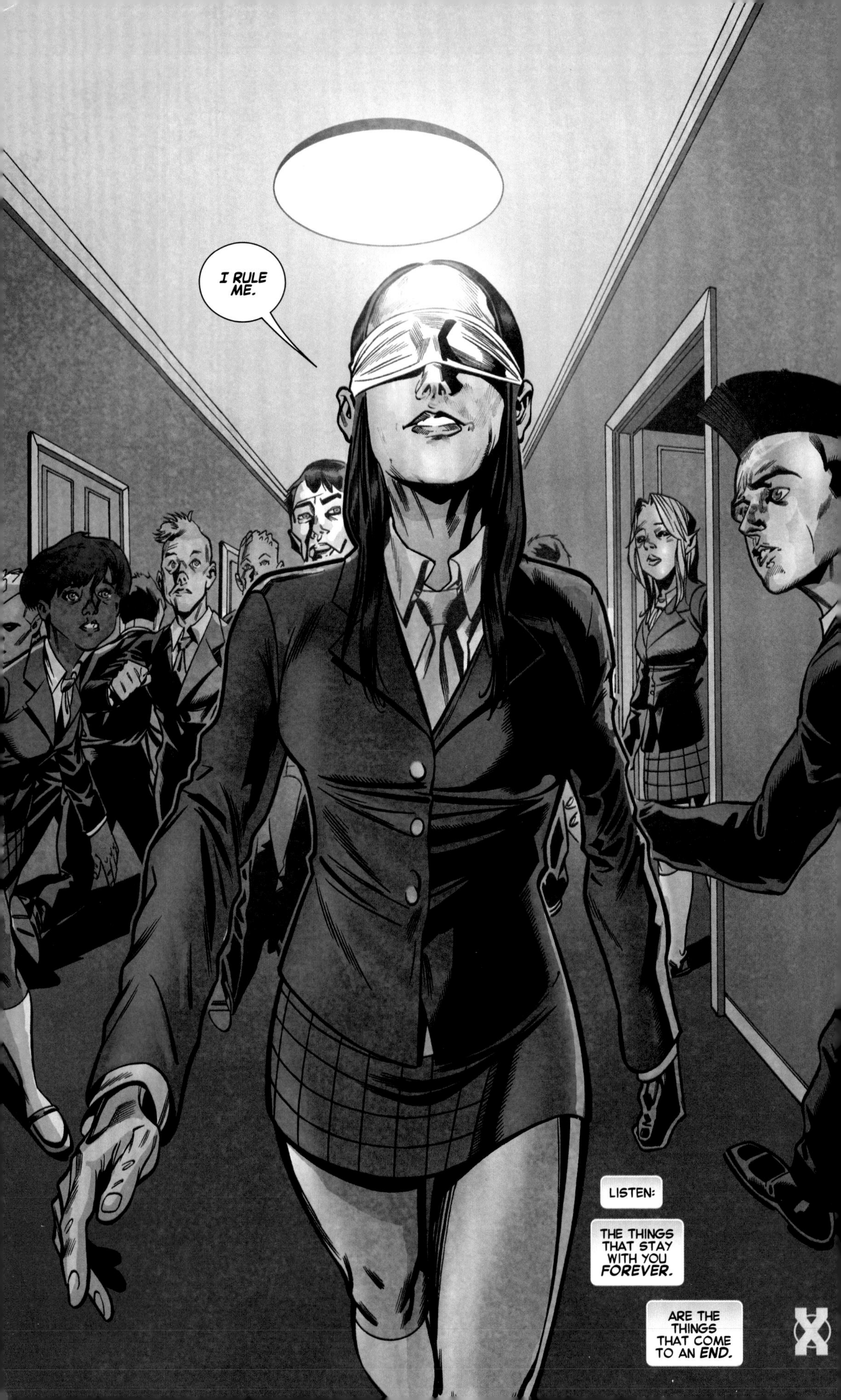
I RULE ME.
LISTEN:
THE THINGS THAT STAY WITH YOU FOREVER.
ARE THE THINGS THAT COME TO AN END.

Hello, folks.

Traditionally this is the part where I provide a last word on the preceding tale. A sculpted aphorism, perhaps, to unlock a narrative puzzlebox nobody realised was there. I shan't, sorry. Just as a story must have its end so must it be capable of standing alone: propped by neither defence nor explanation.

Actually, if you'll permit me one cautious cheat, I'll steal a swift word not on the story but on its fallout. There will be some, I think, angered by these last few pages, on the grounds that a tale's "importance" can only be weighed according to some grand impact on its Universe. I understand but disagree with that view. Indeed I wouldn't have chosen quite such a perversely bittersweet ending if I didn't think it the best way to emphasise a very important point: even when nothing else has changed, when all the explodo and punching seems to have been for nothing, it's the lesson learnt — even the merest echo of it — that renders the journey valuable. Our memories remain. Nobody will ever be able to corrupt what David did today: taking control of his own story at any cost.

Perhaps one day other creators will find some ingenious way to restore him to the Marvel Universe. Perhaps they'll just ignore these adventures. That, reader, is the prerogative of the writer — it's no less than I've done myself to details enshrined by previous Legion-centric tales — and no reason for our outrage. As David put it, lives still matter whether they happened or not. Or if you prefer, as Ruth has just discovered: if you cherish something it will warm you even if everyone else seems oblivious.

Just because something's not real
doesn't mean it's not important.

There. It turns out there was a sculpted aphorism in here after all. I am a dreadful hypocrite.

Thank you. Thank you for sharing this journey. Thank you for taking a punt on a title, a character, a creative team and above all a vibe so bloodymindedly unlike its fellows. I'd ask that you keep an eye on the subsequent works of all the incredible artists who've brought David and Ruth to life, and join me in thanking editors Nick, Jennifer, Xander and above all the irreplaceable Daniel Ketchum, without whom David's adventures would have been even more obtuse and impenetrable, if they'd even happened at all.

Which, of course, they didn't.

-Si Spurrier, 2014.

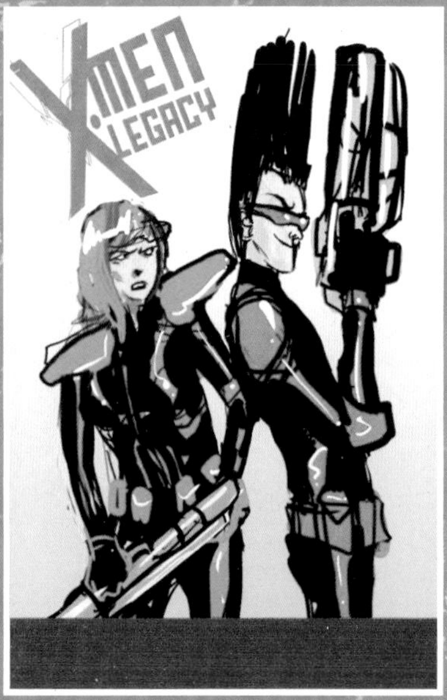
X-MEN
LEGACY

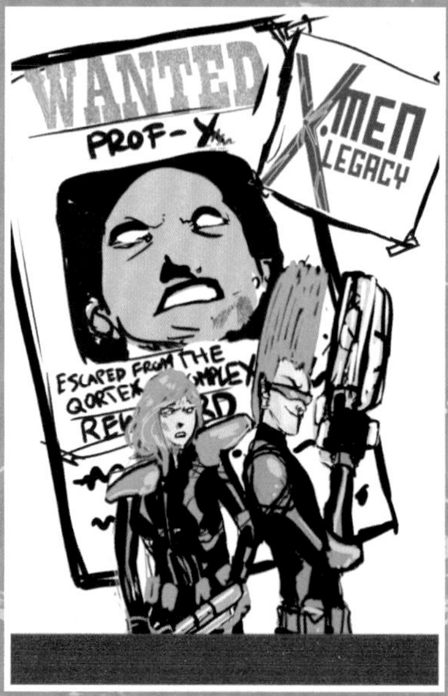
WANTED
PROF-X
X-MEN
LEGACY
ESCAPED FROM THE

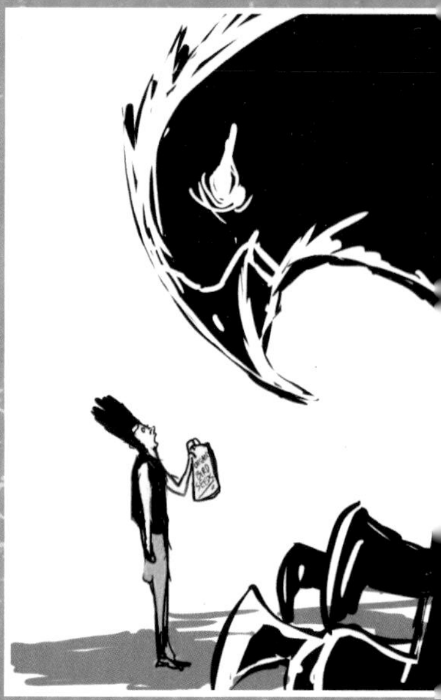

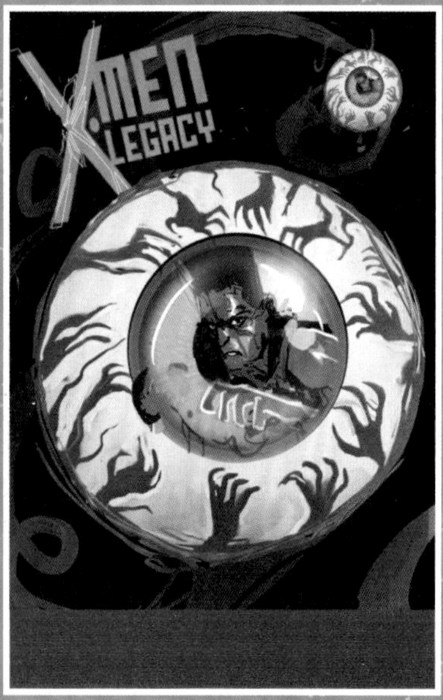
X-MEN
LEGACY

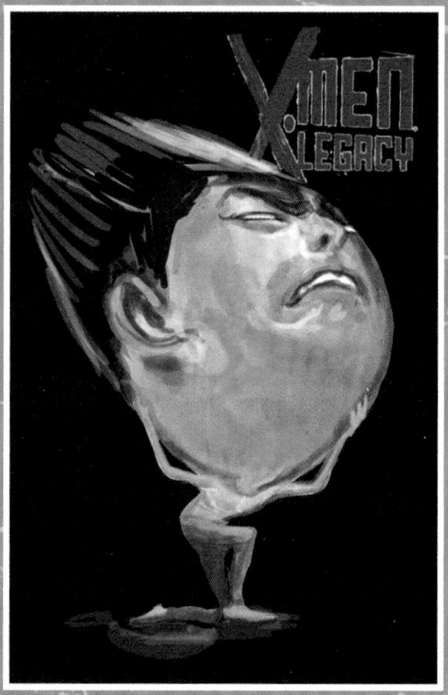
X-MEN
LEGACY

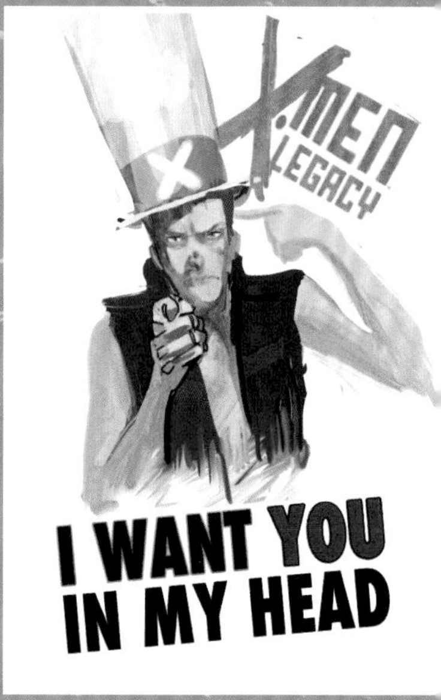
X-MEN
LEGACY
I WANT YOU
IN MY HEAD

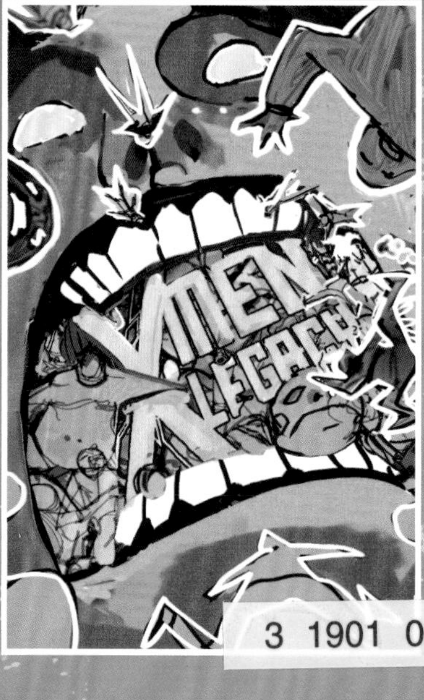
X-MEN
LEGACY

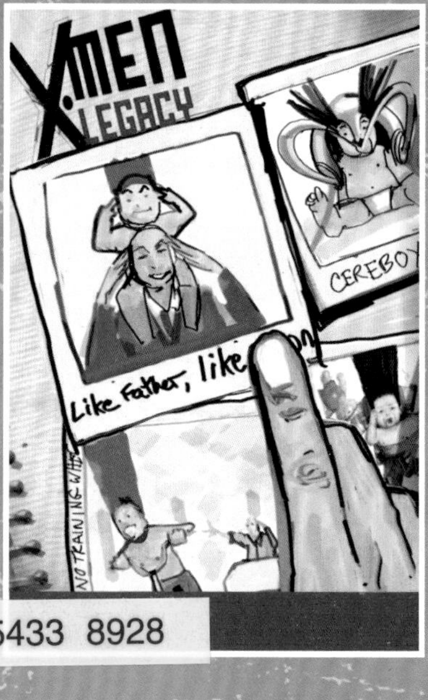
X-MEN
LEGACY
CEREBOY

UNUSED COVER SKETCHES by Mike Del Mundo